The Aus

The
Australian Legend

RUSSEL WARD

Melbourne
OXFORD UNIVERSITY PRESS
Auckland Oxford New York

OXFORD UNIVERSITY PRESS

Oxford New York Toronto
Delhi Bombay Calcutta Madras Karachi
Kuala Lumpur Singapore Hong Kong Tokyo
Nairobi Dar es Salaam Cape Town
Melbourne Auckland
and associates in
Beirut Berlin Ibadan Nicosia

OXFORD is a trademark of Oxford University Press.

© *Russel Ward 1958*

First published 1958

Reprinted 1960, 1962, 1964
Second edition 1966
First paperback edition 1966
Reprinted 1970, 1974, 1977, 1980, 1981, 1983, 1984, 1985

NATIONAL LIBRARY OF AUSTRALIA CATALOGUING IN
PUBLICATION DATA

Ward, Russel Braddock, 1914-.
The Australian legend.

Index.
First published, Melbourne, 1958.
Bibliography.
ISBN 0 19 550286 8.

*1. Australia—History—1800-1900.   2. National
characteristics, Australian. I. Title.*
994

PRINTED IN HONG KONG BY NORDICA PRINTING COMPANY
PUBLISHED BY OXFORD UNIVERSITY PRESS, 7 BOWEN CRESCENT, MELBOURNE

Foreword

THIS book attempts to trace the historical origins and development of the Australian legend or national *mystique*. It argues that a specifically Australian outlook grew up first and most clearly among the bush workers in the Australian pastoral industry, and that this group has had an influence, completely disproportionate to its numerical and economic strength, on the attitudes of the whole Australian community.

The book sprang initially from an interest in Australian folk-ballads, the old 'anonymous' bush songs of the last century, but it grew naturally into a study of the life, outlook and influence of those who sang them. A few ballads and popular songs have been used as background material to help illustrate the pastoral workers' ethos.

What follows is an abbreviated and revised version of a doctoral thesis written in the History Department of the Australian National University. In this book it has been necessary to curtail or omit most of the detailed evidence originally brought forward in support of points made in the narrative. However, the original thesis may be consulted, by those interested, in the library of the National University, Canberra.

I have been helped by hundreds of men and women living all over Australia, and would like to acknowledge especially the aid of three old folk-singers, Mrs Mary Byrnes, Mr Joseph Cashmere and the late Mr John Henry Lee. For particularly valuable encouragement and criticism I am indebted to the late Miss Margaret Kiddle and Professor R. M. Crawford of the University of Melbourne, Professor C. M. H. Clark of the Canberra University College, Mr R. McD. Chapman of Auckland University College, Professor H. C. Allen of the University of London and Dr R. A. Gollan of the Australian National University. I am grateful also to staff members of all the Australian state libraries who often took considerable pains to find information and send it by letter, and especially to Mrs W. D. Fanning of the National Library Canberra, Miss Mander Jones of the Mitchell Library Sydney, Mr John Feely of the Melbourne Public Library, Mr Edgar Waters of the

Sydney Public Library and Mr A. G. Macdonald of the National University Library, in which places most of the work was done. Grateful acknowledgement is made also to Mr John Manifold of Wynnum, Queensland, for permission to quote in full his fine poem, *The Tomb of Lt John Learmonth A.I.F.*, and to the National University which granted me a three years' scholarship to do the work.

University of New England, Armidale, N.S.W., 1958.

Foreword to the Second Edition

THIS new edition of *The Australian Legend* provides the opportunity to correct a few mis-prints which appeared in earlier impressions, and to make other minor changes in the text to allow for additions to historical knowledge since 1958. For example Alexander Harris, author of *Settlers and Convicts* and other books about early Australian life, is now known to have been the real name of the uncommonly percipient man who worked in New South Wales between 1826 and 1841. Accordingly, wherever his name occurs, it has been divested of his self-imposed quotation marks. There seemed no reason for any other, or more substantial, changes.

Since the book was first published it has been the subject of a good deal of critical attention. This was naturally pleasing to the author and publishers since most critics praised the book generously and, more importantly, showed that they understood very well what it tries to do. It seems to me that the dissentient minority misunderstood the book's aim. These critics have rightly stressed that it does not give a balanced or complete view of Australian history; but the first page of Chapter One emphasizes that this is not at all what it seeks to do. At the risk of tedious repetition: *The Australian Legend* does not purport to be a history of Australia, or even primarily an explanation of what most Australians are like and of how they came to be that way. It does, as the title suggests, try to trace and explain the development of the Australian self-image—of the often romanticized and exaggerated stereotype in men's minds of what the *typical*, not the *average*,

Australian likes (or in some cases *dis*likes) to believe he is like. Typical and not average because, in the nature of things, such a national self-image can be built only on those character-traits which differ most dramatically from the general English-speaking, or even European, norm. The average Australian is necessarily much more like the average American than is the typical Australian like his opposite number. If it be conceded that Englishmen and Americans and Australians do differ in certain ways, in their modes of pronouncing their common language for instance, surely it is clear that we shall never identify these 'typical' or characteristic differences by concentrating our attention on the much more numerous and important traits which men of these nationalities hold in common.

Thus when Professor J. M. Ward, in his chapter of *The Pattern of Australian Culture* (ed. A. L. McLeod, 1963), writes that 'More needs to be known about the middle classes and the non-Labor parties', all Australian historians may agree and applaud—if he means that more needs to be known about these things *per se* and for the purpose of writing balanced and complete Australian history. But in context J. M. Ward is criticizing *The Australian Legend* and Dr Robin Gollan's *Radical and Working Class Politics 1850-1910* for not having been addressed to topics quite other than those indicated by their titles. As well might one criticize J. M. Ward's own admirable book, *Earl Grey and the Australian Colonies, 1846-1857*, for not having been written about something else—the pastoral industry of the period for instance.

More directly he writes that the major premise of *The Australian Legend*

> is itself doubtful; do Australians really and distinctively think of themselves as practical men, rough and ready, quick to decry affectation, willing to improvise, unwilling to work hard without good cause, and so on? . . . Some critics have wondered whether his 'legend' existed even among bush workers.

I can only reply here by inverting J. M. Ward's questions. Has anyone ever thought of Australians as being 'really and distinctively' impractical theorizers, quick to admire affectation and pretentious manners, unwilling to make the best of things or to 'give it a go', anxious to work hard and long for the sheer joy of it, and so on? As for the un-named critics who wonder whether these 'legendary' attitudes *ever* existed among the pastoral workers, I refer them to Friedrich Gerstaecker's observations made in the Riverina in 1850 and quoted on page 157:

> If you get the bushmen to talk—which requires a longer time than a few hours' acquaintance—you learn more in one hour of the wild life of the bush than by a year's residence with the swells.

R. H. Tawney once said that a tolerable pair of boots should figure prominently among the essential equipment of the historian. Those who follow Gerstaecker's excellent example by tramping, or hitch-hiking, through the back country today will certainly find that the 'legendary' outlook *still* lives vigorously among bushmen.

University of New England, Armidale, N.S.W., February 1965.

Contents

Contents

THE entire man is, so to speak, to be seen in the cradle of the child. The growth of nations presents something analogous to this; they all bear some marks of their origin; and the circumstances which accompanied their birth and contributed to their rise, affect the whole term of their being.

—De Tocqueville

Shame on the mouth
That would deny
The knotted hands
That set us high!
    —Dame Mary Gilmore

I

THE LEGEND AND THE TASK

For I'm a ramble-eer, a rollicking ramble-eer,
I'm a roving rake of poverty, and a son of a gun for
beer.

IN the last seventy-odd years millions of words have been written
about Australian nationalism and the 'Australian character'. Most
writers seem to have felt strongly that the 'Australian spirit' is
somehow intimately connected with the bush and that it derives
rather from the common folk than from the more respectable and
cultivated sections of society. This book seeks, not to give yet another cosily impressionistic sketch of what wild boys we Australians are—or like to consider ourselves—but rather to trace and
explain the development of this national *mystique*.

Nearly all legends have some basis in historical fact. We shall
find that the Australian legend has, perhaps, a more solid sub-
stratum of fact than most, but this does not mean that it comprises
all, or even most, of what we need to know to understand Australia and Australian history. It may be, however, a very important means to this end, if only because we shall certainly be wrong
if we either romanticize its influence or deny it.

National character is not, as was once held, something inherited;
nor is it, on the other hand, entirely a figment of the imagination of
poets, publicists and other feckless dreamers. It is rather a people's
idea of itself and this stereotype, though often absurdly romanticized and exaggerated, is always connected with reality in two
ways. It springs largely from a people's past experiences, and it
often modifies current events by colouring men's ideas of how they
ought 'typically' to behave.

According to the myth the 'typical Australian' is a practical man, rough and ready in his manners and quick to decry any appearance of affectation in others. He is a great improviser, ever willing 'to have a go' at anything, but willing too to be content with a task done in a way that is 'near enough'. Though capable of great exertion in an emergency, he normally feels no impulse to work hard without good cause. He swears hard and consistently, gambles heavily and often, and drinks deeply on occasion. Though he is 'the world's best confidence man', he is usually taciturn rather than talkative, one who endures stoically rather than one who acts busily. He is a 'hard case', sceptical about the value of religion and of intellectual and cultural pursuits generally. He believes that Jack is not only as good as his master but, at least in principle, probably a good deal better, and so he is a great 'knocker' of eminent people unless, as in the case of his sporting heroes, they are distinguished by physical prowess. He is a fiercely independent person who hates officiousness and authority, especially when these qualities are embodied in military officers and policemen. Yet he is very hospitable and, above all, will stick to his mates through thick and thin, even if he thinks they may be in the wrong. No epithet in his vocabulary is more completely damning than 'scab', unless it be 'pimp' used in its peculiarly Australasian slang meaning of 'informer'. He tends to be a rolling stone, highly suspect if he should chance to gather much moss.

In the following pages we shall find that all these characteristics were widely attributed to the bushmen of the last century, not, primarily, to Australians in general or even to country people in general, so much as to the outback employees, the semi-nomadic drovers, shepherds, shearers, bullock-drivers, stockmen, boundary-riders, station-hands and others of the pastoral industry.

This was so partly because the material conditions of outback life were such as to evoke these qualities in pastoral workers, but partly too because the first and most influential bush-workers were convicts or ex-convicts, the conditions of whose lives were such that they brought with them to the bush the same, or very similar, attitudes.

In nineteenth-century Australia this particular social group developed a surprisingly high degree of cohesion and self-consciousness but, in isolating it for the purposes of study, some distortion may be inevitable. In fact, of course, pastoral workers were constantly influencing, and being influenced by, other sections of colonial society. A convict often spent months or years on government constructional work in the city before being assigned to the service of a country settler, or he might be returned to the city after some years 'up the country'. Small farmers and selectors often sought work as shearers on the western runs to supplement their incomes, and many a city wage-earner did the same for a few seasons, especially during bad times when work was scarce on the sea-board. Bullock-drivers, especially before railways began to creep farther and farther into the interior after about 1870, regularly flogged their teams from the colonial capitals and coastal ports to outback stations and back again. They carried news, gossip, manners and songs, as well as stores, wool and hides. One of them, Charles Macalister, wrote of Sydney in the 1840's:

> A chief house of call for us country folk then was the old Blackboy Hotel, at the corner of George and King Streets. A kind of theatre or people's music-hall was kept in connection with this Hotel, where the leading comedians and singers were Jim Brown and 'Micky' Drew; but, as the platform of the Blackboy 'theatre' was somewhat free and easy, sometimes a strong sailorman, just off a six months cruise, would favour us with 'Nancy Lee' or other jolly sea-song; or an ambitious carrier or drover would 'rouse the possum' by giving some long-winded ditty of the time.

Drovers brought not only cattle and sheep to the city markets but also exotic styles of dress, speech and behaviour, wherewith to impress respectable citizens and newly arrived immigrants. And many a bushman from the interior settled down in the agricultural areas or the city, after a happy marriage or old age had terminated his roving habits. As Alan Marshall wrote, in 1955, of his father:

> After he started work he drifted round from station to station horse-breaking or droving. His youth and early manhood were spent in the outback areas of New South Wales and Queensland, and it was these areas that furnished the material for all his yarns. Because of his tales, the saltbush plains and the red sand-hills of the outback were closer to me than the green country where I was born and grew to manhood.

In some ways it is difficult to consider the pastoral workers apart from their employers, those who came to be known in and after the late 1830's as squatters. Right through the nineteenth century there is abundant evidence of class hostility between pastoral employers and employees. It culminated in the disastrous and bitter strikes between 1890 and 1894. This hostility was itself a very important factor in shaping the distinctive ideology of the pastoral employees and yet, except towards the absentee landlords who multiplied exceedingly towards the end of the period,[1] the hostility was always qualified and conditional. The differences between master and man were economic and often political, but not social in some cases. In the 1840's one squatter wrote of a neighbour:

> He was a native-born white, and had been a stockowner all his life. His parents had given him a few cows and brood-mares at his birth, and he was now, by dint of time and industry, the owner of many thousands of cattle. But though fully possessed of the means, he had no wish to alter his style of living for the better, or to rest in any way from his hard and laborious employment . . .[2]

At least in the earliest pioneering stage, before the squatter's wife arrived to define more rigidly the barrier between 'the house' and 'the huts', conditions forced a certain degree of understanding between the occupants of both. As Samuel Sidney wrote in 1854: 'Now, living in the Bush, and especially while travelling, there is not the same distance between a master and a well-behaved man, although a prisoner, as in towns . . .'[3]

Moreover, although climate, economic factors and the effects of land legislation[4] generally combined to make it difficult for a poor man to become a squatter, it was by no means impossible. An occasional unknown workman like James Tyson or Sidney Kidman, by superior industry, temperance, or skill in cattle-duffing, became a 'shepherd king' and, especially in times of drought or depression like the early 1840's or 1890's, many a squatter was reduced to working for wages at one of the bush trades.[5] The truth seems to be that the working hands, while feeling strongly opposed to their masters in general and in principle, were prepared to take each individual squatter as they found him.[6] Also, as the work of the dispossessed squatter's son, A. B. Paterson, no less than that of Furphy shows, 'there was a region, or so it seemed, where the thought and feeling of the station was identical with that of the shed.'[7] The region was that in which the interests of both conflicted with those of absentee squatters, pastoral companies, banks, and other institutions domiciled in the cities or in Great Britain. The rather complex relationship between masters and men was thus described by an English visitor in 1903:

> It is sometimes said that in Australia there are no class distinctions. It would probably be truer to say that in no country in the world are there such strong class-distinctions in proportion to the actual amount of difference between the 'classes'. . . . The 'classes' collectively distrust and fear the 'masses' collectively far more than is the case at home. . . . Individually, it is true, relations are for the most part amicable enough between capitalists and workmen; and the lack of deference in the tone of employees, their employers, being unable to resent, have grown to tolerate, and even perhaps in some cases secretly rather to like. . . .[8]

Up to about 1900 the prestige of the bushman seems to have been greater than that of the townsman. In life as in folklore the man from 'up the country' was usually regarded as a romantic and admirable figure. The attitude towards him was reminiscent, in some interesting ways, of that towards the 'noble savage' in the eighteenth century. We shall see that, in general, he had more influence on the manners and *mores* of the city-dweller than the latter had on his. The tide turned somewhere between 1900 and 1918. Even today the tradition of the 'noble bushman' is still very strong in both literature and folklore, but, at least since the publication in 1899 of *On Our Selection*, it has been counterpoised by the opposing tradition of 'Dad and Mum, Dave and Mabel'. True, Dad and Dave were not pastoral workers, bushmen proper,[9] but poor selectors, 'stringybark cockatoos', who were sneered at by the men from farther out long before it became fashionable for townsmen to regard them as figures of fun. It is also true that the original creations of A. H. Davis ('Steele Rudd') were real comic characters and not the semi-moronic, burlesque puppets which they have since become in popular imagination. Nevertheless their appearance in literature fifty years ago was symptomatic of a real change in Australian attitudes towards the 'bush'. Since the early days of federation the capital cities have grown rapidly both in prestige and in their relative share of state populations, and bushmen are now usually willing to be taken for city-dwellers where formerly the reverse was the case.

In making generalizations about the bush-worker a difficulty springs from the fact of separate origins of the colonies which later became the federated states of the Commonwealth. There have always been, and still are, differences between them in speech, manners, tradition and outlook. But compared with similar differences in, say, Canada or the U.S.A., they are slight indeed, tending to be differences of degree and emphasis rather than of substance. They are more noticeable among middle-class than among working-class people, and in and near the state capitals than in the back country. We shall see that the convict-derived bush ethos grew first and flourished in its most unadulterated form in the mother colony of New South Wales, but that it early spread thence, by osmosis as it were, to become the most important basic component of the national *mystique*.

Two recent newspaper reports will indicate how strong the tradition still is today, and also the extent to which it has been regionally modified. A semi-editorial article in the *Sydney Morning Herald* of 19 July 1953 declared:

> One of the ugly features of Australian city life is the refusal of bystanders to help, in fact their inclination to hinder, a policeman in trouble. There have been some bad cases in Sydney. Melbourne is no better, judging by an incident last week. A man who turned out to be an escaped mental patient had kicked one policeman unconscious and was struggling with another. A gathering crowd yelled, 'Why don't you give him a go, you big mug?'
>
> Only onlooker to intervene was a New Australian, Steve Ovcar, who secured the escapee's hands with a tie. Said Ovcar afterwards, 'People are terrible here. They just watched. They were all against the policeman.'

A report in the Adelaide *Advertiser* of 12 December 1953 modified the picture slightly:

> The attitude of the police to the public in such matters as traffic control did much to establish the regard in which the Police Department was held in the community, Mr John Bonython, a director of the *Advertiser*, said yesterday. . . . Mr Bonython said that the public's attitude to the police in S.A. was such that he was sure a recent incident in Sydney where members of the public failed to assist two constables who were being attacked, could not happen here. . . .

Many South Australians may feel that Mr Bonython was over-stating his case. Inter-colonial and inter-state population move-ments have gone far towards establishing a general Australian outlook which, in this as in other ways, naturally derives mainly from traditions which early struck root in New South Wales, the oldest colony and, except during the last half of the nineteenth century, the most heavily populated. As R. W. Dale wrote in 1889:

> The development of the typical Australian character has at no time been subjected to any violent disturbance. Among the people of New South Wales I thought that I found those qualities of life and temperament which distinguish all the colonies from the mother country; and I did not observe those secondary characteristics which belong to the special types exhibited in Victoria and South Australia.

The fact that no convicts and relatively few Irishmen emigrated directly to South Australia explains some real differences in out-look which are still discernible, especially in Adelaide and the thickly-settled agricultural districts near it.[10] But the dry, pastoral interior of the state is separated from the station country of New South Wales and Queensland by nothing but a line on the map. Since occupation of the interior began a hundred and fifty years ago almost every observer of outback life has been forcibly struck by the extreme mobility of the pastoral population, and especially of the wage-earning part of it in which we are interested. This mobility has naturally resulted in a diffusing of attitudes and values throughout the interior regardless of state boundaries, and it is to be doubted whether Mr Bonython's re-marks are as true of South Australian station-hands as they are of the solid citizens of Adelaide. The songs of the bushmen graphi-cally reflect both their nomadic habits and their disrespect for policemen and the law they were employed to enforce. As one version of *The Overlander* has it:

> No bounds have we to our estates
> From Normanton to Bass's Straits;
> We're not fenced in with walls or gates—
> No monarch's realms are grander.
> Our sheep and cattle eat their fill,
> And wander blithely at their will
> O'er forest, valley, plain or hill,
> Free as an Overlander.

> We pay no licence or assess,
> Our flocks—they never grow much less—
> But gather on the road I guess,
>   As onward still we wander.
> We vote assessments all a sham,
> Nor care for licences a flam,
> For free selectors, not a d—n,
>   Says every Overlander.[11]

South Australia and Western Australia were most completely insulated, by distance as well as by their lack of convict origins, from the social attitudes emanating from 'Botany Bay'. Yet, even in these colonies, almost from the moments of their founding, the manners and *mores* reflected in the convicts' and pastoral workers' ballads rapidly gained strength among the lower orders.

In part this was no doubt due to like conditions having like effects. The early labour shortage in Western Australia, for example, unalleviated by convicts, would alone have been enough to evoke in working men the saucy and independent attitude so much deplored by their masters on the other side of the continent. The Advocate General and Judge of the Colony's first Civil Court complained constantly that masters there were such only in name, being actually 'the slaves of their indentured servants'. He wrote:

> In my absence, —— does nothing, and if I speak to him — exit
> in a rage. I could send him to gaol, but I do not like this extremity,
> and yet I cannot afford to lose the advantage of his time, and pay
> £30, besides diet, to another in his place.[12]

But when we hear that, within two years of the first landing at Fremantle, workmen had 'got into the habit of demanding' a daily rum ration, we may suspect that manners were being directly influenced by those of early New South Wales and Van Diemen's Land. At the end of the following year, 1831, the Judge Advocate noticed:

> Great visitings among the neighbouring servants; seven or eight
> of them patrolling about; and all this is sure to end in drunkenness
> and mischief—they talk of forming a *club*! They have too much
> control over their masters already; and club-law would be a terrible
> exercise and increase of their power.[12]

And 'a man who had come from Van Diemen's land' seems to have been largely responsible for 'trouble' with the Aborigines. Relations had been fairly good until early in 1833 when this man saw some unoffending natives in the way: ' "Damn the rascals," said he, "I'll show you how we treat them in Van Diemen's Land," and immediately fired on them.'[12]

Samuel Sidney recorded in 1852:

> The timber of Australia is so different from that of Europe that English workmen are very helpless until instructed by bush hands. The first South Australian colonists could not even put up a fence until the overlanders and Tasmanians taught them how.[13]

Even before they set foot on the mainland some South Australian pioneers were taught, in 1836, how to bake a damper by two 'frontiersmen'—sealers named Whalley and Day who had lived with kidnapped Aboriginal women on Kangaroo Island since 1818.[14] In the early 1840's George French Angas found that bush men to the south-east of Adelaide and, even more surprisingly, in the doubly isolated wilderness of Eyre's Peninsula, had already acquired a perfect familiarity with Australian slang, which was largely convict-derived, and with the art and terminology of bush cooking. Bush slang was also established, at the same early date on the then pastoral frontier of Western Australia south of York.[15]

Nineteenth-century observers were no less struck by the essential mobility of the outback pastoral workers than they were by their unity. Anthony Trollope travelled extensively in the outback and spent some months in 1871 and again in 1875 staying on sheep stations, including that of his son Frederick, in western New South Wales. To him it seemed that:

> . . . the nomad tribe of pastoral labourer—of men who profess to be shepherds, boundary-riders, sheep-washers, shearers and the like— form altogether one of the strangest institutions ever known in a land, and one which to my eyes is more degrading and more injurious even than that other institution of sheep-stealing. It is common to all the Australian colonies . . . [16]

Trollope thought that these itinerant workmen were degraded by their customary right to receive free rations and shelter for the night in station 'huts', but he was not blind to their virtues. As Harris had noted of them half a century earlier when the convict element still predominated among them, though they might cheat and rob respectable people, they were honest and loyal to each other.[17] Also they were still, as in the time of Harris, very capable at performing practical bush tasks, and very prone to vary long periods of hard work by short bouts of tremendous drunkenness. As Trollope further wrote:

> The bulk of the labour is performed by a nomad tribe, who wander in quest of their work, and are hired only for a time. This is of course the case in regard to washing sheep and shearing them. It is equally so when fences are to be made, or ground to be cleared, or trees to be 'rung'. . . . For all these operations temporary work is of course required, and the squatter seldom knows whether the man he employs be married or single. They come and go, and are known by queer nicknames or are known by no names at all. They probably have their wives elsewhere, and return to them for a season. They are rough to look at, dirty in appearance, shaggy, with long hair, men who, when they are in the bush, live in huts, and hardly know what a bed is. But they work hard, and are both honest and civil. Theft among them is almost unknown. Men are constantly hired without any character but that which they give themselves; and the squatters find from experience that the men are able to do that which they declare themselves capable of performing. There will be exceptions, but such is the rule. Their one great fault is drunkenness—and yet they are sober to a marvel. As I have said before, they will work for months without touching spirits, but their very abstinence creates a craving desire which, when it is satisfied, will satisfy itself with nothing short of brutal excess.[18]

A just understanding of the distinctive ethos of the 'nomad tribesmen' is of cardinal importance for the understanding of many aspects of Australian history, both in the last century and subsequently. The pastoral industry was, and still is, the country's staple. Its nature, the nature of Australian geography, and the great though decreasing scarcity of white women in the outback, brought into being an itinerant rural proletariat, overwhelmingly masculine in composition and outlook. In the United States the cattle industry, during the stage of 'the open range', produced in the cowboys a not dissimilar social group, but its existence was brief[19] and, relative to the total population, its numbers were small. Throughout the nineteenth century as a whole the typical American frontiersman was a small individualist agricultural proprietor or farm labourer, not a cowboy or ranch-hand. In

Canada and New Zealand, too, the farmer was the typical frontiers-man. In South Africa the pastoral industry, though not relatively as important as in Australia, was the staple, but the working hands were Hottentots or Bantus, whose culture was so different from that of their Boer and British masters that any useful comparison between their life and influence, and those of the pastoral workers in Australia, is scarcely possible. For these reasons it is not too much to say that those whom Trollope designated the 'nomad tribe' constituted a singular social group possessing an ethos which, though similar to those of certain other communities distant in time and place, was in some ways unique.

Among the influences which shaped the life of the outback community the brute facts of Australian geography were probably most important. Scanty rainfall and great distances ensured that most of the habitable land could be occupied only sparsely and by pastoralists. In combination with nineteenth-century economic conditions, climatic factors ensured too that the typical station should be a very large unit employing many casual 'hands', but owned by a single man or company of substantial capital. If Australia had been occupied by the French or any other western European people, it is likely that somewhat the same kind of pastoral proletariat would have been shaped by the geographical and economic conditions. Still, there would have been important differences.

As it happened, the interior was occupied by British people who naturally brought with them much cultural luggage. Moreover, in the early period of the 'squatting rush', when the nomad tribe was forming, the vast majority of its members were British people of a certain type. At first convicts and ex-convicts tended the flocks of the advancing 'shepherd-kings', and at least until 1851 these pioneers predominated in influence and prestige, if not in numbers. But the germ of the distinctive 'outback' ethos was not simply the result of climatic and economic conditions, nor of national and social traditions brought with them by the 'government men' who first opened up the 'new country' beyond the Great Divide. It sprang rather from their struggle to assimilate themselves and their *mores* to the strange environment. We shall find much evidence to suggest that the main features of the new tradition were already fixed before 1851. A considerable number of the gold-seekers and of the later immigrants who found their way to the western plains differed from most of their predecessors in having a middle-class background. They influenced the 'bush' outlook in certain ways, but in the upshot its main features were strengthened, modified in certain directions perhaps, but not fundamentally changed.

Although the pastoral proletariat formed a recognizably distinct social group it was obviously not, as has been said, completely isolated from the rest of colonial society. From 1813 when Blaxland, Lawson, young Wentworth and their convict 'hands' struggled back across the Blue Mountains, there was a constant coming and going of men, and resulting exchange of manners and ideas, between the coastal cities and the hinterland. But the strength of outback influence is indicated by the very phrase used, in the first half of the nineteenth century, to describe Sydney roughs. These rowdy, 'flash' plebeians took some pains to stress the differences between themselves and respectable immigrants. Many were Australian born and all liked to behave in what they considered truly 'Currency' or colonial ways. This involved their imitating 'up-country' manners, for the bushman was axiomatically more 'Australian', and hence differed more from the Simon Pure Briton, than the flashest Currency Lad in the whole of Sydney Town. Life in a bark hut on the Bogan necessarily changed a newcomer's manners and ideas more rapidly than life in a George Street cottage. Hence the roughs of early Sydney, affecting outback styles of dress and behaviour, were known as the 'Cabbage-tree Hat Mob'.

The cabbage-tree palm (*Livistona australis*) grew only in the rain-forests between the Great Dividing Range and the Pacific, being very common in the Illawarra district which was one of the earliest 'frontier' areas. The heart or bud at the growing tip of the palm was a substitute for cabbage among the early settlers and cedar-getters, and the pinnate fronds were woven into broad-brimmed, flat-crowned, 'cabbage-tree hats'. When the 'squatting rush' to the interior began in the late 1820's, this indigenous hat had already become standard wear among bushmen and, like the stockwhip, a potent symbol of outback values. Thus the cabbage-tree hat migrated with the frontier to the western plains, many hundreds of miles from the nearest source of the raw material from which it was made. Plaiting these hats was a favourite pastime among shepherds, whose occupation was an extraordinarily lazy and lonely one. They remained standard wear for stockmen and others until nearly the end of the nineteenth century, though by about 1880 a cabbage-tree hat might cost up to five pounds.[20]

From the beginning, then, outback manners and *mores*, working upwards from the lowest strata of society and outwards from the interior, subtly influenced those of the whole population. Yet for long this was largely an unconscious process recorded in folklore and to some extent in popular speech, but largely unreflected in formal literature. Towards the end of the nineteenth century, when the occupation of the interior had been virtually completed, it was possible to look back and sense what had been happening. Australians generally became actively conscious, not to say self-conscious, of the distinctive 'bush' ethos, and of its value as an expression and symbol of nationalism. Through the trade union movement, through such periodicals as the Sydney *Bulletin*, the *Lone Hand*, or the Queensland *Worker*, and through the work of literary men like Furphy, Lawson or Paterson, the attitudes and values of the nomad tribe were made the principal ingredient of a national *mystique*. Just when the results of public education acts, improved communications, and innumerable other factors were administering the *coup de grâce* to the actual bushman of the nineteenth century, his idealized shade became the national culture-hero of the twentieth. Though some shearers are now said to drive to their work in wireless-equipped motor-cars, the influence of the 'noble bushman' on Australian life and literature is still strong. In the next chapter we shall consider some of the most important elements which contributed to the birth of his tribe.

CHAPTER I

1   B. Fitzpatrick, *The British Empire in Australia*, Melbourne 1941, pp. 384-8; N. G. Butlin, 'Company Ownership of New South Wales Pastoral Stations', *Historical Studies: Australia and New Zealand*, May 1950; and cp. 'Times Special Correspondent', *Letters from Queensland*, London 1893, pp. 70-2.

2   H. W. Haygarth, *Recollections of Bush Life in Australia during a Residence of Eight Years in the Interior*, London 1848, p. 96 ff.

3   *Gallops and Gossips in the Bush of Australia*, London 1854, p. 58.

4   B. Fitzpatrick, *op. cit.*, p. 59; E. G. Shann, *Economic History of Australia*, Sydney 1948 ed., pp. 207-11, 233.

5 John Henderson, *Excursions and Adventures in New South Wales; with Pictures of Squatting Life in the Bush*, etc., 2 vols., London 1851, vol. 2, p. 244; 'Many most distressing cases came within my own knowledge; and when we hear of such things as of an old military officer reduced to the necessity of letting himself out to hire as a bullock driver; or of a shepherd suing his master for a year's wages . . . the pass at which things had arrived can be imagined.'

6 'Tom Collins' (Joseph Furphy), *Such is Life*, Sydney 1948 ed., p. 205 ff.

7 Vance Palmer, *Legend of the Nineties*, Melbourne 1954, p. 109.

8 Percy F. Rowland, *The New Nation*, London 1903, p. 119 ff.

9 cp. F. Adams, *The Australians: A Social Sketch*, London 1893, pp. 12-13; 'In another hundred years the man of the Interior—the veritable "bushman"—will be as far removed from the man of the sea-slope as the Northern Frenchman from the Southern, as the Castilian from the Andalusian . . . ', and *passim*.

10 R. E. N. Twopeny, *Town Life in Australia*, London 1883, p. 99. Discussing larrikinism (in 1883) the author wonders, in vain, how it can be combated in 'communities whose sympathies are so essentially democratic as those of Victoria and New South Wales—for in Adelaide the police has still the upper hand'.

11 This version is from *The 'Native Companion' Songster*, Brisbane 1889.

12 G. F. Moore, *Diary of Ten Years' Eventful Life of an Early Settler in Western Australia*, etc., London 1884, pp. 91, 183-5, 196-7.

13 *Three Colonies of Australia*, etc., London 1852, pp. 307-8.

14 *First Report of South Australian Company*, London 1837, 2nd Supplement, p. 25.

15 E. W. Landor, *The Bushman: or, Life in a New Country*, London 1847, p. 263.

16 *Australia and New Zealand*, Melbourne 1876 ed., p. 69.

17 'An Emigrant Mechanic' (Alexander Harris), *Settlers and Convicts*, ed. C. M. H. Clark, Melbourne 1953 (first published 1847), p. 24.

18 Anthony Trollope, *op. cit.*, p. 202.

19 From about 1866 to 1885. See W. P. Webb, *The Great Plains*, Oxford 1931, pp. 205-7.

20 'An Emigrant Mechanic', *op. cit.*, p. 26; Andrew Crombie, *After Sixty Years, or Recollections of an Australian Bushman*, Brisbane 1927, pp. 109-10.

THE FOUNDING FATHERS

I'll give the law a little shock—remember what I say:
They'll yet regret they sent Jim Jones in chains to
Botany Bay.

ENGLAND has her Angles, Saxons and Jutes, and America he₁
Pilgrim Fathers. Probably the central American republic of San
Salvador, with a population approximately equal to that of Melbourne, romanticizes the memory of certain sixteenth-century
conquistadores. But we Australians often display a certain
queasiness in recalling our founding fathers. Even to-day many
prefer not to remember that for nearly the first half-century of
its existence White Australia was, primarily, an extensive gaol.
Yet recognition of this fact is basic to any understanding of social
mores in the early period when an Australian tradition was forming. In this chapter we shall find reason to think that convict
influence on Australian society was very much more important
than has usually been supposed. The following table gives the
number of convicts, of ex-convicts or emancipists, of colonial-
born or 'Currency' persons, and of free immigrants in the New
South Wales population in 1828, 1841, and 1851:[1]

TABLE I

	Convicts	Emancipists	Currency	Free Immigrants
1828	15,668 (43%)	7,530 (20%)	8,727 (24%)	4,673 (13%)
1841	26,453 (23%)	18,257 (16%)	28,657 (24%)	43,621 (37%)
1851	2,693 (1·5%)	26,629 (14%)	81,391 (43%)	76,530 (41%)

Most writers who have touched upon early Australian demo-
graphic changes have tended to concentrate attention upon the

'swamping' of those whom Mudie christened the 'felonry'[2] of New South Wales by the rapidly increasing number of free persons, colonial-born and immigrant. Often the emancipists also are added to these latter groups. It may be that this approach stems from a conscious or unconscious desire to minimize the influence of convicts in Australian history, rather than from a desire to understand it. We shall see that in manners and social outlook, even more than in the political struggles of the time, the Currency Lads tended to align themselves with the emancipist class rather than with the more respectable of the free immigrants.[3]

If we take the Currency population as having more in common, socially and traditionally, with the convict and emancipist body than with that of the respectable free immigrant and official classes, we may draw from Table I the following figures:

TABLE II

	Convicts, Emancipists and Currency	Free Immigrants
1828	31,925 (87%)	4,673 (13%)
1841	73,367 (63%)	43,621 (37%)
1851	110,713 (59%)	76,530 (41%)

If these figures be expressed (very approximately) as ratios, we have:

TABLE III

	Ratio of Convicts, Emancipists and Currency to Free Immigrants
1828	7 : 1
1841	3 : 2
1851	3 : 2

The approximately constant proportion between the two groups for the last pre-Gold-Rush decade is very interesting. It is consistent with the idea that certain distinctively Australian attitudes may have then been formed, and have become stabilized enough to persist through the more real 'swamping' of the felon strain by the tidal wave of immigrants which arrived during the subsequent decade and later. It need hardly be said that the physical transmission of criminal or other traits from parents to children is not being implied. Unlike eye and hair colours, social attitudes and traditions are not physically inherited, but learnt from parents, playmates, friends and teachers. In this way the children of even the most highly respectable free immigrants often absorbed ideas and manners from the felonry. As Charles Darwin noticed in 1836:

> There are many serious drawbacks to the comforts of a family. the chief of which, perhaps, is being surrounded by convict servants. How thoroughly odious to every feeling, to be waited on by a man who the day before, perhaps, was flogged, from your representation, for some trifling misdemeanour. The female servants are, of course, much worse; hence children learn the vilest expressions, and it is fortunate if not equally vile ideas.

The reminiscences of the son of a Moreton Bay pioneer show that the ideas thus imbibed were not always vile, at least by current Australian standards. Hatred of the tell-tale and informer is not, of course, a trait uniquely Irish or Australian, but there is evidence to suggest that it is a much more widely held sentiment here than, for example, in contemporary U.S.A.[4] This passion was felt all the more strongly by the convicts because so many of them were Irishmen like 'poor Kelly', a convict clerk who tutored young Tom Petrie:

> Poor Kelly . . . would never tell on me. Although I used to get many a thrashing from father for not knowing my lessons, and Kelly got many a scolding for not getting me along better, he would never 'split' on me. I used to take him now and again a bit of tobacco and a little tea and sugar, or a piece of bread, all unknown to my father, and sometimes I gave the other prisoners some, so that I was a great favourite among them, and no matter what I did they never let it out. . . . My brothers, like myself, were in great favour with the convicts, as they used also to bring food and tobacco to them. The prisoners would do anything for us.
>
> A convict called 'Joe Goosey', an odd job man, was much disliked by the others, because he told tales about them. . . . The convicts could not stand a 'tell-tale' at any price, and poor 'Joe Goosey', a soft sort of a fellow, had anything but a pleasant life among them.[5]

If the children of prominent free families were thus influenced by the prisoners' outlook, we may take it that the feeling of emancipists and colonial-born people was affected not less strongly.

Up to 1851 in the mother colony of New South Wales proper (then including Queensland) this broad group of people, more or less directly influenced by convict attitudes, formed quite a large majority of the population. It is equally clear that the smaller group of free immigrants included almost all officials, magistrates and other persons possessed of formal power and prestige. Nevertheless, as a distinctive Australian ethos developed, it drew far more upon the habits and outlook of the larger and socially inferior group than upon those of the smaller and more powerful one, for two reasons.

First, the colonial *élite* tended to keep up respectable connections with 'home', to send their sons there to be educated, perhaps to return there themselves. Even as late as the 1880's an English observer, speaking of squatters and other 'good fellows' in Queensland, wrote: 'every other man is an Englishman . . . and nearly all intend to go home some day.'[6] Their natural bent was to preserve intact, or with minimum modifications, the values of contemporary British society. The career of the first W. C. Wentworth shows that this was sometimes true even of the wealthier people among the native-born; and the novels of Henry Handel Richardson and Martin Boyd reflect the tendency for this tradition to persist in well-to-do families even after the lapse of several generations in Australia. Members of the emancipist-Currency-Lad group, on the other hand, nearly always regarded Australia as their home. When, as early as 1820, Bigge observed: 'of the older inhabitants there are very few who do not regard the colony as their home,' the context makes it clear that he was including all the colonial-born, old or young, among the self-elected Australians.

By the middle 1840's this group, which knew and wished to know no other home than Australia, far outnumbered convicts and emancipists combined. Along with the fashion for stockwhips and cabbage-tree hats there grew up manners and values which were largely a direct response to the new environment, and which hence were much more likely to flourish than transplanted, and relatively unadulterated, British values. *The Emigrant Family*

(1849), the novel by Harris, provides a vivid contemporary caricature of what was happening:

> 'What a queer lot most of these emigrants are,' said Charlie. 'They seem like a set of children. They have no notion how to help themselves till they've been here half the length of a man's life.'
> 'Not all of them, Charlie. Look at all those old commissaries: how soon *they* feather their nests.'
> 'Ay, ay: but that's a different thing: it's in a manner their trade. This old chap at the Rocky Springs, the men tell me, never gives an order himself; and he looks just as if he'd done nothing all his life but sit and munch roast beef between the muzzles of two cannon.'

The second reason for the prevalence of the convict-derived ethos is perhaps less obvious but more far-reaching. Australia is one of the very few countries whose whole development has taken place since the beginnings of the Industrial Revolution. In all English-speaking countries the nineteenth century saw the dilution and partial conquest of traditional and aristocratic values by those of the middle and lower classes. In pre-Gold-Rush Australia this process was intensified because there was no *traditional* aristocracy and a relatively very small 'middle class'. The exclusionist 'upper class' in early Australia was composed mainly of middle-class Britons, possessed often of quite modest amounts of capital. Between this group of 4,477 squatters, importers, bankers and professional men and the 50,158 mechanics, labourers, servants and so on, there were listed in the New South Wales census of 1841 only 1,774 'shop-keepers and other retail dealers'. These figures give a 'middle class' of only 3·1 per cent. In 1843 John Hood wrote in his *Australia and the East*:

> At the two meetings I have attended, the two opposite principles advocated, though both were covered under the cloak of great moderation, were ultra-Toryism and ultra-Radicalism. There does not seem to be any middle class in the colony of sufficient weight to take a leading part; or if such a class exists, it appears, at present, to have no inclination to mix itself up in public matters.

Thus the erosion of aristocratic traditions was accelerated here by the disproportionate weight of the lower-class group, embracing the vast majority of convicts, emancipists, Currency people and even after a few years spent in Australia, of the working people among the free immigrants. Mundy, the conservative Adjutant-General of New South Wales, sensed what was happening when he wrote sadly, about 1848:

> I have always thought the song or whistle of man or maiden a sort of indirect compliment to those they serve under; and I wonder why I so seldom heard in Australia, these tokens of a cheerful heart. 'The milkmaid's song!' 'The ploughboy whistling o'er the lea!'—in New Holland! As well might you expect to hear the robin or the black-bird warbling in a gum-tree! Can it be that the original character and temper of labour has been engrafted permanently on the soil—that the sullen tone of the original convict serf has descended to the free servant of to-day? Or is it that the foedality of feeling existing between master and man has departed altogether out of the land?—is departing out of *all* lands? I have been inclined to think so ever since the last groom and valet I had at home—a modernising fellow, who attended his club twice a week—taught me to look upon my-self, not as his master but as his *employer*. There was a good deal of significance, me thought, in that substitution of title.

The same phenomena were hailed with delight by the radical spokesman, J. D. Lang, who recognized that when the Gold Rush began Australia was 'a land where already perhaps more than in any other part of the world "a man's a man for a' that" '.[7]

If convict and lower-class influences on manners were as signifi-cant as has been argued above, it becomes important to examine their nature. After the convict period itself had closed, most writers were for long inclined either to avoid the subject or to assume, at least tacitly, that the influence of these first pioneers had been almost wholly deplorable. The climate of prevailing opinion is vividly implied by the half-apologetic, half-defiant air with which a clergyman introduced discussion of the subject in 1867:

> It is not easy escaping the conviction, and it has never been, I presume, attempted to be denied, that convictism has tended in no small degree to give a distinct character and complexion to certain phases of Australian life which it would not have otherwise worn, and a knowledge of this constitutes no small part of that much-vaunted 'Colonial experience', extolled as the foundation of success. 'What is the use of a friend,' I have heard one man say, 'but to take the use of him?'[8]

About thirty or forty years ago opinion swung towards the

opposite extreme. 'The greatest English criminals remained in England,' wrote G. A. Wood in 1921, and he meant, not those raised to the eminence of Tyburn tree, but those raised above their fellows by birth, wealth or position, 'the men who plundered their country in habitual political robbery'. To-day we should be able to see the first Australian pioneers as they were. The truth is that most of them were habitual criminals, whether great or small. It is also true that economic and social conditions in Britain were such as to drive a great many people to crime.

In view of the state of British society during and after the Napoleonic Wars it would have been surprising indeed if there had not been a great many hardened criminals. During the eighteenth century the Agrarian Revolution and its accompanying enclosure acts multiplied the number of dispossessed peasant farmers and unemployed farm-hands as fast as it increased primary production. The demand for 'hands' in the rising industrial towns seldom kept pace with the growth in numbers of those seeking work. Not infrequently men had to steal or starve.[9] One result, as Fitzpatrick has pointed out, was that between the Glorious Revolution of 1688 and the day, a century later, when the First Fleet discharged its wretched cargo on the shores of Port Jackson, the number of capital crimes on the English statute book increased from fifty to about a hundred and fifty. It is true that after 1820 the reforms of Peel, Brougham and Lord John Russell mitigated the severity of the laws, though but slightly by modern standards. On the other hand it is a commonplace of historical writing that during the first half of the nineteenth century, particularly up to and including the decade 1830-40, living conditions for the poor were probably harder than at any other period in Britain since the Middle Ages.[10]

There is ample testimony that, for unskilled men with large families, even if they were fortunate enough to have constant work, it was almost impossible to keep body and soul together. But these facts hardly validate Wood's remark that 'the greatest English criminals remained in England'. Mass poverty and misery were perhaps inevitable accompaniments of the beginning of the industrial system. At all events they have accompanied its early stages not only in England but in every country where industrialization has taken place. On the other hand recognition of social evils which tended to manufacture criminals, while it may, in the final analysis, absolve most of them from emotionally charged moral blame, should not lead the historian to suppose that the transports were filled with virtuous men and women. Even if they were not confirmed in vicious courses on conviction, many of them were corrupted by the conditions in the transports, and by the effects of the 'system' on those who drew an unlucky ticket in the lottery which it was.[11] Perhaps the best prisoners merited Vance Palmer's description of them 'as people distinguished from their neighbours only by a lighter regard for property or a fainter capacity for self-control in the presence of a landlord'.

The vast majority of the convicts were unskilled or semi-skilled working-class people, as probably were the vast majority of the assisted immigrants of the 1830's and 1840's.[12] Most of the immigrants were townsmen,[13] though some of these may have had a not very remote rural background, being redundant farm-workers or the children of countrymen forced to the towns in search of work. Generally speaking the townsmen were the more cunning and adaptable, the countrymen stronger but duller, or at least more set in their traditional ways. There is even some reason to think that townsmen, because of their adaptability and because they had nothing to un-learn about rural work, often made the better bush-workers.[14] Cunningham gives an amusing picture of the two groups as he saw them on the transports in the early 1820's:

> The cockneys are, of course, beyond all dispute the worst, and a leaven of a dozen of these is enough to infect a thousand of the country *yokels*, with whom peace is generally the order of the day. Such a number of these *townies* will keep a hundred of the others in subjection, from the manner in which they cling together, and from their overwhelming *oratorical* abilities. The less gifted *yokels* have not a chance with them, if the strong hand of power is not stretched out for their protection. A ship which took in her *yokel* cargo in the river, sailed round to Portsmouth to fill up with a *dunnage* (a sea-phrase signifying a kind of make-weight) of thirty *townies*, when the whole boast of the simple *yokels*, while proceeding round, was, how they would 'serve out' the *townies* on the voyage: but before they were a week together, the handful of *Spartans* left the others scarcely a pair of decent trousers to clothe their nakedness.

Most desperate combats sometimes take place between the two parties in badly regulated ships, and murder has often nearly ensued; for when the bristles of the *yokels* are fairly up, they level the cockneys as if they were playing at ninepins; *bullying* being the chief qualification of the latter.

The predominance of the 'cockneys' in numbers, prestige, and 'oratorical abilities' probably accounts for the basic qualities of what Mitchell calls 'Broad Australian' speech, but it would be misleading to exaggerate the difference in outlook between the urban and rural labouring classes from which most of the convicts were drawn. The songs sung by both groups were usually interchangeable, and there is little doubt but that they mirrored faithfully the social outlook of those who sang them. A London Ragged School master wrote in 1851:

> [The poor] have a literature of their own, though they seldom read, and . . . that literature represents correctly their feelings and ways of thinking. . . . The form of literature which best suits the alley is the ballad—a striking proof of the influence which poetry combined with music possesses over the human mind, even when most hardened and depraved . . . and the people are influenced by their ballads to an extent which a casual observer would not readily credit.[15]

There is also no doubt but that the prisoners brought their songs with them in the transports to Australia. Cunningham, who conducted four shiploads of felons to New South Wales, without, he was proud to claim, losing a single individual, wrote of their embarkation:

> Before leaving the hulk, the convicts are thoroughly clothed in new suits and ironed; and it is curious to observe with what nonchalance some of these fellows will turn the jingling of their chains into music whereto they dance and sing.

He encouraged them to keep it up throughout the voyage, 'all day long if they pleased', as he sensibly believed it was good for their health. Another naval surgeon, T. B. Wilson, recorded that his maxim was 'never to permit the slightest *slang* expression to be used, nor *flash* songs to be sung, nor swearing'; but he added

sadly that it was 'nearly impossible to restrain their almost unconquerable propensity [for song and ribaldry] while below'. The
schoolmaster, quoted above, also states that many ballads were
'songs of transports, and felons of various grades', and he quotes
a few lines of one as an example:

> It was a few hours after her father did appear,
> And march'd me back to Omer gaol in the county of Tyrone,
> And there I was transported from Erin's lovely home;
> When I heard my sentence it grieved my heart full sore,
> And parting from my true love it grieved me ten times more.

In 1954 the whole of this ballad was sung to me by Mrs Mary
Byrnes, a lady of old Irish-Australian stock. She had learnt it from
folk-singers on the western slopes of the Blue Mountains during
her girlhood in the 1890's. The equivalent lines had become:

> It's when we thought all danger past her father did appear,
> Which soon did separate me from the arms of my dear.
> He marched me off to Honeford gaol in the county of Tyrone,
> From which I was transported from Erin's lovely home.
> When I received my sentence, it grieved my heart full sore,
> To leave my home behind me, it grieved me ten times more.

Although in the first half of the nineteenth century many,
perhaps most, ballads were especially written for the market by
professional street ballad-singers or 'chaunters', it would be a mis-
take to imagine that therefore they were not folk-songs but self-
conscious, literary work. The chaunters were poor, semi-literate
men who shared fully the living conditions and attitudes of their
customers. In his *London Labour and the London Poor* Henry
Mayhew gives a thumbnail autobiography of a typical chaunter.
In 1848 this man told Mayhew:

> I am what may be termed a regular street ballad-singer. When I
> was thirteen years old . . . I turned into the streets in consequence
> of the harsh treatment I met with [at home]. . . . I lived at this time
> upon the refuse I picked up in the streets—cabbage-stumps out of
> the market, orange-peel and such like. . . . Having a tidy voice of
> my own . . . I was going on for fourteen when I first took to [ballad-
> singing] and I have stuck to the business ever since. Of the regular
> street ballad-singers there are not less than 250 in and about Lon-

don . . . who live solely by ballad-singing and selling ballads and
song-books. . . . There are five known authors for the Seven Dials
Press, and they are all ballad-singers. I am one of these myself. The
little knowledge I have I picked up bit by bit, so that I hardly know
how I came by it. I certainly knew my letters before I left home,
and I have got the rest off the dead walls and out of the papers and
ballads I have been selling. I write most of the Newgate ballads now
for the printers in the Dials, and indeed, anything that turns up. I
get a shilling for 'a copy of verses written by the wretched culprit
the night previous to his execution'. I did the helegy . . . on Rush's
execution. It was supposed, like the rest, to be written by the culprit
himself, and was particular penitent. I didn't write that to order—I
knew they would want a copy of verses from the culprit. The publishers read it over and said, 'That's the thing for the street public.'
I only got a shilling for Rush. Indeed they are all the same price,
no matter how popular they may be. . . .

It is natural to suppose that transportation ballads would have
been especially popular among our pioneers, and there is evidence
to show that this was, in fact, the case. As late as 1888 a Sydney
Bulletin correspondent, writing on *Bush Songs*, recorded:

Over twenty years back . . . at the station hut and during shearing time where a very representative gathering of bushmen was to
be found, the nasal quaver of the 'old hand' might be heard as he
vaunted the glories of some old-time bushranger . . . or gave a
doggerel reminiscence of the ill-famed island prison . . . where

'They yoked us up like horses
All in Van Dieman's [*sic*] Land.'[16]

And since 1950 I have talked with many surviving ballad-singers
who remember transportation ballads, or fragments of them, which
they learnt from even older Australians in the last decade or two
of the last century. Judging by the number, variety, and widespread provenance of extant versions of 'Van Diemen's Land', this
song was perhaps the most popular and typical of all transportation ballads; but we may take as an example 'Adieu to Old England' which, though hardly less typical, is much less well known.
It's 'Come-all ye' invocation to 'wild young native lads' points
also to the direct derivation, suggested above, of Currency
attitudes from convict ones:

Adieu to Old England

or

The Transport's Farewell

(*Air*: 'Native Lad')

Come all you wild young native lads
    Wherever you may be,
One moment pay attention
    And listen unto me.
i am a poor unhappy soul,
    Within those walls i lay
My awful sentence is pronounced,
    I am bound for Botany Bay.

I was brought up in tenderness,
    My parents' sole delight.
They never could be hapy
    But when i was in their sight.
They nourished my tender yrs
    And Oft to me would say,
Avoid all evil company
    Lest the lead you astray.

My parents bound me prentice
    All in fair Devonshire
To a linen Draper,
    The truth you soon shall hear.
I bore an excellent character,
    My master loved me well,
Till in a harlot's company
    Unfortunately I fell.

In the gayest of splendour
    I maintained this lofty dame,
But when my money spent
    She treated me with disdain.
She said go robe your master,
    He has it in great store,
If some money you don't get
    You'll see my face no more.

To her bad advice I yielded
    And to my Master went;
To plunder him of what i could,
    It was my full intent.
Of costly robes and money too
    I took as you shall hear
All from the best of masters,
    As to me did appear.

The next robbery i committed,
    It was on a gentleman,
Of full 500 sovereigns
    He placed them in my hand.
Taken i was for this sad crime,
    To Exeter sent me;
The Harlot then foresook me quite
    In this extremely.

The assizes then drew near,
    Before the Judge i stand.
My prosecutor then swore that
    I was the very man.
My aged parents dear, they
    So bitterly did cry,
Oh must we with a bleeding heart
    Bid our fair boy good bye.

My master and friends
    As they stood in the hall,
What floods of tears they shed,
    And for mercy did call.
The cruel jade no mercy shew'd
    But unto me did say,
My lad you're transported—
    And to Botany Bay.[17]

During the twenty or thirty years prior to 1840, when the export of convicts to Australia was at its height, the living and working conditions of the poor in Great Britain were probably changing more rapidly than at any other period for a century before or afterwards. Nevertheless it was an age of reform, not of revolution. The people who listened to the chaunters and sang their songs were an integral part of an old society, and one which has proved, since the seventeenth century, to be perhaps the most stable in the world. Yet the Ragged School master of 1851 thought 'the principles introduced into these ballads most immoral, and dangerous to society'. Looking back now, it is difficult at first glance to see why. In the above transportation ballad, or in 'Van Diemen's Land', or in 'Botany Bay', there is surely no fundamental conflict, in principle, with the famous lines from a hymn of the Victorian age:

> The rich man in his castle, the poor man at his gate,
> God made them, high or lowly, and order'd their estate.

Another quotation from the schoolmaster's diary will help in understanding:

> Throughout these songs there is not the least expression of remorse, nor do their authors attempt to make the victims of the law give vent to feelings of contrition or sorrow for the past, nor do they ever suggest that the criminal loses more than his liberty by the punishment awarded for his crimes. He is always made to speak of returning to his friends, as if nothing out of the way had happened; and I have remarked, in a former part of my diary, that this is the actual state of the case in their society. They have little or no feeling of shame; their behaviour would lead to the belief that they rather gloried in their degradation than otherwise. This is, perhaps, the most unpromising feature in their character. . . .

The judgement is at once both penetrating and superficial. 'Adieu to Old England' carries a heavier burden of conventional moralizing than do most transportation ballads, but even so the distress of the hero and his friends clearly springs from the fact that he has been discovered, and not in the least from anything approaching truly felt moral penitence. By members of the social class to which they belonged, poachers and pickpockets were obviously accepted as normal, though unlucky people, and it was this fact which respectable middle-class contemporaries found shocking. Seeing the conventional moralizing for what it was, as little more than part of the rogues' professional stock-in-trade, they completely failed to see that it was also an indirect, and indeed largely unconscious, tribute to the prestige of middle-class morality, and so to the stability of contemporary society. While many poor men lived by breaking the rules and took it for granted that they should do so, they tended to take it equally for granted that the rules themselves were an immutable part of the natural order of things. In their ballads working-class people complained of their hard lot, but rarely indeed did they question the basic assumptions on which society rested.

However the stability of English society was not, and could not have been, carried intact across half the world by the new colonists. Respect for the squire, based on traditional obligations which were, or had been, at least to some extent mutual, was not often transformed into respect for a commercial slave-master whose wealth was often ill-gotten and nearly always recently acquired. James Backhouse wrote in 1843:

> People in England maintaining a good character are little aware how much of what gains them this character they owe to the oversight of those by whom they are continually surrounded, and how little to principle. When they emigrate to a country where this oversight is withdrawn, too generally but little that has the appearance of principle remains.

And in 1847 E. W. Landor noted exactly the same tendency in the then non-convict colony of Western Australia. Many of the convicts and paupers who made up the cargoes of transports and emigrant ships must have been demoralized to the point of becoming uninterested in, and even incapable of, honest work. Yet, lazy, drunken and dissolute though so many of them were, the conditions in which they existed undoubtedly fostered the growth of some positive qualities which they brought across the oceans with them.

First among these was a certain group or class solidarity indicated by the maxim that 'there is honour among thieves'. After all, this strong collectivist sentiment of group loyalty is, apart from his own individual cunning, the criminal's sole means of defence against the overwhelmingly powerful organs of state authority. On the other hand the very fact of his criminality presupposes his possession of unusually strong individualist leanings. He is, by definition, anti-social. But when the criminal becomes a long-term convict, his scope for exercising individual cunning is very severely limited, while the forces impelling him towards social, collectivist behaviour (within his own group) are correspondingly strengthened. All that we know about the convicts shows that this egalitarian class solidarity was the one human trait which usually remained to all but the most brutalized of them after the 'system' had done its best or its worst. A 'Resident of Twelve Years' Experience' wrote in 1849:

> Perhaps the worst trait in the character of the convict population is the ill feeling they display to all except their own class. A spirit of freemasonry exists among them to a great extent, and the greater the ruffian the greater pet he is. A man who endeavours to become reformed, or to give satisfaction to his master, is barely tolerated, while he who has been subjected to excessive secondary punishments at the penal settlements of Morton Bay or Norfolk Island is considered a hero.

There is abundant evidence that the following vignette from Marcus Clarke's *Term of His Natural Life* reflects faithfully the strength of the sentiment. Gabbet, the utterly debased cannibal prisoner, has just been re-captured after 'bolting' from the Macquarie Harbour penal establishment. Clarke almost certainly based the character of Maurice Frere on that of the real-life John Price,[18] Commandant of Norfolk Island (1848-53):

> 'How many mates had he?' asked Maurice, watching the champing jaws as one looks at a strange animal, and asking the question as though a 'mate' was something a convict was born with—like a mole, for instance.

There is some reason to think that this freemasonry of felonry may have been, to a certain extent, institutionalized. Many of the stories of William Astley ('Price Warung') about convict life were based on sound research, and their author also learnt directly from ex-convicts with whom he was friendly much about the 'system'. His story, *The Liberation of the First Three*, describes an 'underground' brotherhood whose organization centred round the 'convict oath':

> The five agreed . . . and . . . took the Convict Oath. They chanted the eight verses, which began:
>
> > 'Hand to hand,
> > On Earth, in Hell,
> > Sick or Well,
> > On Sea, on Land,
> > On the square, ever.'

And ended—the intervening verses dare not be quoted—

'Stiff or in Breath,
Lag or Free,
You and Me.
In Life, in Death,
On the Cross, never.

They chanted them with crossed and re-crossed hands, and the foot of each pressed to the foot of another. . . . So was fealty to their leader, honour to one another, plighted. The Convict Oath was a terrible thing; it was never broken without occasioning death to someone—not necessarily the violator. John Price died in 1857 because of a Convict Oath registered at Norfolk Island in the Forties.[19]

It would be easy, but probably wrong, to dismiss this as entirely the product of Astley's imagination, for in February 1830 a convict bolter from a road-gang described in court 'his swearing with their hands crossed to stand by them',[20] when he joined a gang of bushrangers. And in 1840 T. P. Macqueen declared roundly that convicts serving in road-gangs invariably established 'regulations of secrecy and fellowship' to which all were liable.

Another marked convict trait was resourcefulness, the ability to make piecemeal adjustments to changing circumstances, to make rough but serviceable implements from whatever scanty materials were to hand, and to be equally at home in a London tenement or gutter, an iron-gang on the Cowpastures road, or a bark hut beyond the Bathurst Plains. C. E. W. Bean notices this faculty for improvisation as being, at a much later period, an established characteristic of bushmen, and explains it, correctly enough, as a necessary response to outback conditions.[21] But the most successful improvisers among the first bushmen tended to be 'old hands'. Thus, when J. C. Byrne in 1839 drove nearly 1,000 head of cattle overland from Yass Plains to Adelaide, he chose for the enterprise:

chiefly 'old hands', many having been convicts long inured to every description of hardship, and caring little whether they lay down to rest within the hollow of a monster gum-tree, or the walls of a human habitation. Several years previously, two of the number had dwelt for some time amongst the aborigines, and were most experienced bushmen.[22]

That prisoners were often conspicuously untrustworthy and un-resourceful in relation to the work assigned them by their task-masters was only the reverse side of the medal. In their relationship with each other they were equally often loyal and enterprising.

However, the century-long preoccupation with the question of whether the convicts were, or were not, the sort of people one would like to have had for grandparents, has diverted attention from another matter not less interesting and important. Granted that most of the convicts were habitual criminals, whether petty or great, how did they and their offspring react to the unfamiliar Australian environment?

There is good reason for thinking that, generally speaking, the convicts changed markedly in many ways, most of which were for the better. Some were incorrigibles who ended their lives in the cells, or on the scaffold at Norfolk Island or some other place of secondary punishment. With many more, reformation, in any deep or spiritual sense, was certainly more apparent than real. Yet the fact remains that the great majority of the convicts became free men and women who at least kept out of prison and performed useful tasks in society. A letter from the Convict Department to the Colonial Adjutant-General, dated June 1850, stated that of the 60,000-odd prisoners transported to New South Wales during the whole period of the 'system',

> 38,000 are now filling respectable positions in life, and earning their livelihood in the most creditable manner. . . . Of the residue, death and departures from the colony will account for the greater part; and I am enabled to state that only 370 out of the whole are now undergoing punishment of any kind.[23]

Although the lawful earning of bread is not evidence of a changed and contrite heart, it may indicate a standard of morality not inferior to that of the 'untainted' gentlemen of the 'Rum Corps', their associates and successors. In 1843 John Hood wrote:

> If the truth must be told, the fortunes of many of the exclusionists themselves were not acquired by the purest means; close contracts, the gin or rum-shop, embarrassments wilfully created by insidious loans and ejectments, and other crooked paths, were used equally by both parties, bond and free.

And, after nine years as Governor, Macquarie wrote in 1819 to
J. T. Bigge:

> You already know that Nine-tenths of the population of this
> Colony are or have been Convicts, or the Children of Convicts. You
> have Yet perhaps to learn that these are the people who have
> Quietly submitted to the Laws and Regulations of the Colony, altho'
> informed by the *Free Settlers* and some of the Officers of Government
> that they were illegal! these are the Men who have tilled the Ground,
> who have built Houses and Ships, who have made wonderful Efforts,
> Considering the Disadvantages under which they have Acted, in
> Agriculture, in Maritime Speculations, and in Manufactures; these
> are the Men who, placed in the balance as Character, both Moral
> and political (at least since their Arrival here) in the opposite Scale
> to those Free Settlers (who Struggle for their Depression) whom you
> will find to preponderate [*sic*].[24]

How did this reform, or at least this change, come about? Not,
as has been too often implied, by the influence of virtuous emana-
tions from the southern sun or from the aromatic leaves of the
gum-trees. Contemporary observers were quite clear about the
much more mundane and material reasons for the metamorphosis.
Judge Therry wrote in his *Reminiscences*:

> Even in the class of the more depraved convicts transported for a
> serious crime, the instances of a reformed character were numerous
> and gratifying. London pickpockets and convicts from Dublin, Liver-
> pool and the large towns of the United Kingdom, who from their
> childhood upwards, had been brought up in ignorance, and had led
> lives of habitual crime, if not from principle, from obvious motives
> of interest in the prospect of becoming independent in a land of
> abundance, altered their course of conduct and became industrious
> members of society. . . .

Charles Darwin, after his visit to New South Wales in 1836, stated
a similar view:

> The worst feature in the whole case [the transportation system]
> is, that although there exists what may be called a legal reform, and
> comparatively little is committed which the law can touch, yet that
> any moral reform should take place appears to be quite out of the
> question. . . . On the whole, as a place of punishment, the object is
> scarcely gained; as a real system of reform it has failed, as perhaps
> would every other plan; but as a means of making men outwardly
> honest—of converting vagabonds most useless in one hemisphere

into active citizens of another, and thus giving birth to a new and splendid country—a grand centre of civilisation—it has succeeded to a degree perhaps unparalleled in history.

Judged from the viewpoint of its effect on the people, the greatest single difference between the old environment and the new was that in Australia there was a perennial labour shortage. Even during the country's first major depression of 1840-3, though there were workless men in Sydney, there were still jobs to be had 'up the country' if one went far enough. Moreover, the working people enjoyed a vastly higher standard of living than they had known in Britain. There, millions tasted meat once or twice a week if they were lucky. In Australia three square meals a day, including too often a surfeit of meat, was the unquestioned portion of everyone. Even convicts serving their sentences usually worked for fewer hours and ate more and better food than did labouring people at home. In 1812 ex-Governor Hunter was asked by the House of Commons Select Committee on Transportation, 'Could you judge at all what number chose to settle in the country?' He replied: 'I cannot say what proportion, but there were many who did return to this country. When I returned to England numbers applied to me for permission to go out again, for they said they could live there, but they could not live here.'[25]

Mundy wrote in 1846: 'In England and Ireland the permission to work hard from Monday morning to Saturday night, is a great boon; in Australia, the artisan and labourer has *leisure* as well as work.' Under these circumstances it is small wonder that the convicts' outlook, and that of their offspring, changed so rapidly. A condition of affairs in which jobs are more plentiful than men to do them always tends to evoke an attitude of 'manly independence' or, according to the point of view, insubordinate insolence in working people.

Many of the qualities which the pioneers brought with them were retained, or even accentuated by the comparatively bounteous environment. There is a wealth of testimony to the passion for gambling, and to the careless improvidence of many early Australians. 'A Gentleman Just Returned from the Settlement' wrote in 1808:

> To such excesses was the pursuit of gambling carried among the convicts that some have been known, after losing money, provisions,

and all their cloathing, to have staked their cloaths upon their wretched backs, standing in the midst of their associates naked, and as indifferent about it as the unconscious natives of the country. They have been seen playing at their favourite games of cribbage and all-fours, for six, eight, and ten dollars each game; and those who are not expert at these, instead of pence tossed up for dollars.[26]

To judge from contemporary accounts, no people on the face of the earth ever absorbed more alcohol per head of population, or swore so foully and fluently. In April 1850, when the oceanic tide of rum had long been ebbing, an intelligent world traveller, freshly arrived from the 'Barbary Coast' of California, wrote: 'I have really never been in any place yet where I saw so many drunkards as in Sydney, and, more disgustingly still, drunken women.' A few years earlier another observer had explained:

> The two most glaring vices, intoxication and profane swearing, prevail throughout the interior of New South Wales to an extent hardly conceivable but by those who have actually witnessed it. . . . From the force of constant example which is always so very contagious in this particular, the native-born youths often inherit this way of talking and grow gradually callous to its enormity, thus handing down to succeeding generations one of the most pernicious legacies of the old Botany Bay convicts.[27]

Pioneering conditions accentuated not only the dissolute habits, but also the toughness and adaptability of the pioneers; and the loneliness of bush life, no less than the brutalities of the system, accentuated their group solidarity. But much of their lip-service to conventional morality, and of their psychological acceptance of an inferior position in society, disappeared along with the abject poverty which in Britain had helped to condition these traits.

Very early the convicts had established for themselves a customary right to the more euphonious and dignified title of 'government men'. Charles Rowcroft wrote in 1843:

> But first I must warn you that we never speak of the convicts in this country by that term; we always call them 'government men', or on some occasions, prisoners; but we never use the word 'convict', which is considered by them an insulting term, and the expression therefore is, by all right-minded persons, carefully avoided.

By the 1820's the convicts had also composed many ballads which probably reflected their changing outlook.[28] Unfortunately, no Australian folk-song which can be dated with certainty before about 1820 appears to have survived, but 'Jim Jones', which refers to the notorious bushranger Jack Donahoe as though he were alive when it was composed,[29] probably belongs to the late 1820's. Its deep melancholy reminds the reader of the mood of 'Van Diemen's Land', and yet instead of the *pro forma* moralizing of that ballad or of 'Adieu to Old England', it shows a spirit of open and implacable defiance. Instead of an implicit acceptance of the rules of society, there is an explicit assumption that society itself is out of joint, and even a hint that in the new land society may be remoulded nearer to the heart's desire. Charles Macalister's *Old Pioneering Days in the Sunny South* gives the only surviving text of this interesting ballad:

O, listen for a moment lads, and hear me tell my tale—
How, o'er the sea from England's shore I was compelled to sail.

The jury says 'He's guilty, sir,' and says the judge, says he—
'For life, Jim Jones, I'm sending you across the stormy sea;

And take my tip, before you ship to join the Iron-gang,
Don't be too gay at Botany Bay, or else you'll surely hang—

Or else you'll surely hang,' he says, says he—'and after that, Jim Jones,
High up upon th' gallow-tree the crows will pick your bones—

You'll have no chance for mischief then; remember what I say,
They'll flog th' poachin' out of you, out there at Botany Bay.'

The winds blew high upon th' sea, and th' pirates came along,
But the soldiers on our convict ship were full five hundred strong.

They opened fire and somehow drove that pirate ship away.
I'd have rather joined that pirate ship than have come to Botany Bay.

For night and day the irons clang, and like poor galley slaves
We toil, and toil, and when we die must fill dishonoured graves.

But bye-and-bye I'll break my chains: into the bush I'll go,
And join the brave bushrangers there—Jack Donahoo and Co.;

And some dark night when everything is silent in the town
I'll kill the tyrants, one and all; and shoot th' floggers down:

I'll give th' law a little shock: remember what I say,
They'll yet regret they sent Jim Jones in chains to Botany Bay.

Obviously the outlook of Jim Jones, and of those who sang about him, differed from that of their like in Britain not only because of the better food and greater security which even prisoners enjoyed in Australia, but also by reason of the repeated injustices and brutalities which many of them suffered. It was not uncommon for prisoners at Norfolk Island, Moreton Bay and other penal stations to murder a comrade deliberately for no other reason than to end his sufferings at once and their own, shortly afterwards, on the gallows.[30] Charles Macalister records vividly the hardening effect which repeated flagellation had on some of the convicts:

[They] were made of the sternest human stuff possible, and men of that type never flinched under the lash. On two occasions I saw men—after undergoing, one a flogging of fifty, and the other seventy-five lashes, bleeding as they were, deliberately spit, after the punishment, in the flogger's face. One of them told Black Francis 'he couldn't flog hard enough to kill a butterfly'.

Black Francis was the official flagellator at Goulburn for three years in the late 1830's, until one day he was found near Run-o-Waters Creek with three bullets in his carcase.

It was argued at the beginning of this chapter that the outlook of 'government men' tended to influence strongly that of the emancipists and of the colonial-born population, but there is much evidence to show that the whole of colonial society, including even the purest of 'pure merinos'[31] was deeply affected by 'the system'. It has to be remembered that up to 1840 practically every employer of labour was *ipso facto* a gaoler, and it did not need modern psychology to show that those possessing nearly absolute powers over their fellow men are inevitably more or less corrupted by the relationship. John Turnbull wrote in 1805:

The circumstances under which the colony was settled, and the very purpose of the settlement, has had a very visible effect upon the general manners, or what may be called the national character, of Botany Bay. The free settlers are not without something of the contagion. . . . From upwards of a hundred families who have been sent out from England, there are not above eight or ten between whom and the convicts the smallest degree of discrimination could be drawn. . . .

And thirty years later J. D. Lang thought that the position had in no way altered: 'From their great number and comparative concentration, the prison population have uniformly given the tone to society, throughout this community—and a low tone it is. . . .'[32] In the character of Maurice Frere, Marcus Clarke gives an imaginative picture of the process. Later still in 1895 an old colonist wrote:

When we look back, and recollect what a thorough barbarian the average 'Government man' was, and how the free immigrant, yielding to the contemptuous assumption of the 'old hand', too often sank in the scale by adapting himself to the ruling standard of the 'men's huts'; when we picture over again old scenes, and recall the fact that, among the working classes there prevailed habits and language which now characterize the lowest grades only, we begin to realise how much our world of Australia has changed.

And these are not the only facts we can recall as proving the extent of the change.

At the other extremity, the other pole of the social system, there was to be found another index, and as true a proof of the prevalent barbarism.

It would seem as if the first efforts European Australia made to evolve a leading caste, resulted at times like the experiment of Frankenstein—the product was not a feudal hybrid, but a mongrel of original stamp. . . .

Such 'gentlemen' were simply the natural reflex and counterparts of their congenors [sic] clothed in grey felt and marked with the broad arrow, whom they treated with so much contempt and cruelty.[33]

Class divisions in early nineteenth-century Britain were of course very much more rigidly marked than they have become since, but the difference in this respect between early and present-day Australia is even more striking. The fact that, initially, practically all 'lower-class' Australians were also convicted criminals strongly underlined the dividing line between them and their masters and intensified mutual hostility. In 1822 James Dixon wrote that the immigrant to New South Wales would:

> land in a country possessing two distinct sorts of mankind. He will find that he can hardly avoid attaching himself to one party: if to the free, the other will say, 'Let him alone awhile; the swells will pluck him, and then he will come to us.' . . . Perhaps in all societies, it is in some measure the same, but here it is more strongly felt.

And Hood wrote in 1843: 'Caste in Hindostan is not more rigidly regarded than it is in Australia: the bond and free, emancipist and exclusionist, seldom associate together familiarly.' The testimony of most contemporary writers makes it clear that this comparison of early Australian society with that of India was not wholly absurd, but the same testimony demonstrates too that the affectations and vulgarity of the rich, in their strivings after gentility, often were. Cunningham relates an amusing anecdote in illustration of the point:

> The pride and dignified *hauteur* of some of our *ultra* aristocracy far eclipse those of the nobility in England. An excellent Yorkshire friend of mine, in command of a merchant-ship, unaware of the distance and punctilio observed here, very innocently stepped up to one of our 'eminent lawyers' (to whom he had been casually introduced but a few days previous), to ask some trifling question, which he prefaced with 'Good morning Mr. . . . .' The man of the law, however, recoiled as if a toad had tumbled in his path, and ejaculated with a stern frown, 'Upon my life, I don't know you, sir.' This proved a subject of much merriment afterwards to my friend, who would receive my usual 'How d'ye do's,' when we met, with a disdainful toss of the head, and 'Upon my life, I don't know you, sir.'

Possibly the 'eminent lawyer' was not a 'pure merino' but one of the almost incredibly vulgar wealthy emancipists described by Mrs Meredith,[34] but of these Hood observed, in about 1840: 'their children [are] sent to the colleges of England, and their daughters' fortunes get them husbands from among the free.' It may be suspected that this ludicrous straining after exclusiveness and gentility was in reality a measure of the perilously slight differences in taste between the classes, and that it was exacerbated by the almost total absence of any middle class already noted. In fact few of the colonial 'upper class' were persons of what would have been accepted, by the contemporary English landed gentry, as real birth and breeding.

The effort to emphasize class differences artificially points also to the much greater fluidity of colonial society. This was caused partly by the breaking of old ties and traditions, inseparable from physical up-rooting from the mother country, but partly too by the much greater economic opportunities open to those possessing even a modest amount of capital—or unusually sober habits. Mundy wrote of the last pre-Gold-Rush decade:

> In England there are instances of individuals—especially among the manufacturing classes—who, in the course of one life-time, have raised themselves and their families from moderate means to enormous wealth; but in Australia all the stages between adventurous beggary and inordinate possessions have, in some cases, been traversed in a quarter of a man's usual existence.

George French Angas was even more explicit. He wrote in 1847:

> An individual who is pining in Great Britain—struggling . . . to be a 'somebody', upon a very limited income—may, by changing his abode to the genial climate of South Australia, live like a little prince, and become a 'somebody' with the same amount of income upon which he could barely exist in England.

There is little doubt that the lower orders were singularly unimpressed by the self-proclaimed superiority of the colonial 'gentry'. Australians acquired a cynical attitude towards the pretensions of wealthy citizens long before the Gold Rush underlined the point for them. Hood wrote of Sydney in 1843:

> Many of the private houses in the vicinity of the town are delightful little retreats, placed amid beautiful gardens and scenery, wood and water. Many are magnificent in their architecture and dimensions. When you inquire the names, however, of some of them, you are amused at hearing, in reply, a nickname generally indicative of the calling, or origin of its possessor or builder. 'Frying-pan Hall', for instance, a very handsome chateau in the neighbourhood, belonged to a person who, after serving his term of bondage for seven years, followed the useful calling of an ironsmith.

It is worth noting, in passing, that the nickname imputes no blame to the ironsmith for having come out to Australia at government expense, but only for his having become rich and, it is implied, pretentious.

One important result of 'upper-class' exclusiveness was that the great majority of free immigrants, who came from a working-class background at home, tended, after a few years' acclimatization, to adopt the attitudes and outlook of the old hands. For instance John Russell, assistant-surgeon to the Sixty-Third Regiment in Van Diemen's Land from 1829 to 1833, observed: 'the lower orders . . . [of] the free emigrant population who have resided in the colony for a number of years, appeared to be very much on a par, in point of habits, with the convicts.'[35]

For masters accustomed to lording it over convict servants it was natural to treat free men, performing the same tasks, in much the same way. J. C. Byrne also drew attention to the evil in 1848 when he wrote:

> Nearly all the great flock-masters of the colony of New South Wales have at some period been accustomed to employ convict labour. Slaves, subject to the lash, to chains, and the penal settlements, have served them; they have become accustomed to such, and with these habits, they forget the rights of free men. Newcomers often fall into this mode of proceeding from example . . .

The free employees would have been less than human if they had not frequently reacted to such treatment by making common cause with their unfree fellow workmen.

In conclusion it may be said that the attempt, only partly conscious, to establish an English pattern of life was distorted by the various factors considered above. The distance between upper and lower classes was not at first sensibly lessened. Indeed, in many ways it was increased, but at the same time movement up and down the social ladder became easier and the lower class, placed in a strong position to do so by the insatiable demand for labour and by the need for adaptation to new conditions, came more rapidly and trenchantly than in Britain to question the assumptions on which the old society rested.[36] Generally speaking, the new Australian conditions had a levelling effect. As Cunningham wrote of New South Wales in the 1820's:

> Thieves generally affect to consider all the rest of mankind equally criminal with themselves, only being either lucky enough not to be found out, or committing actions which (though equally bad in the

eye of the Divinity) are not so tangible in that of man. It is their constant endeavour to reduce everyone in fact, to the same level with themselves.

Without diminishing class consciousness and hostility, the new environment made society much more fluid and, while it tended to vulgarize and debase the rich, it tended equally to augment the integrity and self-reliance, though not to polish the manners, of working people. And poor men generally, indeed the whole of colonial society, were strongly influenced by the convict system and by the outlook which it evoked among its primary victims.

CHAPTER II

1   In this and following tables the figures for 1828 are taken from T. A. Coghlan (N.S.W. Govt. Statistician), *General Report on the Eleventh Census of N.S.W.*, Sydney 1894, pp. 71-3. Those for 1841 and 1851 are from the Census Returns in *Votes and Proceedings of the N.S.W. Legislative Council*, 1841 and 1851.

All figures refer to the colony of New South Wales, excluding Van Diemen's Land and the Port Phillip District, but including what later became Queensland. The 1841 figures exclude also the 2,130 persons on board colonial vessels on the day of the census, since no particulars about them, other than their whereabouts, were recorded.

Of his 1828 figures Coghlan observes that the muster of that year, from which he drew them, was thought to have been particularly inaccurate, and that it was difficult to allow justly for the number of convict 'bolters' at large in the bush.

Commenting (*op. cit.*, p. 91) on the 1851 census, Coghlan writes: 'It is important to remember that the act did not permit of any direct questioning in regard to civil condition, and some of the emancipists probably took advantage of this provision to return themselves as either Born in the Colony or Arrived Free.' The number of emancipists given is certainly too small, as it was also in the 1828 and other earlier censuses. (cp. J. D. Lang, *Historical and Statistical Account of N.S.W.*, etc., 2 vols., London 1834, vol. 1, pp. 271-2.) Comparison of figures given in the various censuses makes it seem likely that, of those emancipists who falsified their returns, the vast majority chose Currency status rather than that of 'Arrived Free'.

2   James Mudie, *Felonry of New South Wales*, etc., London 1837-38, p. vi.

3   See, for instance, *House of Commons Select Committee on Transportation, Report with Minutes of Evidence, 1837*, p. 153 (Evidence of Lt Col. H. Breton).

4   *Canberra Times*, 21 September 1955, p. 4: 'The Vice-President of the Executive Council, Sir Eric Harrison, yesterday called Mr E. J. Ward a

"sucker" who had accepted incorrect information from "the lowest form of human life—an informer".' Perusal of the United States press shows that this is anything but the accepted attitude or language of contemporary Americans.

5 Tom Petrie, *Reminiscences of Early Queensland*, etc., Brisbane 1932 ed. (first published 1904), p. 246; and cp. 'A Gentleman Just Returned from the Settlement', *An Account of the English Colony at Botany Bay*, etc., London 1808, p. 64: 'The difficulty of bringing the people to bring evidence against each other was unsurmountable, and by far the greater part of the acquittals were occasioned by a wilful suppression of evidence.'

6 A. W. Stirling, *The Never Never Land*, etc., 2nd ed., London 1884, p. 21.

7 Quoted W. K. Hancock, *Australia*, Sydney 1949 ed., p. 42.

8 'A Clergyman, etc.' (Rev. John Morison), *Australia As It Is*, etc., London 1857, pp. 222-3.

9 Pauline Gregg, *Social and Economic History of Britain 1760-1950*, London 1950, ch. 1; J. L. and B. Hammond, *The Village Labourer 1760-1833*, London 1913, p. 195 and *passim*.

10 J. L. and B. Hammond, *Rise of Modern Industry*, London 1925, pp. 205-6 and ch. 12, 13, and *The Bleak Age*, London 1947 (rev. ed.), esp. ch. 1; G. D. H. Cole and R. Postgate, *The Common People 1746-1946*, London 1946, pp. 138-9, 142, 686-7; J. R. M. Butler, *History of England 1815-1918*, p. 69 and ch. 3 *passim*. Sir John Clapham (*Economic History of Modern Britain*, London 1926) and disciples like F. H. Hayek and T. S. Ashton have dissented from the majority view; but in a recent work edited by Hayek (*Capitalism and the Historians*, etc., Chicago 1954), Ashton admits that N. J. Silberling's statistics, on which Clapham largely based his argument, are unreliable. Ashton also admits that during the Napoleonic Wars the 'economic status of labour' was 'almost certainly worsened' (p. 135). He argues that the marked downward trend in the terms of trade from 1814 to the middle 1830's 'did not represent any worsening' of working-class living standards (p. 141), but admits that 'throughout the twenties the cost of the staple diet moved to a higher rather than a lower level' (p. 156). In conclusion he suggests that the real living standard of skilled workers improved, unlike that of the 'unskilled and poorly skilled' (pp. 158-9).

11 *Report, House of Commons Select Committee on Transportation, 1837-38*, pp. xx-xxi ff., and cp. *Historical Records of Australia*, Series 1, vol. 17, p. 322.

12 R. B. Madgwick, *Immigration into Eastern Australia, 1788-1851*, London 1937, p. 242 ff.

13 J. T. Bigge, *Report . . . State of the Colony of New South Wales*, London 1822, p. 75; and A. G. L. Shaw, *Sydney Morning Herald*, 27 June 1953.

14 George Bennett, *Wanderings in New South Wales*, etc., London 1834, 2 vols., vol. 1, p. 90, and see Alexander Marjoribanks, *Travels in New*

South Wales, etc., London 1847, p. 35 ff., which makes it quite clear that though, as Bigge said. townsmen might make poor *agricultural* workers in the new land, they often made the best pastoral workers.

15 *English Journal of Education*, vol. 9, 1851, p. 33 ff.

16 Sydney *Bulletin*, 10 March 1888, p. 14.

17 I have supplied rudimentary punctuation but otherwise reproduced this text exactly from a MS. scrap-book, kindly given me by the grandson of its compiler, M. J. Conlon. (See *Cyclopedia of New South Wales*, Sydney 1907; pp. 477-8.) The scrap-book is now held by the National Library, Canberra.

18 cp. Clarke's 'Maurice Frere' with the character of the real John Price, as sketched by John Singleton in his *Narrative of Incidents in the Eventful Life of a Physician*, Melbourne 1891, pp. 154-69.

19 In *Tales of the Old Regime*, etc., Melbourne 1897, p. 91; Price, then head of the penal department at Melbourne, was battered to death by his convict charges with quarrying tools on 26 March 1857 (*Australian Encyclopaedia*, 2 vols., Sydney 1926, vol. 2, p. 333).

20 George Hobler, *Diary 1827-1871*, 23 February 1830 (in Mitchell Library, Sydney).

21 *Dreadnought of the Darling*, London 1911, p. 322 ff.

22 *Twelve Years' Wanderings*, etc., 2 vols., London 1848, vol. 2, p. 216 ff.

23 Quoted G. C. Mundy, *Our Antipodes*, etc., London 1855, 3rd ed., pp. 44-5.

24 *Historical Records of Australia*, Series 1, vol. 10, pp. 220-4, and cp. vol. 9, p. 238; G. F. Davidson, *Trade and Travel in the Far East*, etc., London 1846, p. 136; J. D. Lang, *Historical and Statistical Account of New South Wales*, etc., 2 vols., London 1834, vol. 2, p. 19 ff.

25 *Report, House of Commons Select Committee on Transportation, 1812*, Appendix 1, p. 23; and cp. T. B. Wilson, *Narrative of a Voyage Round the World*, etc., London 1835, p. 326; T. Potter Macqueen, *Australia As She Is and As She May Be*, London 1840, p. 6.

26 *An Account of the English Colony at Botany Bay*, etc., London 1808, p. 65; and cp. David Collins, *An Account of the English Colony in New South Wales*, etc., 2 vols., London 1802, vol. 1, pp. 359 ff., 377 ff.; Edward Curr, *An Account of the Colony of Van Diemen's Land*, etc., London 1824, p. 14; and James Atkinson, *An Account of the State of Agriculture and Grazing in New South Wales*, etc., London 1826, pp. 28 ff., 106 ff.

27 F. Gerstaecker, *Narrative of a Journey Round the World*, etc., 3 vols., London 1853, vol. 2, pp. 285-6; H. W. Haygarth, *Recollections of Bush Life in Australia*, etc., London 1848, p. 26 ff.; and cp. *Historical Records of Australia*, Series 1, vol. 21, p. 719; Mrs Charles Meredith, *Notes and Sketches of New South Wales*, London 1861 ed., p. 77.

28 P. Cunningham, *Two Years in New South Wales*, etc., 2 vols., London 1827, vol. 2, p. 198.

29 Donahoe was shot by the police on 1 September 1830 (*Sydney Gazette*, 7 September 1830).

30 R. Therry, *Reminiscences of Thirty Years' Residence in New South Wales and Victoria*, London 1863, pp. 20-24; W. Ullathorne, *The Catholic Mission to Australasia*, 2nd ed., Liverpool 1837, p. 41; H. S. Russell, *The Genesis of Queensland*, etc., Sydney 1888, pp. 61-5, 212; and *Report, House of Commons Select Committee on Transportation, 1837-38*, p. xiv ff.

31 R. Therry, *op. cit.*, p. 58: 'The term *pure merino*, a designation given to sheep where there is no cross-blood in the flocks, was applied to mark a class who were not only free and unconvicted, but who could boast of having no collateral relationship or distant affinity with those in whose escutcheon there was a blot. These *pure merinos* formed the topmost round in the social ladder.'

32 *Op. cit.*, vol. 2, p. 410; and cp. evidence of John Russell, *Report, House of Commons Select Committee on Transportation, 1837-38*, pp. 58-9; J. C. Byrne, *op. cit.*, vol. 1, p. 224; and R. Therry, *op. cit.*, pp. 47-8.

33 George Ranken (ed.), *Windabyne, a Record of By-gone Times in Australia*, etc., London 1895, p. 51 ff.; and cp. G. F. Davidson, *op. cit.*, p. 136; and *Hogan Papers* (MS.), Letter from J. R. Macleay to T. Hogan, 12 May 1830.

34 *Op. cit.*, pp. 50-1, 82.

35 *Report, House of Commons Select Committee on Transportation, 1837-38*, pp. 60-1.

36 Here, as throughout, I am trying to deal with commonly held *social* attitudes, rather than *political* attitudes and actions, though the latter often proceeded from the former. In the sphere of political thought and action colonial working men, before the gold discoveries, were usually less militant than their fellows in Britain.

CELTS AND CURRENCY

═══

Then hurl me to crime and brand me with shame,
But think not to baulk me my spirit to tame,
For I'll fight to the last in old Ireland's name.
   Though I be a bushranger,
   You still are the stranger,
      And I'm Donahue.

THE convicts and lower-class immigrants, whose influence on early Australian manners we have examined, were not an undifferentiated group. They came from England, Ireland, Scotland and Wales, and the traditions they brought with them differed accordingly. In this chapter we shall consider the ways in which Celtic and native Australian influences modified the basically English tradition of the majority.

A leading authority on Australian ballad music, Dr Percy Jones, says that some of the songs were sung to tunes popular in the British Isles a hundred years or more ago, while others were set to original melodies composed for the new ballads in Australia. Of the former group he writes:

> they indicate to some extent the proportionate extent of the various racial influences among the balladists and their friends. The honours seem to be fairly evenly divided between England and Ireland. Numerically there is a slight preponderance of English tunes, but quite a few of these were, so to speak, common property, so that an accurate estimate is very difficult. . . . One rather interesting fact is the almost complete absence of any Scottish songs.[1]

The scarcity of Scottish tunes and ballads among Australian folk-singers was no accident. In this chapter we shall find many reasons for thinking that the Irish influence on the early Australian working class was disproportionately strong while that of the Scots was disproportionately weak. There were so few Welsh convicts and immigrants that, for the purposes of a broad sketch like the present one, they can be disregarded. In the census of 1841, for instance, of 51,680 persons in New South Wales who had been born south of the Tweed only 558 gave Wales as their birthplace.

Although Australian census returns do not record the national ancestry of citizens, they do record their religions. Of course there are many Presbyterian Irishmen in Ulster and a few Catholic Scotsmen in the Highlands, and there are Catholic and Presbyterian Englishmen. Nevertheless these exceptional cases tend to balance each other, and the body of professing Catholics in Australia was, until the large-scale immigration after World War II, probably approximately equal to, though not identical with, the body of people of Irish descent. In the same way the Presbyterian body serves as a rough index to the number of Australians of Scottish ancestry. The following table gives a picture of the population, from the above viewpoint, at the censuses of 1841, 1851, and 1947:[2]

TABLE IV

	Roman Catholic	Presbyterian	Church of England plus Remainder of Population	Roman Catholic	Presbyterian
				Per cent of Total Population	
1841	33,249	11,109	72,630	28·4	9·5
1851	56,899	18,156	112,188	30·4	9·7
1947	1,569,726	743,540	5,266,091	20·7	9·8

It is immediately clear that the 'racial' composition of the Australian population differs markedly from that of the British Isles. As Fitzpatrick says, of the 1933 census figures, in his *Australian People*:

> The Australian percentage of twenty Roman Catholics compares with not much more than half that percentage in the combined populations of Britain and Ireland, and the eleven per cent of Australians who are Presbyterians are about half as great again a proportion as Presbyterians are in the whole of the British Isles.

One might expect to find then that Irish influence has been about twice as strong here as in Britain, and Scottish influence half as strong again. Fitzpatrick suggests that this has in fact been so in the political and other spheres. The figures also show however that, in the formative period of the 1840's, there were proportionately not twice but about three times as many people of Irish descent in New South Wales as there were in the British Isles. Before 1851 more than half of the assisted immigrants reaching New South Wales were Irish. The actual figure is forty-eight per cent, but this excludes many Irish who emigrated by ships clearing from English or Scottish ports.[3] Moreover, it is certain that people of Irish and Scottish descent were not scattered more or less evenly through the different strata of colonial society. Generally speaking, Irish convicts and immigrants became unskilled labourers in Australia, while a very high proportion of Scotchmen, even of those who landed with little or no capital, became rich or at least 'successful'.

The reasons for this state of affairs are not far to seek. First of all, relatively very few Scottish convicts were sent out and those few, owing to differences between the English and Scottish legal systems, were likely to have been unusually hardened criminals; although there were, of course, honourable exceptions such as the 'Scottish Martyrs'. There was more than a germ of truth in the remark of a *European Review* writer: 'a man is banished from Scotland for a great crime, from England for a small one, and from Ireland, morally speaking, for no crime at all.'[4] Scotchmen were not more wicked than their fellow subjects. A report from the Inspector of Scottish Prisons in 1845 to the Home Secretary explains the situation:

> In England and Wales the average number of persons sentenced to transportation in each of the last three years has been 3,900; while in Scotland, with a population of about one-sixth of that of England and Wales, the number has been less than 300. In other words, there have been more than twice as many persons sentenced to transportation in England and Wales, in proportion to the population, in the last three years, as in Scotland. . . . This great difference . . . is, I think, chiefly attributable to the power of awarding it being much more confined in Scotland than in England; being in England possessed not only by the judges, but by the numerous recorders and by the courts of justices in quarter sessions; whereas, in Scotland it is limited to the judges.[5]

Even among the few Scottish convicts, some like Macquarie's protégé, Andrew Thompson, rapidly became rich. Among Scottish immigrants, both assisted and unassisted, the proportion was undoubtedly much higher.[6] There were probably three main reasons for this. A high proportion of Scottish migrants were of middle-class, or tenant-farmer stock. Their Presbyterian faith, in practice, often came near to equating virtue with material success, but it did instil into their minds the habits of hard work and frugality. And the average standard of education, as much above that of England as England's was above Ireland's, also gave the Scottish immigrants an advantage in the race for colonial 'success'. As Margaret Kiddle writes:

> The Scots farmers . . . represent the middle-class immigrants who came to Australia. They were the men who came with varying amounts of capital. . . . In . . . the Victorian Western District, no less than two-thirds were of Lowland farming stock. . . . And in 1845, according to Dr. Lang, there was a concentration of Scots squatters around Moreton Bay. The New England district too, was largely settled by Scots.[7]

G. F. Davidson noted that even paupers from Scotland often rapidly made good by frugality, sobriety and hard work:

> Several ships with emigrants from the Highlands and Islands of Scotland arrived at Sydney during the years 1838 and 1839. These people were, in general, unwilling to accept of employment in any shape, but preferred taking clearing-leases of land on their own account. This plan, many of them succeeded in carrying into execution, much to the disappointment and annoyance of the community at whose expense they had been brought to the colony; and it was reasonably complained, that these men, in place of supplying the labour-market, as was intended, actually created an increased demand for labour, by requiring aid in their own operations before the first twelvemonth had passed over them. Be this as it may, they are a hard-working, industrious set of men . . .

Since so many Scottish immigrants quickly became rich, it is not surprising that they should have had little influence on the outlook and songs of Australian working people. With the Irish the case was very different. We have seen that during the two pre-Gold-Rush decades about a third of the whole population and more than half of the immigrants were Irish, and there is much more than the evidence of the folk-songs to show that the great majority of these were extremely poor working people. In Australia most of them joined and remained in the unskilled and semi-skilled labour force, and the working-class character of most Irish colonists was clearly recognized by Catholic spokesmen of the time.[8]

There is nothing discreditable to the Irish people in this fact. At home political, social and economic factors had combined to reduce their standard of living to rock bottom. De Beaumont wrote, with little exaggeration: 'in all countries, more or less, paupers may be discovered, but an entire nation of paupers is what never was seen until it was shown in Ireland.' So wretched was their food, clothing and shelter that even the hold of a convict transport could be a haven of luxury by comparison. Cunningham observed:

> The Irish convicts are more happy and contented with their situation on board than the English, although more loth to leave their country, even improved as the situation of the great body of them is by being thus removed—numbers telling me they had never been half so well off in their lives before.

To illustrate the point he went on to quote some passages from convicts' letters which it was his duty to censor. Typical of many, he says, was the following: 'Many a *Mac* in your town, if he only knew what the situation of a convict was, would not be long in following my example! Thank God for the same! I never was better off in my life!'

Most observers of the Australian scene in the 1840's commented upon the large numbers and pervasive influence of Irish working people. When, as in most cases, the writer was a respectable English or Scottish Protestant, he more or less openly deplored the situation. We may take John Hood's comments in 1843 as typical:

> Throughout my wanderings in New South Wales, I have observed that the lower classes are chiefly Irish . . . the poorest, most useless, and most dissolute part of the population from the southern counties of the Emerald Isle have been exported hither, more as articles of commerce than with a view to the benefit of this country. . . . Few of the Irish emigrants land with anything except the clothes on their backs; whereas, from England and Scotland the generality have a little stock wherewith to commence their colonial career. . . . I shall

be borne out by the present state of the populace of New South Wales when I say that the lower Irish character, in some of its worst features, is deeply imprinted upon this colony, and that it would be well for it if the tide *of a similar description of its population* were to cease to set in here from the shores of Ireland.

Hood's gloom was occasioned partly by the fact that the Irish who at home were willing to work, or at any rate did work, for next to nothing, rapidly became 'discontented' and 'independent' towards their employers in Australia. 'They can live at home on simple and scanty fare, but on reaching the shores of this country their character changes,' he complained. 'They are found to be indolent at their tasks, and troublesome and discontented as to their food.' Davidson, a rather pious old China sea-captain and opium-trader wrote in 1846: '[It was] remarked all over the Colony . . . that the man who had been worst fed at home, was the most difficult to please abroad. An Irishman is generally found the chief grumbler here . . .' Yet, as we have seen, Cunningham, the Scottish surgeon, stressed that, in the most unpropitious circumstances, the Irish were 'happy and contented with their situation', and even that they possessed 'an anxiety to oblige' and 'a lighthearted civility . . . of which the English are *totally destitute*'. Davidson also noted that, although the Irish were so hard to please in New South Wales, a friend of his who was a major in an Irish regiment thought that the reverse was true in the army.

It is not very difficult to reconcile these apparently conflicting views. At home the Irish peasant worked for a handful of potatoes because he had to do so or starve. Comparatively, life in a well-conducted convict ship or an early nineteenth-century army barracks might be secure and even luxurious. Naturally the Irishman in these circumstances became light-hearted and cheerful. Yet the rigid discipline, never very far in the background, prevented him from seriously challenging the slightest whims of those who regarded themselves as his 'betters'. But, as Hood complained, his character changed in Australia. There, after serving his time if a convict, at once if an immigrant, he found himself free of rigid legal or other restraints, and placed in a very strong economic position by the perennial labour shortage. With plenty of good food and no worry about obtaining another position if he should offend his employer he could afford to become 'troublesome and dis-

contented'—from his employers' point of view. From his own, no
doubt, he was merely living for the first time as a free man should.
The extent to which, in comparison with his English fellows, he
tended to glory insultingly in his new-found confidence was a
measure of his previous degradation. As John Sidney wrote in his
Voice from the Far Interior (1847):

> The sweepings of English workhouses and Irish beggars, who
> have never eaten a good meal or done a good day's work in their
> lives, grow fat and saucy as soon as they exchange their rags and
> potatoes, or parish uniform and parish allowance, for our fine climate
> and Bushfare.

Another contemporary summed up the position not inaptly
when he wrote: 'Of all the colonial devils the English is the strongest, the Irish the merriest, and the Scotch the keenest and best
educated.'[9]
In the last chapter we saw that the social outlook of colonial
working people was very strongly influenced by that of the convicts. It is now clear that Irish working-class attitudes formed
another important ingredient in the distinctive Australian ethos
which was developing. Even though Irishmen seemed usually to
retain a greater sentimental attachment to their native soil than
did the English immigrants, other powerful factors tended to
attach them also more quickly and closely to that of their adopted
country. The brute fact that their standard of living at home was
so much lower than that of the English must have tended to make
them more appreciative of conditions in the new land of plenty.
Though they continued to sing sentimental songs about 'the
shabbit island where the dear little shamrocks grow', Caroline
Chisholm's 'Voluntary Statements' from immigrants show that
they were, if anything, even more anxious than English immigrants
to persuade relatives and friends to follow them to Australia.
Marjoribanks tells the story of one Irish convict girl who, after
serving her seven years, returned to Dublin but then committed
another crime for the express purpose of re-emigrating at government expense. When sentenced, she exclaimed joyously to the
court: 'Hurrah for Old Sydney, and the sky over it!'
The other factor which made Irishmen specially prominent
in developing a distinctive Australian outlook was more complex
and more important. We saw in the last chapter that what was

new in this outlook tended to spread upwards and outwards, from the convicts initially, and then from the 'lower' sections of society generally. The mere fact that a disproportionately large majority of Irish convicts and immigrants were very poor working people tended to place them naturally in the vanguard of the movement, but more important was the anti-British attitude which so many Irishmen brought across the oceans with them. It would have been astonishing if, in the earlier part of the nineteenth century, most peasant and working-class Irishmen outside Ulster had not hated England and English rule. Irishmen convicted and transported under English laws, or forced to emigrate by the appalling poverty which they felt to be 'made in England', were likely to be doubly and trebly Anglophobe. The influence of Irish immigrants in the United States and the history of the later Fenian movement underline the point.

The strength of this Irish-Australian hatred of England is vividly suggested by the composition here of Irish revolutionary folk-songs and their survival, in some cases, right down to the present day. The most famous and popular of all early Australian folk-bards was one 'Frank the Poet' or Francis Macnamara, an Irish convict who is said to have prefaced his public performances by declaiming a sort of 'signature stanza' which went:

> My name is Frank Macnamara,
> A native of Cashell, County Tipperary,
> Sworn to be a tyrant's foe—
> And while I've life I'll crow.[10]

From the internal evidence of the verses themselves it seems not unlikely that 'Frank the Poet' may have been the original author of the following effusion, though it has also been ascribed to the most celebrated of pre-Gold-Rush bushrangers, Jack Donahoe himself:

> A life that is free as the bandits' of old
> When Rome was the prey of the warriors bold,
> Who knew how to buy gallant soldiers with gold,
> Is the life full of danger
> Of Jack, the bushranger,
> Of brave Donahue!

If Ireland lies groaning, a hand at her throat,
Which foreigners have from the recreants bought.
Forget not the lessons our fathers have taught.
　　Though our Isle's full of danger,
　　And held by the stranger,
　　Be brave and be true.

I've left the old Island's hospitable shores,
The land of the Emmets, the Tones and the Moores;
But Liberty o'er me her scalding tear pours,
　　And she points to the manger,
　　Where *He* was a stranger,
　　And perished for you.

Then hurl me to crime and brand me with shame,
But think not to baulk me my spirit to tame,
For I'll fight to the last in old Ireland's name.
　　Though I be a bushranger,
　　You still are the stranger,
　　And I'm Donahue.[11]

This ballad, more clearly than most in the same *genre*, reflects the ambivalence of early Irish-Australian working-class feeling. Stanzas two and three, except for the reference in the latter to transportation, could come from a purely Irish ballad of the period. They struggle to express something deeper than a merely sentimental patriotism. But in the first stanza there is a clear recognition of the greater freedom and plenty of life in Australia, greatest of all for bushrangers, who are conceived of as continuing in the new land the old patriotic fight against English tyranny. The same *motif* is emphasized in the last stanza, and carried a stage further. Irishmen in Australia are continuing, more success-fully and joyously, the battle against British authority, and they already feel that the new land belongs truly to them, that they are at home in it while their rulers are still 'strangers', just as had been the case in Ireland.

This Irish-Australian hatred of England cut very deep, and no doubt it was a major component in the general Australian working-class disdain for Englishmen. Fifty years after Donahoe's death it found incoherent, but volcanically forceful, expression in Ned Kelly's life and death, no less than in the remarkable document known as the *Jerilderie Letter* which he bequeathed to posterity. Why should men obey the laws of England, the *Letter* asks, under which so many Irishmen were starved to death?—and it goes on:

> more was transported to Van Diemand's [*sic*] Land to pine their young lives away in starvation and misery among tyrants, . . . were doomed to Port McQuarie Toweringabbie Norfolk island and Emu Plains and in those places of tyranny and condemnation many a blooming Irishman rather than subdue to the Saxon yoke were flogged to death and bravely died in servile chains . . . [12]

The importance of ballad singing as a vehicle of folk-tradition is strikingly instanced by the fact that this particular passage clearly springs from Kelly's memory of a stanza in one of 'Frank the Poet''s most popular songs, 'Moreton Bay'. The relevant lines are:

> Early one morning as I carelessly wandered by the
> Brisbane waters I chanced to stray,
> I saw a prisoner sadly bewailing, whilst on the
> sunbeaming banks he lay.
> He said: I have been a prisoner at Port Macquarie,
> at Norfolk Island and Emu Plains;
> At Castle Hill and cursed Towngabbie—at all those
> places I've worked in chains;
> But of all the places of condemnation in each penal
> station of New South Wales,
> Moreton Bay I found no equal, for excessive tyranny
> each day prevails.[13]

Finally it is worth noticing that before 1851 there were, relative to the total population, many more Irishmen in New South Wales than elsewhere in Australia. This state of affairs seems to have stemmed largely from the fact that few, if any, Irish convicts were sent to Van Diemen's Land between 1824 and about 1840. Giving evidence to the New South Wales Legislative Council's Select Committee on Immigration in 1838, the Colonial Secretary, Alexander Macleay, stated: 'All the convicts transported from Ireland are without exception sent direct to this colony, and since Van Diemen's Land was made a separate government, no Irish convicts have been transported from hence to that island.'[14]

For once J. D. Lang, the paladin of anti-popery, and Therry,

a leading Catholic layman, agreed in thinking there was something sinister, or at least unexplained, about this arrangement.
T. Potter Macqueen, an ex-Member of Parliament, ascribed it to
'the influence which Sir George Arthur possessed in Downing
Street'.[15] Whatever the true explanation, this concentration of
Irish convicts in the mother colony was one more factor tending to
make New South Wales the major seed-bed of the emerging
Australian ethos. It also helps to explain the traditional feeling
that Tasmania, which still has a lower percentage of Catholics in
its population than any other state except South Australia, is 'more
English' than the rest of Australia.

It would be misleading to seek to isolate completely the Irish
component in the budding Australian national sentiment. The
latter, as we have seen, tended to spring up first among the
convicts and lower-class immigrants, and it is true only to say that,
among these elements of the population, people of Irish birth or
ancestry tended to acquire the new outlook most readily and to feel
it most deeply. Since World War I home-front battles over con-
scription have faded into the background of consciousness it has
become more and more clear to everyone that Australian patriotism
does not usually or necessarily involve weakening of attachment
to Britain, but rather the reverse. Before that time it was by no
means clear. In the nineteenth century Australian patriotic sentiment was usually more or less deeply tinged with 'disloyalty', with
radical notions of complete republican independence. Prisoners
and assisted immigrants had less reason to love Britain than did
more prosperous persons and were less able to maintain their
connections with 'home' however much, in many instances, they
may have wished to do so. Still, to love the new land more seemed
often to mean loving the old one less, in so far as Australian
national sentiment was felt to weaken the attachment to Crown
and Empire. For English and Scottish working-class immigrants,
patriotic and class feelings seemed to pull in opposite directions.
For Irish-Australian working people the reverse was true. To love
Australia more was also to strike a blow for 'Old Ireland', just
in so far as the development of an Australian national feeling was
felt to weaken the British connection.

It is not suggested, of course, that such considerations were consciously present in the minds of many. An incident recorded by G. C. Mundy illustrates with extraordinary aptness both the complete lack of self-consciousness with which the embryonic national feeling was held, and the organic connection between it and the convict-lower-class-Irish elements of the population. On 3 December 1846 Sir Charles Fitzroy's party, on tour of the Western districts, stopped for luncheon at the Summerhill inn. Mundy writes:

> [We] passed out of Summerhill under a pair of gorgeous banners sustained by two standard bearers standing, or, more properly, staggering opposite each other, and apparently on the worst of terms. I heard one of them, a little old native of the land of pat-riotism, conclude a volley of abuse discharged at his *vis-à-vis* by contemptuously denouncing him as 'a bloody immigrant!'—thereby leaving the hearer to infer that the speaker himself was a 'Government Man', that his rival was a free man, and that it was disgraceful for anyone to come to this country except in pursuance of the sentence of a court of criminal jurisdiction.

The hyphen in 'patriotism' suggests that the more aggressive of the two standard bearers was an Irish ex-convict who, by virtue of these qualifications and of an at least relatively long residence in the colony, felt ineffably superior to the free immigrant.

Nevertheless, even an old Irish lag obviously could not have felt as completely at home as did the native-born Australians. Of these Harris noted that by the 1830's 'fellowship of country' had 'already begun to distinguish them in a most remarkable manner'.[16] In 1820 Commissioner Bigge wrote:

> They are generally tall in person, and slender in their limbs, of fair complexion, and small features. They are capable of undergoing more fatigue, and are less exhausted by labour, than native Europeans.[17]

Only three or four years later Cunningham wrote:

> They grow up tall and slender like the Americans, and are generally remarkable for that Gothic peculiarity of fair hair and blue eyes which has been noticed by other writers. Their complexions, when young, are of a reddish sallow, and they are for the most part easily distinguishable—even in more advanced years—from those born in England.

In their accounts of the physical characteristics of the Currency people most writers agree at least to the extent of believing that Australians were typically tall, slender, and fair or 'sallow'. But Hood also says flatly that 'the eye is generally black in both sexes', and it is noticeable that the more detailed the descriptions are, the more the general impression conveyed diverges from the stereotype. It would indeed have been a remarkable 'sport' in the laws of heredity if a really distinctive physical type had sprung up in the first native-born generation. One suspects that many later writers had Bigge's picture in their minds when they came to put down on paper their own impressions. Yet twenty years before Bigge wrote, a visiting sea-captain had observed: 'the children born in the colony are very fair and healthy.'[18] Probably more and better food and an active, out-door life did make the average 'Cornstalk' taller and more slender than the average Briton, and it may be that when visitors described the Australians as 'fair' or 'sallow', they meant simply that, as Cunningham noted, they lacked the rosy cheeks which have always been held a prime sign of good health in the cold British climate.[19]

However it is clear that, in matters not so intimately connected with Mendelian laws, the Currency population early developed distinctive traits. As has been suggested above, these characteristics sprang largely from working-class, particularly Irish working-class, attitudes; and it is not usually possible to distinguish sharply between these and Currency attitudes proper, except in so far as the native-born tended to exhibit the common outlook in a heightened form. Its basic component was simply a feeling of being at home, of 'belonging' in the country. The corollary, of course, was that the country belonged to the people who felt thus. When Alexander Harris first went 'up the country' seeking work in the late 1820's, he slept near Bulli Pass in a hut of 'two Irishmen, brothers, who . . . refused nobody a feed and shelter for the night'. Most of his fellow guests, he tells us, had been convicts and they chaffed him 'not very sparingly, but I must say with very good humour . . . for having come to the colony "to make a fortune", or for being "a free object" (subject), or for having "lagged myself for fear the king should do it for me"'. A few days later his mate, an assigned servant, apologized for Harris to a visiting bushranger by saying that he had been 'hardly a month in the country'. The reply was: 'Oh! we know that; he's one of the free objects—bad luck to 'em! What business have they here in the prisoners' country?'[20] Even wealthy emancipists often shared in the feeling. In 1834 George Bennett wrote:

> It is well known that free emigration is detested by most of the convict party, and a wealthy individual of this class once remarked, *'What have the free emigrants to do here? the colony was founded for us, they have no right here'*; and that individual, from his wealth, would probably be elected a member of a future House of Assembly.

Not only prisoners and emancipists, but Currency Lads and poor settlers generally shared in the conviction that the new land belonged, morally, to them. This feeling was deepened, though not initiated, by the official practice of granting (after 1831 of selling) large estates to immigrants with capital. In 1818, for instance, one Benjamin Singleton, a 'dungaree settler' at Windsor, discovered most of the overland route to the Hunter River valley. There he obtained, three years later, a grant of 240 acres at Patrick's Plains.[21] He was made a constable and, by the end of 1823, was depasturing on this very modest holding and on the neighbouring estates of James Mudie and others between two and three thousand head of cattle most of which were believed to have been stolen. When the wealthy immigrant settlers, his neighbours, complained of these depredations, and of Singleton's familiarity with their assigned servants and with ex-convict small settlers, he is reported to have replied that—

> they would take as many Cattle as they liked and run them wherever they thought proper in spite of any of us, and that Government had no right to give so much Land to Free Settlers and so little to those that are borne in the Country, and threatened that if Government did not alter their plan that they would not submit to it long, for they would help themselves . . . [22]

James Macarthur was voicing the common 'pure merino' opinion when he wrote that the origin of the feeling 'that the colony was *theirs by right*, and that the emigrant settlers were interlopers upon the soil', could be traced to Macquarie's pro-emancipist policy. No doubt Macquarie's long reign accentuated the feeling, but there is reason to suppose that basically it was an inevitable response to the conditions under which the new land was settled. Indeed, some of Macquarie's actions, such as his spreading of his own and other old country names across the map, were felt by contemporaries to militate against the already emerging national feeling. In 1824 Edward Curr wrote:

> There is already a degree of nationality in Van Diemen's Land; people begin to talk of the good old times with which the old names are connected; and a governor might as well abolish the English language by proclamation, as the names which are associated with former days.
>
> We still talk of the Fat Doe River, Gallows Hill, Murderer's Plains, and Hell's Corners. These names were principally bestowed upon them by bush rangers and the hunters of the kangaroo, who in fact have been the discoverers of all the good districts in the island.

And James Dixon, who visited Australia in 1820, observed that a distinctive type of Australian speech had already appeared. Oddly enough he found it more euphonious than have most visitors. Dixon wrote:

> The children born in these colonies, and now grown up, speak a better language, purer, and more harmonious, than is generally the case in most parts of England. The amalgamation of such various dialects assembled together, seems to improve the mode of articulating the words.[23]

The early feeling of 'nationality', of which Curr wrote, is difficult to define though his paragraphs give its flavour very aptly. The young W. C. Wentworth dreamed of 'a new Britannia in another world',[24] but in a very important sense, 'a new *Britannia*' was the last thing which convicts and many immigrants, especially if Irish, wished to build in Australia. As one immigrant girl said to Caroline Chisholm in 1846:

> Oh, what a difference there is between this country and home for poor folks. I know I would not go back again. I know what England is. Old England is a fine place for the rich, but the Lord Help the poor.[25]

Wentworth's poem also saw 'the early blot' of convictism as the main impediment to a true national development. This view, of course, was the absolute antithesis of the strong lower-class feeling, which we have noticed, that Australia was peculiarly 'the prisoners' country'. As Hood wrote:

> The fact of being a drunkard, or a convict, is not looked upon in this country, amongst the *class*, as any disgrace; on the contrary . . . no shame whatever is evinced by the very best amongst them; and they look upon all 'self-imported devils' as beneath them, and not worth consideration.

Similarly that arch-radical, J. D. Lang, with his plans for a democratic Australian republic ruling imperially over the Pacific Islands, was far too individualistic, too doctrinaire, too sectarian, too 'political', and above all too respectably bourgeois, really to touch the imagination of early Australian working people. Even the first native-born poet of any significance, Charles Harpur, failed almost completely to touch that in men's hearts which was really new and distinctive of the new country. His play, *The Bushrangers* (1853), is Australian in setting but in little else. In style, construction and characterization, it is pseudo-Shakespeare with a dash of Gay's *Beggar's Opera*. The 'bushrangers' remind one of pompous aides to Falstaff, incomprehensibly transported to the Upper Hawkesbury scrubs. In a comprehensive study of the growth of Australian national sentiment, the tendencies represented by such middle-class people as Wentworth, Lang and Harpur would have an important place, but they have not much bearing on the unselfconscious but deeply-felt outlook of the common folk which is our proper concern.

Before 1850 this sentiment had little to do, directly, with political programmes, and perhaps even less to do with visionary aspirations of a glorious national future. The key to its understanding is that it was a lower-class outlook which, towards the end of the century, emerged in somewhat changed form as the main ingredient of a myth truly national in the sense that it was believed, at least to some extent, by all classes. Before the Gold Rush most middle-class immigrants, like Henry Kingsley's 'Geoffry Hamlyn', thought of Australia as a place in which to make their fortunes before returning 'home' to live in comfort and honour. The point is only underlined by the fact that many of them, like Niel Black, insensibly became more and more involved with their Australian interests until the cherished dream of a permanent return 'home' receded into the background.[26] Even

Wentworth, most illustrious of the native-born, and most prominent in developing nationalism on the political plane, retired to England for the last ten years of his life. But the strength of the attachment to Australia among working people, and the extent to which it had already begun to affect some members of the middle class, are suggested by the report of a Sydney court case in 1854. A solicitor, who had referred to events in Britain as having occurred 'at home', was rebuked by the police magistrate who said: 'You may call it *at home*, but we Currency Lads call it *abroad* and this is our home.'[27] This story, however, probably shows a greater degree of quasi-political awareness in the speaker than was common among his social inferiors. More characteristic is a scene from Harris's novel. Reuben Kable and a fellow Currency Lad, Charlie, are driving some cattle along a bush track when they see a young magistrate and two mounted soldiers nearing them from behind at full speed:

> 'I wonder what's up, Reuben. I'll be hanged if the lobsters haven't got their shells off. There's something afoot that's not easy.'
>
> 'They know their own best, Charlie,' said his countryman, as, after a short, careless gaze, he took his hand off his horse's crupper, and threw himself square again in his saddle.
>
> Nothing further passed between them for the instant. The Australians uniformly take pains to exhibit a contemptuous dislike of the British military. But suddenly Mr Hurley reined up at their very heels, his horse and himself almost breathless.
>
> 'Hollo! young fellow,' said Charlei [*sic*], 'don't ride into the cattle, without you want to be driven the rest of the way with them.'
>
> Reuben Kable, who saw that the newcomer was a gentleman, though acting rather unaccountably, merely rode on without remark, moving his horse a little away.
>
> 'In the Queen's name I require your assistance, sir,' cried Mr Hurley.
>
> 'I believe so,' responded Charlie; 'by-and by. Me first; next time you, mate.'
>
> Reuben took very little notice, beyond one of his half audible laughs, followed by a shout to one of his dogs not to go 'possum-hunting before the day's work was done'.

Currency sentiment expressed itself mainly in a very high valuation of 'practical' virtues so necessary for pioneering a new country, in a marked dislike of authority, particularly of soldiers and policemen, in contempt rather than hatred of 'new-chums', especially of those with polished or pretentious manners, and in the ancestral form of what later came to be known as larrikinism.

Samuel Sidney, in 1852, neatly summed up colonial feeling about the first of these matters:

> *Gentlefolks* . . . with little money and much pride, are the least likely to succeed as emigrants because . . . although poverty drives them from Europe, they cling to European prejudices, and continually sacrifice their independence to a short struggle to maintain appearances. . . . Action is the first great requisite of a colonist: to be able to do anything, to need the least possible assistance, to have a talent for making shift and being contented—these are golden talents. . . . I have known men of an active, energetic disposition, with a rich flow of animal spirits, who, although bred up in luxury and refinement, succeeded better than old fashioned farmers, who were always hankering after the market ordinaries of Old England.[28]

But, thirty years before Sidney wrote, colonial conditions had already evoked in the native-born what Cunningham called an 'open manly simplicity of character'. Harris was strongly impressed by the same trait when he wrote of the 'manly independence of disposition' shown by emancipist workmen, and he noted too the practical bent of the colonists:

> I was awakened by our host coming in from his work to breakfast. It was about eight o'clock, and his brother, who had also been up some time, had lit the fire, boiled a piece of salted beef, baked a cake on the hot hearth, and made the tea. This sort of readiness and activity is a remarkable feature in the character of the working population of the Australian colonies.[29]

The Currency attitude towards authority was, at least from a conventional point of view, less praiseworthy. A colonial Adjutant-General deplored the fact that native-born youths scorned to enter the Government service in any capacity, much preferring to be stockmen, or even shepherds.[30] Cunningham thought that it was 'a sense of pride . . . as much as the hostile sentiments instilled into them by their parents, that makes them so utterly averse to fill the situation of petty constables, or to enlist as soldiers'. In 1930 a nonagenarian Currency Lass recalled the Sydney of the 1840's:

Often quarrels arose between the soldiers and the civilians. At these times the soldiers would take off their belts with buckles and use them on the civilians. These fights became so frequent that at last the soldiers were not allowed to wear belts when they were going out at night. . . . They were sent to the colony to protect the people, but the civilians had very often to be their own protectors.[31]

'It cannot be denied,' wrote Harris, 'that the infusion of so much military character and agency into our civil courts in Australia, produces amongst the native race, universally, a most untoward feeling toward the common course of the law.'[32] And Melville affirmed that the military barracks were moved 'at a cost of £60,000' from George Street, in the centre of Sydney, to Surry Hills, because of 'the continued squabbles that occurred between the soldiers and the populace'. One feels that other reasons may have been at least equally weighty in the minds of the military authorities. Melville is more convincing when he writes of the army band's performances at the Sydney Domain:

> [They were] not so well attended as they were in former times, for the military and the inhabitants are on anything but good terms with each other. There is likewise a city band, all the performers are native youths, or what are sometimes called 'currency lads'; these young men perform in an excellent style, and on public festivals they willingly offer their services.

The Currency feeling of scorn for new chums, who were so obviously not at home in Australia, is again well illustrated by Harris. Martin Beck, the Negro overseer who is the hero of Harris's novel, explains to his employer, the new chum, gentleman squatter:

> . . . the emigrants are flats and the others [freed men and natives] are sharps. Of the two I think the sharps are a great deal best worth their wages; they want good looking after, but there's something to be got out of them. The emigrants they send out here always seem more dead than alive, till they've been five or six years in the country; then they begin to be like the rest of the people.

That this sentiment of the native-born was largely convict-derived is suggested by a remark of Frank Fowler's. Writing of the middle 1850's he notes that Victoria, 'not having had the equivocal advantage of convict labour, . . the battle of "oldhandism" against "new-chumism" is not everlastingly waging' there as it was in New South Wales, 'where the natives are more intolerant and intolerable than the bowery boys of America'. Fowler continues:

> The young Australian is systematically insolent to the new-chum; so is everyone indeed. How I, who had pretty well run the gauntlet of London life, was branded and fleeced during the first three months of my residence in Sydney! A new-chum is fair game for anyone. Your villainous bullock-driver in the interior, when he cannot by any stratagem, get his cattle to budge, culminates his oaths and imprecations by striking the leader of the refractory beasts over the head and grunting from the depths of his stomach—'Oh! you ——— NEW CHUM! move on!'

Contempt, good-natured or otherwise, could hardly go farther. Yet visiting Englishmen often felt a not less justified contempt for the ill-bred behaviour by which many Currency Lads felt it proper to demonstrate their heritage. This peculiarly Australian form of hooliganism was closely associated with another widely noticed trait, the precocity of the native-born youth. Most writers ascribed the latter to the influence of the climate but some, perhaps more realistically, thought it a natural result of the endemic labour shortage. Mundy tells of a twelve-year-old boy who filled 'the posts of waiter and *laquais-de-place*' at the Marine Hotel, Wollongong, and of another mite who, at the age of four, was not thought too young to begin acting as a carpenter's mate. Lads of seven or eight often drove bullock drays under supervision, and it was common for youths in their early teens to make long cross-country journeys in charge of teams or stock.[33] Fowler draws a vivid picture of the less happy results on the young of this forcing process:

> The Australian boy is a slim, dark-eyed, olive-complexioned, young rascal, fond of Cavendish, cricket, and chuck-penny, and systematically insolent to all servant-girls, policemen, and new chums. His hair is shiny with grease, as are the knees of his breeches and the elbows of his jacket. He wears a cabbage-tree hat with a dissipated wisp of black ribbon dangling behind, and loves to walk meditatively with his hands in his pockets, and, if cigarless, to chew a bit of straw in the extreme corner of his mouth. . . . He can fight like an Irishman or a Bashi-Bazouk; otherwise he is orientally indolent, and will swear with a quiet gusto if you push against him

in the street, or request him politely to move on. Lazy as he is
though, he is out in the world at ten years of age, earning good
wages, and is a perfect little man, learned in all the ways and by-
ways of life at thirteen . . . for shrewdness, effrontery, and mannish
affectation, your London gamin pales into utter respectability before
the young Australian. I should add that your thoroughbred gum-
sucker never speaks without apostrophising his 'oath' and interlard-
ing his diction with the crimsonest of adjectives. . . . One is struck
aghast with the occasional blasphemy of his language.

Such manners were understandable, if not excusable, in children. When carried on into manhood, they often provoked
respectable immigrants and visitors to fury. The urbane and well-
read Mundy was moved to wish that persons of this class had but
one collective nose, in order that it might the more easily be
rendered a bloody one. He wrote:

> These are an unruly set of young fellows, native born generally,
> who, not being able, perhaps, to muster coin enough to enter the
> house, amuse themselves by molesting those who can afford that
> luxury. Dressed in a suit of fustian or colonial tweed, and the
> emblem of their order, the low-crowned cabbage-palm hat, the main
> object of their enmity seems to be the ordinary black headpiece
> worn by respectable persons, which is ruthlessly knocked over the
> eyes of the wearer as he passes or enters the theatre.

Yet even at its worst, such behaviour should be seen in perspective as the perhaps inevitable concomitant of the 'readiness',
'activity', and 'manly independence' noted above. The descriptions
quoted, and nearly all other such, are of town roughs, and in all
towns of any size rowdyism exists. We have tried to show the main
reasons why it took this particular form in Australia.

Some allowance should also be made for the fact that nearly
all reports on the insufferableness of the 'Cabbage-tree Hat Mob'
come from educated, middle-class immigrants, whose own more
polished manners may often have been such as to arouse the very
worst in the native-born. Here, as so often elsewhere, the testimony of Harris is particularly valuable, because, almost alone
among contemporary writers on Australia, he seems to have
looked at life quite naturally from a working man's point of view.
On the night of his first landing in Sydney, in 1826, he went into
the tap-room of a Market Street tavern. His description of the

drinkers might almost serve as a microcosm of the developing Australian society:

> Most had been convicts: there were a good many Englishmen and Irishmen, an odd Scotchman, and several foreigners, besides some youngish men, natives of the colony. . . . The chief conversation consisted of vaunts of the goodness of their bullocks, the productiveness of their farms, or the quantity of work they could perform.

Harris goes on to describe their rough clothes, their almost animal-like force and crudity, and their vast consumption of rum and tobacco smoke, but what impressed him most deeply was 'one remarkable peculiarity common to them all—there was no offensive intrusiveness about their civility; every man seemed to consider himself just on a level with all the rest, and so quite content either to be sociable or not, as the circumstance of the moment indicated as most proper'.[34] This thorough-going egalitarianism, based on a relatively absolute though minimum economic security, was perhaps the most striking difference between the outlook of ordinary colonial working men and that of working men 'at home'. In ordinary circumstances most Currency Lads apparently did not feel called upon, in the manner of the 'Cabbage-tree Hat' roughs, to protest too much their independence.

Finally it is interesting to notice that, in the early period as since, Australians took inordinate pride in their sporting prowess. They early achieved the reputation of being excellent swimmers, and of being passionately fond of boxing, horse-racing and cricket. In this last, wrote an observer of the 1840's, 'The young Australians think themselves unrivalled . . . and wish Lord's players would come out and be stumped out.' Moreover, though their relative popularity has declined since, in the last century, both before and after the Gold Rush, rowing and yachting were no less keenly loved than cricket and horse-racing, at least in the two old coastal cities of Sydney and Hobart. Describing a Port Jackson regatta in the 1840's, an English visitor wrote: 'Then it is that the pride of the country oozes out; then it is two to one the "Natives" against the Yankees—"them Englishmen can't pull for a spurt like the Natives".'[35]

The Currency ethos was vividly summed up by E. S. Hall, pro-emancipist editor of the *Monitor*, in a partisan letter to the

Secretary of State. Hall's picture, as all brief generalizations must, fails to take account of complexities and exceptions, but enough has been said above to show that it contains an important basis of truth. In November 1828 he wrote:

> The fact is, Sir, the young men of this Colony have feelings just the reverse of those of the Lower Orders in England and Ireland. The circumstances of the parents of most of them having come to the Country in bondage, so far from making them humble, causes them to be the proudest people in the world. They are high-minded even to arrogancy. The circumstance of being *free* is felt by them with a strength bordering on a fierce enthusiasm. Nothing can induce them to enter the army, nor take office in the police; and few of them settle in our Towns. There seems to be an hereditary hatred among them to all professions. A few indeed were originally apprenticed as mechanics, but generally they prefer to indulge their independence in the wilds of their Native forests, where they can brood over their discontents without restraint or contradiction. There they become humble assistants to our large graziers. . . . [36]

In Chapter II we found reasons for thinking that convict and working-class attitudes had a disproportionately strong influence on the nascent Australian ethos. We have now seen that within the Australian working class, before the gold discoveries, Irishmen and native-born Australians exerted a disproportionately strong, and increasing, influence. In the next chapter we shall consider the effect of the 'up-country' environment on those who repaired thither, to 'brood over their discontents without restraint or contradiction', and to become not particularly 'humble assistants to our large graziers'.

CHAPTER III

1 'Australia's Folk Songs', *Twentieth Century: an Australian Quarterly Review*, vol. 1, No. 1.

2 The figures for 1947 refer to the whole of Australia; those for 1841 and 1851 to New South Wales, excluding the Port Phillip District and Van Diemen's Land, whence so many of Victoria's first citizens came. This choice of area has been made, as in the last chapter, for two reasons. First, in the early period New South Wales contained the bulk of the population; and the 'Old Australian', up-country ethos, which is our primary interest, began there and spread thence to the rest of the con-

tinent. Second, as will appear in Chapter V, it is desirable to keep the Victorian figures separate from those of New South Wales, because of the very different rates of immigration to the two major colonies during the decade of the first gold discoveries.

3 Margaret Kiddle, *Irish Paupers c. 1830-1850*, seminar paper, Australian National University, 20 May 1954.

4 Quoted A. Marjoribanks, *Travels in New South Wales*, etc., London 1847, p. 154; and cp. P. Cunningham, *Two Years in New South Wales*, 2 vols., vol. 2, p. 245.

5 Quoted A. Marjoribanks, *op. cit.*, p. 144 ff.

6 (David L. Waugh), *Three Years' Practical Experience of a Settler*, etc., 4th ed., Edinburgh 1838, p. 17; and cp. (Thomas Walker), *A Month in the Bush of Australia*, etc., London 1838, p. 7.

7 *Scottish Lowland Farmers c. 1830-1850*, Australian National University seminar paper, 13 May 1954; and see John Hood, *Australia and the East*, etc., London 1843, pp. 273-4; and R. Howitt, *Impressions of Australia Felix*, etc., London 1845, p. 150.

8 Brisbane to Bathurst, 28 October 1824, *Historical Records of Australia*, Series 1, vol. 11, p. 383; and R. Flanagan, *History of New South Wales*, etc., 2 vols., London 1862, vol. 1, pp. 379-80.

9 Rev. John Graham (ed.), *Lawrence Struilby*, etc., London 1863, p. 165.

10 Geoffrey C. Ingleton, *True Patriots All*, Sydney 1952, pp. 129, 143, 269.

11 Quoted 'An Old Identity' (Thomas Walker), *Felonry of New South Wales*, etc., Sydney 1890, p. 60 ff.

12 Quoted Max Brown, *Australian Son: The Story of Ned Kelly*, Melbourne 1948, p. 280.

13 This version from Jack Bradshaw, *Highway Robbery Under Arms*, etc., Sydney n.d. (about 1929).

14 *Votes and Proceedings, Legislative Council of New South Wales, 1838*, p. 177.

15 See J. D. Lang, *Transportation and Colonization*, etc., London 1837, pp. iv-vi; R. Therry, *Reminiscences*, etc., London 1863, p. 146; and T. Potter Macqueen, *Australia As She Is and As She May Be*, London 1840, p. 17.

16 *The Emigrant Family*, etc., 3 vols., London 1849, vol. 1, p. 3; and cp. *Report, House of Commons Select Committee on Transportation, 1837*, pp. 108, 175-6.

17 *Report on Agriculture and Trade in New South Wales*, etc., London 1823, p. 81.

18 Capt. John Myers, *The Life, Voyages and Travels of*, etc., London 1817, p. 200.

19 *Two Years in New South Wales*, etc., 2 vols., London 1827, vol. 2, p. 54; and cp. J. P. Townsend, *Rambles and Observations*, etc., London 1849, pp. 5-6.

20 *Settlers and Convicts*, ed. C. M. H. Clark, Melbourne 1953 (first published 1847), pp. 23-34.

21 *Royal Australian Historical Society, Journal and Proceedings*, vol. 22, pp. 371-4; and vol. 12, p. 86.

22 N.S.W. Colonial Secretary, *Inward Letters*, Newcastle: Bundles 19-21, 1823 (Mitchell Library MS.).

23 *Narrative of a Voyage*, etc., London 1822, p. 46. For other early accounts of Australian pronunciation cp. George Bennett, *Wanderings in New South Wales*, etc., 2 vols., London 1834, vol. 1, pp. 331-2; P. Cunningham, *op. cit.*, vol. 2, pp. 59-60.

24 *Australasia, A Poem*, etc., London 1823, p. 22.

25 Quoted Margaret Kiddle, *Caroline Chisholm*, Melbourne 1950, p. 243.

26 Black Papers (Public Library of Victoria, MSS.).

27 C. A. Corbyn, *Sydney Revels of Bacchus, Cupid and Momus*, etc., Sydney 1854, p. 128.

28 *Three Colonies of Australia*, etc., London 1852, pp. 22, 231; and cp. F. Lancelott, *Australia As It Is: Its Settlements*, etc., 2 vols., London 1852, vol. 2, p. 72 ff.

29 *Settlers and Convicts*, pp. 20, 24.

30 G. C. Mundy, *Our Antipodes*, etc., 3rd ed., London 1855, p. 155; and cp. J. P. Townsend, *Rambles and Observations*, etc., London 1849, pp. 152-3.

31 *R.A.H.S. Journal and Proceedings*, vol. 16, pp. 315-16.

32 *The Emigrant Family*, etc., vol. 2, p. 219.

33 G. C. Mundy, *op. cit.*, pp. 431-2; 'A Bushman', *A Voice from the Far Interior of Australia*, London 1847, pp. 32-3; J. P. Townsend, *op. cit.*, pp. 68-9; J. C. Hamilton, *Pioneering Days in Early Victoria*, Melbourne n.d. (1913), pp. 17-19; and *Memoirs of Joseph Holt*, ed. T. C. Croker, 2 vols., London 1838, vol 2, pp. 144-6.

34 *Settlers and Convicts*, p. 5.

35 J. P. Townsend, *op. cit.*, p. 260 ff.; John Henderson, *Excursions and Adventures in New South Wales*, etc., 2 vols., London 1851, vol. 2, p. 205; and *Report, House of Commons Select Committee on Transportation, 1837*, p. 108.

36 *Historical Records of Australia*, Series 1, vol. 14, p. 580.

'UP THE COUNTRY'

━━━━━━

*I'll take you round the stations and learn you how to ride
And I'll show you how to muster when we cross the Great Divide.*

THE crossing of the Blue Mountains in May 1813 foreshadowed the end of New South Wales as a predominantly convict colony. Yet it was perhaps symbolic that after twenty years of vain effort the barrier should have been conquered by a party consisting of four convicts, and a young Currency Lad, in addition to the two immigrant leaders, Blaxland and Lawson. For the next forty years there was to be a significantly higher proportion of convicts, ex-convicts, and native-born Australians on the expanding edge of settlement, as it moved into the interior, than there was in or near Sydney. Moreover, young Wentworth realized that distance and transport costs would for long inhibit the development of agriculture on the Western Plains, which were 'much better adapted for all the purposes of grazing and rearing cattle . . . [and] sheep, the wool of which will without doubt eventually become the principal export of this colony'.[1] When the first ten free settlers set out for Bathurst in February 1818 five of them were Currency men and the other five old hands.[2] In their wake came the great 'squatting rush' to the west which reached its flood during the 'thirties and 'forties.

If many of the squatters were, as Governor Gipps thought, 'young men every way entitled to be called gentlemen', most of their working hands were not. From the census returns it can be established that right up to 1851 there were, in the squatting districts beyond the boundaries of location, nearly twice as many convicts, 'old hands' and native-born Australians as there were free immigrants. Of the first three groups the prisoners were the largest in 1841, and the Currency people in 1851, but in this latter year the three groups together still comprised practically two-thirds of outback people. The following table provides, in these terms, a picture of population distribution during the period:

TABLE V[3]

	Convicts	'Other Free Persons'	Born in the Colony	Total Convicts, Emancipists and Natives	Arrived Free	Convict, Emancipist and Native % Total Population
County of Cumberland—						
1841	7,908	7,959	16,257	32,124	25,984	55·3
1851	734	6,546	36,812	44,092	37,022	54·4
Other Counties within the boundaries of Location—						
1841	13,553	7,929	11,114	32,596	14,852	68·7
1851	998	12,836	35,226	49,060	29,372	62·6
Squatting Districts beyond the boundaries of Location—						
1841	3,028	2,360	1,210	6,598	2,447	72·9
1851	961	7,247	9,353	17,561	10,136	63·4

For the sake of brevity, we may refer to convicts, ex-convicts and native-born—the groups among which the embryonic national sentiment was strongest—as 'old Australians'. It will be seen that, throughout the last pre-Gold-Rush decade, the proportion of these people in the population increased with distance from Sydney. Transportation to the mainland ceased in 1840, but for the next ten years new arrivals went far towards keeping pace with the natural increase of Currency people, so that in New South Wales as a whole the ratio of 'Old' to 'New' Australians remained approximately constant at about three to two. 'Up the country' in 1841 this ratio was nearly three to one, and in 1851 at the beginning of the Gold Rush, it was still nearly two to one. In Sydney and its immediate neighbourhood, throughout the decade, the ratio was not much more than one to one. Thus, if there is any validity in the arguments of the last two chapters, there is substance also in the traditional belief that the 'true' or 'typical' Australians were the men of the outback, for it was there that, relative to the total population of each area, most of them were to be found.

What is the explanation of the peculiarly 'Australian' nature of the outback population? Initially, the 'government men' who made up the overwhelming majority of the pastoral labour force, were conscripted to the up-country life. From 1827 onwards government administrative policy consciously aimed at directing convict labour to the hinterland.[4] Scottish and other flockmasters of the interior generally preferred assigned servants to free labourers for the sufficient reason that they were much cheaper, but there is evidence that the government men were preferred for other reasons also.

As late as 1850, at a meeting of Darling Downs squatters called to discuss the re-introduction of transportation, one speaker declared that he 'would rather have the pick of the gaols than the refuse of the workhouses'.[5] There is no doubt but that the hardships of their servitude made the prisoners, generally speaking, better able than the free immigrants to cope with the rough and makeshift conditions of frontier life. As Howitt wrote of two ex-convict splitters whom he employed for a time: 'Their hands were horny with toil; their faces tanned and tawny; their bodies seemed compounds of iron and leather. Hard workers they were, and hard drinkers.'

Moreover the fact that large numbers of convicts reached Australia before there were many free immigrants meant that the former were, generally speaking, more thoroughly 'colonized'. When Cox directed the building of the first road across the Blue Mountains in 1814 and 1815, he chose for the task from among the convicts 'well-inclined hardy men, *who had been some years in the colony*, and accustomed to field labour'. Townsend noted that an assigned servant on the frontier of settlement in the 1830's learnt 'how to maintain himself in a new country', so that later when transportation to the mainland had ceased, settlers preferred 'men so tutored to emigrants; who, on their first arrival, [were] comparatively but "babes in the wood" '. And John Sidney ['A Bushman'], one of the most acute contemporary observers of outback life, undertook to prove, 'if necessary, before a committee of either House of Parliament . . . that for flock-masters and cattle-breeders, prisoners have always been the best servants'.

Naturally, then, the hardest and most highly-skilled kinds of work were usually performed by old hands and native-born youths. Generally speaking, the management of cattle required more skill, and was more spiced with danger and romance, than that of sheep. Harris writes, as though it were the usual thing, of a large group of stockmen who were nearly all ex-convicts,[6] and Haygarth testifies to the skill and prestige of native-born stockmen. Of cattle-mustering he writes:

> . . . our most powerful ally, our sheet anchor, was 'Amos' . . . a native-born white . . . a man who could not be wholly domesticated; his slab hut was all that he required at night, and his home was abroad in the saddle. . . . Sparing of his speech . . . though he was ever most ready to assist, he never interfered with his neighbours. His whole ambition seemed to be to be what he was—an oracle upon all subjects connected with his own peculiar occupation, and the most fearless rider in the district, one who, let the animals pursued go where they might, had never yet failed to 'head them', or refused to follow them down anything 'short of a precipice'.

'Bullock-driving in the bush being almost a science,' wrote Sidney, 'we say, "any man can knock bullocks about, but very few can drive them".' And Byrne recorded:

> Old convicts generally make the best bullock-drivers; their knowledge of the country and their rough habits seem to have formed them for this employment. The wages of bullock-drivers are somewhat higher than that [sic] of other general servants.

The profanity of bullock-drivers was already legendary.[7] Splitters and sawyers, usually known as tiersmen, were also famous for their rough habits, debauchery, skill and hard work. They, too, were usually old hands.[8]

On sheep stations, shearing was the most specialized and skilled occupation. Perhaps because it was also the most completely nomadic of all outback jobs, it seems to have attracted a higher proportion of old hands than any other.[9] In Port Phillip, wrote Joyce, 'there were two classes of shearers, the Derwenters from Van Diemen's Land, and the Sydneys. The former were the better shearers but the latter were the faster.'

The fact that they were the pioneers and their higher average level of skill gave to the old hands and the Currency Lads an influence and a prestige among their fellows out of all proportion to their numbers. There is a description of the proceedings at a Land Commissioner's Court of Inquiry which amusingly illustrates the point. Each of the squatters who were parties to the dispute called in turn on witnesses who swore to their master's prior claim to the land. Finally,

> A. now brings forth his reserve, a man who, by his own account, is of so long standing in the neighbourhood as to have been what is called in the colony a 'first fleeter'. He declares that he has been originally in the service of the actual explorer and earliest occupant of the run, . . . and all the other witnesses are put to silence, and listen in admiration to their more enterprising companion.[10]

Although 'government men' were originally conscripted to the ranks of the pastoral proletariat, a glance at Table V strongly suggests that after becoming free a great many of them voluntarily remained in the outback, and that others purposely went thither. Between 1841 and 1851 the number of old hands in the County of Cumberland fell by about half. During the same decade the number in the twenty counties almost doubled, while in the remote squatting districts it more than trebled. The table shows that native-born people also were drawn in disproportionate numbers to the outback. What caused these men to *choose* the hardships and loneliness of outback life?

First, there was always, even in the depths of the depression of the early 1840's, an absolute labour shortage in the far interior. Looking back a few years, John Sidney wrote in 1847:

> Where ship-loads of emigrants were idling in the government barracks, and starving in the streets of Sydney, at the McIntyre, 500 miles in the Bush, I, in common with many of my neighbours, was badly put to for hands, [and] obliged to leave sheep to pasture without a shepherd.

This picture exaggerates the distress in the capital. A few pages later, referring again to the depression, Sidney himself says that it was felt chiefly by 'the master class', and stresses that the labouring classes in New South Wales had *never known distress in the European sense of the term—want of food or clothing*. But the picture of labour scarcity far 'up the country' is accurate. It meant that wages were usually higher in the bush[11] and this fact, of course, attracted many thither.

Probably more important was the fact that the outback offered something nearly approaching absolute economic security, albeit at what was, from a middle-class point of view, a relatively low level. Gargantuan quantities of mutton, damper and tea, and sufficient rough slop clothing, were always available to a competent workman unencumbered by wife or children. If a man did not like his work, or his employer, he could always leave without trouble or notice, sure of being able to find another position at a neighbouring station. Even if he could not find work or, to a certain extent, if he did not want it, he still had no need to fear starvation. The customary right of every traveller to receive rations, at least of flour, at each station was early established.[12]

This basic economic security meant that pastoral workmen could afford to be even more 'independent' towards their employers than their brothers in Sydney. Almost every contemporary observer of outback manners either lauded the 'independence' or complained of the insubordination of the up-country workmen. A conservative Scottish squatter, Niel Black, wrote in 1840:

> One would almost be inclined to think it a mistake in the arrangements of providence when he sees so many of the most refined in consummate villainy swaggering and bustling about with a parade of independence and boasting themselves free men, while the Master stands quietly by watching their humour and Screwing his wits to get on the Sunny Side of them. Whilst in Scotland many an upright honest man begs a brother of the earth to give him leave to toil.

After six months' more experience as an employer of bush-workers he described them to T. S. Gladstone, on 21 September 1840, as follows:

> The veriest blackguards that move upon the earth and I believe

in circumstances the most independent of any class of labouring men alive . . .

And even Sidney, who understood and sympathized with outback workmen, wrote:

> Within the boundaries labouring men are frequently most grievously oppressed. In the Bush, masters are almost entirely at the mercy of their free servants.

Where labourers were so scarce, and magistrates often several days' or even weeks' journey distant, even the Draconic Masters and Servants Acts were often of little avail to the employers. J. C. Byrne's troubles in 1839, on an overlanding trip from Yass Plains to Adelaide, graphically illustrate the point. He and his friend set out with 973 head of cattle, four drays, and sixteen men who were 'chiefly old hands'. When they came to the bark shanty at the Gundagai crossing of the Murrumbidgee Byrne's workmen fell in with some old companions who were sprawled on a pile of split timber, drinking rum from a bucket in tin pint pots. 'Next day twelve out of the sixteen were uproariously drunk, and loudly expressed their determination not to proceed one step further on their journey without an advance of 2 l. per man, and time to spend it at the inn.' Byrne and his friend finally had to make the best of the matter because, as he says, 'there were no other hands to be obtained', and the nearest police station and magistrate were at Yass, about seventy miles away. Sometimes in frontier districts, the labour shortage was so severe and effective state control so remote that even ticket-of-leave men and assigned servants dared to combine against their masters. A Van Diemen's Land government proclamation of 5 January 1822 reads:

> Complaint having been made to the Lieutenant Governor, that in several instances at the late harvest crown prisoners holding tickets of leave demanded excessive wages or payment for their labour; they are now warned, that . . . any . . . ticket-of-leave man . . . refusing to accept work at a just and reasonable rate of payment . . . will forfeit the indulgence of holding a ticket-of-leave. The settlers are earnestly recommended to . . . act in unison with each other in preventing the imposition . . .[13]

And James Backhouse, the Quaker missionary, who journeyed through the outback pastoral country about a decade before the Gold Rush, wrote in 1843:

One of the prisoners at the house where we lodged, having been flogged by order of a magistrate, for allowing the sheep to ramble over a piece of marshy ground, the whole of those at the establishment refused to come to the reading of the scriptures last evening. I went to them this morning, and gave them some counsel, which was well received.

The very remoteness of the frontier was, in itself, an attraction for some men. Old hands and others who wished to 'keep out of trouble', or to be forgotten, could do so most easily by removing themselves as far as possible from the temptations of the capital, and from the provocation to violence which the sight of a police uniform represented to many of them. The following illuminating incident took place in 1865, a quarter of a century after transportation to the eastern mainland had ended. A. B. Peirce, an American, was skipper of the *Lady Daly*, one of the first river steamers to navigate the River Darling. At Menindie, in a resplendent blue uniform, he went ashore to sell some kegs of beer to the publican, one Quinn, whose customers had just consumed the last drop of alcohol in the shanty. The bar, wrote Peirce, was filled with 'men of the toughest variety',

[many of them] had been sent out for penal servitude. . . . Mistaking the uniforms for those of the police, the dirtiest and drunkenest of the mob rushed up and struck me squarely in the face. . . . A free fight ensued, in which the crowd exerted all its power to show the respect in which it held the representatives of Her Gracious Majesty. The battle was shortly ended, however, by Quinn's forcing his way to me, shouting that the boat was in, and explaining the uniforms. The attack immediately ceased, and abject and profuse apologies were in order, my first assailant wishing to kiss me and make up.

This desire for obscurity no doubt accounts largely for the back-country usage, which persisted well into the present century, by which most working men were known, to mates and masters alike, only by nicknames. As Haygarth reported,

In the bush of Australia, *aliases* are frequently as prevalent among the labouring classes as in the English collieries. . . . A neighbour of ours had a stockman who . . . was only known, probably from his rough-riding feats, by the title of 'Go by 'em'; and I remember that . . . when it was necessary to discover the real name of a man . . . for the purpose of taking out a warrant against him, for having aided and abetted a party of bushrangers . . . we could get no further, for some time, than the sobriquet of 'Terrible Tommy'.

Up-country life had one other attraction which, though immaterial, seems to have been very important. It is easy, and at present fashionable, to wax ironical over the freedom and simplicity of life in the 'wide open spaces' but for certain types of mind these charms were very real, and were felt by masters and men alike. Haygarth communicates the feeling very accurately in the following passage:

> This sensation of absolute freedom, which is one of the chief attractions of this sort of life, some might say its only one, gains a strong hold upon many minds; and it is certain that in a new country, such as Australia, there are few men who, after leading a pastoral life, would be able to content themselves with the less exciting and less independent occupations of agriculture, such as it is pursued in the more thickly populated parts of the colony, or in the vicinity of the capital.

Nearly a hundred years later bushmen in the Northern Territory felt just the same about frontier life. I spent some months there on two occasions in the mid-1930's prospecting, road-making, and 'seeing the country'. Most men I met, when asked why they stayed in the Territory, answered more or less articulately in such terms as the above.

High wages, then, and a vagabond life of freedom from conventional restraints attracted many men to the bush, but more were repelled by its strangeness, hardships and loneliness. Generally speaking, newly arrived immigrants did their best to remain in or near Sydney, at any rate for some years. They feared real difficulties, and some others which were largely illusory. Mundy tells of meeting an Irish immigrant in Sydney:

> [he] seemed much tickled by my account of the life of the provinces, and above all of the Saturday serving out of the weekly rations to the labourers—'the mate, and the tay, and the like';—'but the snakes, my darlin', the snakes!' he continued; and having once stumbled on this unlucky subject, he gave up all idea of rural employment!

'The far bush is not popular with emigrants,' wrote Sidney. 'They are afraid, and prefer lingering at lower wages in the settled districts; if they get up, they are not of much use at first,

lose your sheep and bullocks, and themselves . . .' This low
estimate of newly arrived immigrants' fitness for bush work is
confirmed by Niel Black. Though he hated the arrogant independence of the old hands, he was forced to recognize that most
immigrants were 'very stupid and ignorant respecting the business
at which they are employed, and unless they improve I fear they
will be no great acquisition'.[14]

'The business at which they were employed' was usually shepherding, an occupation held in tremendous contempt by stockmen,
bullock-drivers, shearers and other skilled bush-workers. Their
attitude is given accurately, if colourfully, by 'Rolf Boldrewood'
in his novel, *The Squatter's Dream*, in which a native-born stockman thus replies to a Chinese who has asked whether he is a
shepherd:

> You be hanged! Do I look like a slouchin', possum-eating, billy-
> carrying crawler of a shepherd? I've had a horse under me ever since
> I was big enough to know Jingaree mountain from a haystack, and
> a horse I'll have as long as I can carry a stockwhip.

'Crawler' seems first to have meant any lethargic person.[15] Then
it came to mean a convict employed in an 'iron-gang', and later
a shepherd who 'crawled' *in front of* his flock to stop the leaders
from straying. It acquired its present meaning of 'toady' much
later.

Before the Gold Rush all outback runs were unfenced. The
shepherd's duties consisted of little more than to wander about
with his flock by day, remaining wakeful enough to see that none
of them strayed too far away from the main body, and to count
them at night into a temporary fold made of brushwood hurdles.
Usually he shared his bark hut with a mate, the hut-keeper, who
slept in a kind of portable sentry-box beside the flock to protect
it from dingoes. But much of what active work was required of
both shepherd and hut-keeper was performed by their dogs. The
life was so lazy, lonely and monotonous that many shepherds
became a little mad. These, especially when their eccentricity
took the form of preference for a solitary life, came to be known
as 'hatters'.

Partly because of the extreme loneliness, and partly because
they considered that the inactivity unfitted them for any other

work, experienced bushmen would usually accept employment as shepherds only as a last resort.[16] Thus it was that a good number of the newly arrived immigrants found their way to the bush as 'crawlers'. Mechanics possessing any degree of skill could usually find work in or near Sydney, but unskilled labourers, operatives or clerks, for whose services there was comparatively little demand, sometimes had to go up country to find work, whatever their fears may have been. And there is evidence that many of them made good shepherds, especially townsmen and sedentary workers, who had no old-world preconceptions to unlearn of how rural work should be performed.[17]

If one may apply locally a rather cosmic idea, Professor Toynbee's concept of 'challenge and response' seems apposite to the situation. 'Up the country' greater security, of a kind, and certainly greater freedom or 'independence', awaited old hand, Currency man, or free immigrant alike, *if* he could summon up the physical and spiritual resources necessary for assimilation to the strange and hard environment. For the staid, the timid or the vicious, the settled farming lands near the coast or the slums of Sydney were more tempting. Referring to thoroughly hardened convict prostitutes, Macqueen, who was a magistrate in the Singleton district, wrote:

> As to imprisonment in the third class of the factory [at Parramatta], they laugh at it, well knowing the demand for female servants to be so great, that their turn will soon come round, when they will be again returned to the rum bottles and gin shops of the metropolis. I soon found that the only system they dreaded, was to make an order that they should in future, only be assigned to settlers far in the interior, and entirely removed from large towns.[18]

It seems that outback conditions exercised a kind of natural selection upon the human material. The qualities favouring successful assimilation were adaptability, toughness, endurance, activity and loyalty to one's fellows, just those traits already noticed as being typical of the convict and currency elements of the population. This is not to deny that some newly arrived immigrants made good bushmen. There must have been many cases of 'natural inborn fitness' for outback life, such as that recalled by an old Queensland pioneer.[19] Nor is it to suggest that the typical bush-worker was a noble being *sans peur et sans reproche*. We shall see that he was callously brutal to the Aborigines to whom he owed so much of his knowledge of the country, that he habitually shielded those who stole certain kinds of property from squatters and others felt to be beyond the pale of his tribe, and that he was even more profane, improvident, and (when opportunity offered) drunken, than Australian city-dwellers.

Nevertheless, there is convincing evidence that convicts and old hands were morally improved, if not entirely made over to the Lord, by up-country conditions. George Bennett, who in his earlier chapters takes a very low view of convict and emancipist morals in Sydney, felt constrained to admit that the picture was different along the remote upper Murrumbidgee:

> [I] remarked with some degree of pleasure, that although most of the stations are solely under charge of assigned servants, (convict is an obsolete word in the colony), yet the huts are clean and well arranged. The men in most instances take care of the property entrusted to their charge . . .

Patrick Leslie, a pioneer squatter on the Darling Downs, recalled:

> We had twenty-two men, all ticket-of-leave, or convicts, as good and game a lot of men as ever existed, and who never occasioned us a moment's trouble: worth any forty men I have ever seen since.[20]

Macqueen, during his five years as a large settler, actually kept the following statistical record of the two hundred odd 'convicts and ticket-of-leave men' he employed during the period:

Become free or enjoying their ticket, married, and thoroughly reclaimed	14
Become free or holding ticket, single, and thoroughly reclaimed	49
Become free from expiration of sentence, but worthless	7
Become free, reclaimed, and returned home	1
Well conducted men, as yet under sentence	62
Indifferent—not trustworthy	29
Depraved characters—irreclaimable	7
Sent to iron gangs and penal settlements, for robbery, absconding, etc.	11
Escaped	1
Died—one old age, two casualties	3
Given up at request of Government	2
Returned to Government hospital from ill health	4
	191 [*sic*]

To this number may be added about 15 lately arrived, and not yet classed.

Although Macqueen's pamphlet was largely a piece of partisan pleading for transportation, these figures are (in spite of his faulty arithmetic) broadly consistent with most other contemporary opinion on the point under discussion. As E. M. Curr wrote, justly because realistically:

> Station life not only put a stop to drunkenness and theft by the absence of grog and of anything worth stealing, but the constant absence of temptation had a tendency to throw the convict's mind into a better groove. . . . Probably, also, the possession of a reasonable freedom went towards creating a healthier tone of mind.

Yet, after all, the effect of the outback environment was perhaps not so much to 'reform' those who went thither, as to accentuate and develop certain characteristics which they brought with them. Frontier conditions fostered and intensified the growth of the distinctively Australian outlook whose beginnings we have considered above.

Take, for example, the strongly egalitarian sentiment of group solidarity and loyalty, which was perhaps the most marked of all convict traits. This was recognized as the prime distinguishing mark of outback workers fifty years before Lawson and others wrote so much about mateship. In 1845 Griffith, who had 'always considered the observation of the effects produced on' pastoral workers by the up-country environment 'a most interesting study', wrote:

> They have a strong *esprit de corps*, which is kept up by their speaking a language so full of cant expressions as to become almost a separate dialect. Their best trait is their liberality towards each other. . . . Though amongst this class of men the standard of morality is very low, yet they are not without their rude notions of honour, modified, however, by a kind of public opinion amongst themselves, which exercises a considerable influence over their actions. . . . A man guilty of crimes of a mean and unmanly nature is despised by them; and one who robs from his fellows, but especially from his mate, is regarded as infamous. On the other hand . . . [they are not] very scrupulous on the subject of honesty, if the person injured be not a poor man. Defrauding one not of their own class they seem to regard as a spoiling of the Egyptians.

Harris, in one of his most penetrating passages, pointed to the environmental pressures towards such behaviour. After describing how, to succour him, his mate had walked 'full forty miles' in twenty-four hours, carrying a fifty pound pack across the mountains, he observed:

> Looked at in an abstract point of view, it is quite surprising what exertions bushmen of new countries, especially mates, will make for one another, beyond people of the old countries. I suppose want prevailing less in the new countries makes men less selfish, and difficulties prevailing more make them more social and mutually helpful.[21]

We have already seen that actual 'want'—of the basic necessities of life—was almost unknown in the interior. On the other hand, what Harris called the 'difficulties' of outback life were abundant. They made the practice of a collectivist 'mateship' essential, just as the abundance of basic foodstuffs made it possible. The hazards and hardships, but above all the loneliness of up-country life were such that, to make life tolerable, often merely to preserve it, every man had habitually to treat every other man as a brother. In cases of accident or illness the individual depended completely on whoever was nearest. Even apart from these contingencies, the mateless man was likely to become a 'hatter'.

The strength of this tradition is perhaps best shown by that 'free and easy hospitality' that became everywhere in the interior a sort of public right'.[22] There was, of course, a gulf fixed between the squatter's or superintendent's 'house' and the men's huts, so that bush hospitality flourished on two separate planes, as it were, but it is scarcely an exaggeration to say that it amounted, at least within the circle of the 'nomad tribe', to a kind of primitive Communism, or primitive Christianity as described by Saint Luke: 'Neither said any *of them* that ought of the things which he possessed was his own; but they had all things in common.' 'I really believe,' wrote a German traveller who walked through the Riverina in 1850:

> there is no country in the world where hospitality is carried to a greater extent than Australia. Poor shepherds . . . allow strangers to stay with them maybe three or four times every week. They will never turn them from their doors, nor ask the least remuneration for the shelter and diet they have provided; indeed, they seem ashamed to take money from the traveller, and feel insulted at the offer. Should he chance to have tobacco with him, they will thankfully accept a little.[23]

The evidence of Harris is even more striking:

> Immediately you get into the country parts of the colony every door is without bolt or lock, and every hut ready to receive you for the night. You enter the first that suits you about sundown, whether the owner is there or not, and light your pipe, and unsaddle your horse, and bring in your equipments. When the residents come in, they will neither ask you who you are, nor stare at you; the only notice they take of your trespass is a courteous good evening, and putting down an extra quartpot at the fire. The traveller, on the other hand, does not ask them whether they are free or bond; but if he judges they are prisoners, or free men and in want of anything, he shares his own stock of the article with them. The best accommodation in the hut is usually allotted to the stranger.[24]

So strong was this tradition that it influenced even bush publicans and shanty keepers who, as a class, were by-words[25] for ruthlessness and greed. In the remotest frontier districts they usually charged working men nothing for food, tea and shelter, relying for their profits on the bar trade, and board paid by travelling 'swells'. In 1850 a Darling River shanty keeper explained:

> . . . eating and drinking (that is tea) they did not count upon; a man must have that, and they were not going to take advantage of a poor devil who had to carry his bundle through the world; but if a gentleman travelled on horseback, it was another thing.[26]

Half a century later the same practice still obtained at Dunstan's Hotel on the then mining frontier at Marble Bar, Western Australia, a couple of thousand miles away.[27]

There is a passage in Harris's novel which shows both the strength and the derivation of this outback sentiment so graphically that it must be quoted in full. The scene is a stockman's bark hut not far from the present site of Canberra:

> A voice of that mixed accent which distinguishes the offspring of Dublin parents of the lowest class born in one of our great English cities, was singing, with the richest licence of droll intonation, a composition of which we retain only the concluding verses, but which might be not inaptly entitled 'The Family Man'—a phrase signifying, in the 'flash dialect', a 'thief' or 'cross-man'. The fragment will at once illustrate their sentiments, and identify the melodist

himself with that portion of the population whose right of passage to the colony is presented to them with so many grave public ceremonies at the various Old and New Bailies.

> There's never a chap—Bob, Arthur, or Dan—
> Lives half such a life as the Countryman;
> He scours the city, he sweeps the road;
> Asses laden too heavy he helps to unload.
> He spends all he gets, and gets all he can,
> Does the rattlin', roarin', Family Man.

> There's never a chap—Bob, Arthur or Dan—
> Half such a chap as a Countryman;
> If you've little or none you may share in his mess,
> If you've got too much he'll help you to less;
> He gets all he spends, and that's all he can,
> Does the rattlin', roarin', Family Man.

To these lyric stanzas, a rolling chorus was supplied by six or seven voices repeating the first couplet of each at its conclusion; a short interlude being supplied in the same manner after the chorus by deafening shouts—'Good song, Dubbo!'—'Here whet thee whistle lad!'—'I'll back Mikkey for a strave against all Morrumbidgee!' 'Silence'—'Attention'—'The song, gentlemen.' 'Bob! shut up:—go on, Dubbo.'

These scenes and sounds, which may be supposed to be novel to the reader, were to Martin Beck habitual and familiar in the daily experience of many years . . . almost everyone [of the singers in the hut] had the stockwhip either in his hand, or hung round his neck, or near him on the ground.

The song itself is not Australian, but neither is it an English folk-song of the type of 'Adieu to Old England' or 'Van Diemen's Land'. There is none of the underlying melancholy and overt conventional moralizing, typical of the latter *genre*. 'The Family Man' is a 'flash song', typical of those sung in their 'bowsing kens' by the submerged class of professional thieves and prostitutes of London and other large British cities. The whole passage illustrates strikingly not only the pastoral workers' spirit of easy-come, easy-go egalitarianism and mateship, but also its derivation from convict, Irish and lower-class sources. Harris, in a footnote, says of the term, *Countryman*, 'We apprehend this term must be of similar signification with the other' (i.e., *Family Man*), but as

Countryman does not occur in James Hardy Vaux's glossary of thieves' cant, nor in other available slang dictionaries, it is reasonable to suggest that it may here be a sign of acclimatization, introduced by the singers to give up-country significance to the lines. Though not part of the song itself, the nickname 'Dubbo', and the symbolism of the stockwhip, show how thoroughly at home the singers had already become in their new environment.

Adaptability was another convict trait which was accentuated and developed by frontier conditions. In 1905, on the cover of the first edition of Paterson's *Old Bush Songs*, there appeared the following four lines of an old ballad, the remainder of which had apparently been forgotten:

> Stringy-bark will light your fire
> Green hide will never fail yer,
> Stringy-bark and green-hide
> Are the mainstay of Australia.

If rough and ready improvisation were convict traits they were also, in the outback, often necessary conditions of survival. Where population was so scattered and specialist services of all kinds practically non-existent, a man had to be a jack-of-all-trades who knew how to make do with whatever scanty materials were to hand. In the first stages of settlement masters and men alike sheltered from the elements in bark huts or 'gunyahs', adapted from those of the aborigines.[28] As nails, and indeed ironmongery of all kinds, were very scarce, strips of untanned hide were used to fasten the bark together, and for a hundred other purposes. In his *Ten Years' Experience in New South Wales* (1845), Rev. David Mackenzie listed twenty-nine uses for green-hide, concluding:

> But time would fail me to enumerate half the virtues and uses of green hide. Suffice it to say, that green-hide, horses, and stringy-bark, are the grand support and stay of Australia; without them the whole fabric would totter and fall.

Thus, stringy-bark and green-hide early became a symbol of the outback, or 'Australian', capacity for improvisation. In the 1820's 'inland settlers' were already known by the sobriquet of 'Stringy-barks'.[29] And by the 1840's the saying that 'if it were not for green-hide and stringy-bark the colony would go to [hell]' had already become traditional.[30] The above quatrain obviously derived from the following song, which was apparently composed in 1866:

> I sing of a commodity, it's one that will not fail yer,
> I mean the common oddity, the mainstay of Australia;
> Gold it is a precious thing, for commerce it increases,
> But stringy bark and green hide can beat it all to pieces.

> *Chorus:*

> Stringy bark and green hide, that will never fail yer,
> Stringy bark and green hide, the mainstay of Australia.

> If you travel on the road, and chance to stick in Bargo,
> To avoid a bad capsize, you must unload your cargo;
> For to pull your dray about, I do not see the force on,
> Take a bit of green hide, and hook another horse on.

> If you chance to take a dray, and break your leader's traces,
> Get a bit of green hide, to mend your broken places;
> Green hide is a useful thing all that you require,
> But stringy bark's another thing when you want a fire.

> If you want to build a hut to keep out wind and weather,
> Stringy bark will make it snug, and keep it well together;
> Green hide if it's used by you, will make it all the stronger,
> For if you tie it with green hide, it's sure to last the longer.

> New chums to this golden land, never dream of failure,
> Whilst you've got such useful things as these in fair Australia,
> For stringy bark and green hide will never, never fail you,
> Stringy bark and greenhide is the mainstay of Australia.[31]

A nomadic habit of life was another prominent convict trait which was accentuated by conditions in the interior. Like a soldier or sailor under orders, a convict had, and could have, no permanent abode. If he did not abscond from a bad master, he was always liable, at a moment's notice, to be re-assigned, or 'returned to Government' on account of illness or bad behaviour, or moved from one penal station or road-gang to another, quite apart from being moved to different working parties and different quarters within the same establishment. Tom Petrie tells a significant story of an old hand whose ill treatment during the Logan regime at Moreton Bay had left him 'not quite in possession of his senses in all things'. 'He would never sleep in a bed, but would "camp" beside the kitchen fire, or, if a lime kiln were burning, there for a certainty would he be found, rolled up in a blanket, surrounded by dogs.'

We know that the old hands were the most foot-loose of out-back workers. Charles Griffith wrote:

They are very fond of change, wandering about the country generally in pairs, and rarely remaining more than a year in one service. They are to be found more at the distant stations and in newly-settled country where wages are higher, and there is more difficulty to contend with, than in the more civilised parts where the emigrants have in a great measure superseded them.

Yet even if no 'government man' had ever crossed the Great Divide, other factors would have imposed a wandering habit of life on most bushmen. A pastoral economy always tends to create nomads just as agriculture tends to wed the farmer to his own plot of soil. In Australia this tendency was reinforced by the vagaries of the climate, which were always making it necessary to move stock from one area to another, by the sparsity of settlement, by the temporary and insecure title to runs resulting from the land laws, and by the seasonal or occasional nature of much bush work such as shearing, fencing, splitting, clearing, tank-sinking and so on. Harris noted already in the 1830's 'a peculiar characteristic' of 'the *free* labouring population of Australia'.

. . . it is in a state of constant migration. The man who has a con-tract job and is a hired servant here this year, probably spends the next at the other end of the colony.[32]

And John Sidney, in a more colourful phrase reminiscent of Gipps's famous statement, wrote: 'you can no more change shep-herds and herdsmen into citizens and gardeners, than you can turn wandering Arabs into weavers and drapers.' The stock reason, given by the men themselves, for their endless movement was that they liked 'to see the country'.[33]

Two other aspects of outback life, both of which had important consequences on the outlook of the pastoral workers, were the acute shortages of women and of clergymen. Among the convicts also women had been scarce, and though clergymen had been relatively plentiful, they seem on the whole to have had a negative influence. Cunningham, a very acute observer, wrote: 'the only real signs of religion [he] ever saw among convicts, were amongst a portion of Catholics on board.'

The official status of early Anglican clergymen as chaplains to convict establishments made them, in the eyes of the prisoners, part of the government machinery of repression. The result was that, in Crowley's words, 'the practice of religion was an object of ridicule and part of the punishment.'[34] There is no reason to suppose that Kingsley was exaggerating much when he made one of his characters in *Geoffry Hamlyn*, a well-disposed old hand working on an outback station, say:

> These prisoners hate the sight of a parson above all mortal men. And for why? Because when they're in prison, all their indulgences, and half their hopes of liberty, depend on how far they can manage to humbug the chaplain with false piety. And so, when they are free again, they hate him worse than any man. I am an old prisoner myself, and I know it.

The prisoners' anti-clericalism was increased by the fact that in the early days of the colony several Anglican priests sat on the Bench as magistrates. The Rev. Samuel Marsden, for long the principal chaplain in New South Wales, was notorious among the 'government men' for his severity. In his *Report on the State of the Colony* (1822), J. T. Bigge wrote:

> Without, however, impeaching the moral feelings of Mr Marsden, and without stating it as my opinion that he has acted with undue severity, it is in proof, that his sentences are not only, in fact, more severe than those of the other magistrates, but that the general opinion of the colony is, that his character, as displayed in the administration of the penal law in New South Wales is stamped with severity . . .

The practice of appointing clergy as magistrates seems to have come to an end during Governor Darling's regime, but the tradition of the savagery of 'flogging parsons' persisted for over a century. J. D. Lang wrote in 1834:

> Under so preposterous and so enormous a system, well might the miserable wretch, whose back was still smarting under the Saturday's infliction, join in the oft-repeated prayer of the Litany on the

Sunday morning, 'Lord, have mercy upon us!' and well might he add from the bottom of his heart, 'for his Reverence has none!'[35]

In 1899 it was recorded that the prisoners had thought:

> . . . the clerical magistrates were generally far more cruel than the lay magistrates, and this opinion was crystallised into a cant phrase which was current among the old hands many years later. It was 'The Lord have mercy on you for his reverence will have none.' This phrase was used on all occasions, whether it was appropriate or not to the subject or the circumstances of the time.[36]

And the tradition has been immortalized by a living Australian poet, Kenneth Slessor, in his *Vesper Song of the Reverend Samuel Marsden*, which begins:

> My cure of souls, my cage of brutes,
> Go lick and learn at these my boots!
> When tainted highways tear a hole,
> I bid my cobbler welt the sole.
> O, ye that wear the boots of Hell,
> Shall I not welt a soul as well?
>> O, souls that leak with holes of sin,
>> Shall I not let God's leather in,
>> Or hit with sacramental knout
>> Your twice-convicted vileness out?

Symbolic of the convicts' hatred for the kind of religion offered them was an event which took place during Hunter's governorship. When in 1798 he compelled the convicts to attend religious services, incendiaries burnt down the church. He offered to any informer, even one serving a life sentence, a free pardon and passage home, plus a reward of £50. But the group loyalty of the government men was equal to the occasion. 'One would have thought that irresistible,' Hunter said sadly, 'but it brought no evidence. I never learnt who it was; it was a designed thing.'[37]

The extent to which this hostility, or at best indifference, to organized religion, like other convict attitudes, influenced the whole of early colonial society, may be gauged by the contrast between Melbourne and Sydney Sabbaths in the 1840's. A Presbyterian clergyman observed that in Sydney, Sundays were 'spent by many in "boating", driving, riding, drinking, visiting, &c.', and 'most of the churches' were 'more than half empty'. In Melbourne the churches were 'well attended, the people dressed in their best attire, the shops shut, the streets as quiet as in an English town', and there were 'no visible symptoms of riot or drunkenness'.[38] However, Joyce's *Homestead History* records: 'It was a common saying in those early days that Sunday did not extend any distance out of Melbourne and not at all into the distant bush. . . .' A lay observer, Alexander Marjoribanks, though less disturbed by the facts, thought Sydney's churches even emptier, estimating that not more than 5,000 out of Sydney's then population of 45,000 ever attended church at all. He wrote:

> The people of that country, however, do not seem to trouble themselves much about religion. . . . Instead of dining on cold meat, and anything else, to save the trouble of cooking on the Sunday, and the sin of doing so, as some think in this country, the Sydney people, particularly the working classes, make that the great day for feasting; and the quantity of pies and roasted meats, of every description, to be seen carrying through the streets at one o'clock on the Sundays, from the different ovens throughout the town, would rejoice the heart of many a poor starving creature in this country After three o'clock the nobility (*alias* mobility) and gentry start in their carriages and gigs along the Parramatta Road, for an airing in the country, and the multitudes of people riding on horseback in that country are perfectly astonishing.

The clergyman could attribute the contrast between the two ways of keeping the Sabbath to 'nothing else than the comparative absence of convict influence' [in Melbourne]; but the higher proportion there of members of his own faith, and of newly arrived immigrants from a Britain already feeling the influence of the Evangelical movement, were probably also contributory causes. In spite of the profane influence of the Gold Rush on Melbourne, the same sort of difference between Sundays there and in Sydney is still noticeable to-day. Even at the height of the gold mania in 1853 one observer 'marvelled to witness . . . the air of quiet serenity and decorousness which pervaded the capital on the Sabbath morning'; though he was acute enough to realize that 'in reality, the odour of sanctity was not in the ascendant'.[39]

Most of those who crossed the mountains took this anti-clerical attitude with them to the outback, where it was accentuated by the almost complete absence of religious facilities. In the early 1840's, for instance, there was not a single church nor a resident clergyman in the four hundred odd miles between Yass and Melbourne. Joyce reports one itinerant minister in his district during the period, but observes: 'unfortunately he did not remain faithful to his charge, disappearing one day with the collection and his patron's horse.' To the north-west, once the relatively closely settled Hunter River District and its immediate hinterland were left behind, the situation was no better. Men were born, and lived, without entering a church or hearing a sermon or prayer. Of those lucky enough to find helpmeets, many lived, permanently perforce, in an unhallowed state of concubinage. One man, 'in the simplicity of his heart', went through the form of marriage 'by way of securing the woman', for his brother who had been detained 'up the country'.[40] Even in death the vast majority of bushmen had to do without professional spiritual assistance. This description from the *Geelong Advertiser* of 24 March 1848 of a typical bush-worker's funeral was truthful, if melodramatic: '. . . splints of green wood for his coffin, a bush carpenter his undertaker, a bullock dray his hearse, reckless and hardened men his mourners, and the wild forest or open plain his burial place'.

It cannot be said that most bushmen consciously deplored the situation. If they did so sub-consciously, the result was to make them more actively scornful of the defaulting clergy and, perhaps, to reinforce their already strong feeling of mateship and their propensity to mutual aid. On his walk through the Riverina in 1850, Gerstaecker came to a station where the squatter had put forward a plan to bring to the district an itinerant minister whose salary was to be supplemented by donations from the working hands. 'On this subject,' he wrote, 'I heard opinions so very freely expressed that I am quite sure the Murray Scrub is not a soil favourable for preachers.' But Harris gives on this subject, as on so many others, the most penetrating evidence. Writing of the 'society' of outback working people, he says:

Very few of its members cherished any religious thoughts; and those who did said nothing about them. Those who had none were the chief orators upon the subject; and they, of course, would suffer

nothing like expression of pious sentiments to pass without malig-
nant jeers. Perhaps, had the question been made a practical one,
divested of all ingredient of the conventionality of sects, it would
have been given in favour of the claim of religion to respect. But,
unfortunately, it was the fanatical form into which religious sentiment is sometimes thrown, that was assumed to be the true and
intrinsic manifestation of its character. And this no one who regarded
his reputation for sound sense cared to be the advocate of.

It is worth noting that Harris goes on to make a partial exception of Catholic bushmen, many of whom were sincerely religious,
he says. They were not usually mocked, because of a feeling that
their religion was both so deeply ingrained, and yet so purely
formal, that ordinary canons of judgement did not apply to them.[41]
No doubt their relative immunity from the mockers derived also
from the fact that itinerant Catholic priests were seen in the bush
more often than were those of any other denomination.[42]

The famine of females in the interior was remarked even more
widely, and deplored more deeply, than that of clergymen.
Sidney records, for example, that in the early 1840's both sides
of the 'Barwen' river for 300 miles were occupied by stations
and that 'there was not one white woman in the whole distance'.
These creatures were, he adds feelingly, 'as scarce as black swans
in Europe'. From the census returns may be drawn figures which
show that the position was not quite so black as that.

TABLE VI

Proportion of Males to Females in White Population in 1841 and 1851
(N.S.W. excluding Port Phillip)

	Males	Females	Total	Per cent of Males
County of Cumberland—				
1841	33,763	24,345	58,108	58·0
1851	42,035	39,079	81,114	51·8
Other Counties within the Boundaries—				
1841	33,322	14,126	47,448	70·2
1851	44,975	33,457	78,432	57·3
Squatting Districts—				
1841	7,551	1,494	9,045	83·5
1851	19,219	8,478	27,697	69·4

Assuming women to be distributed more or less evenly through the different economic groups of the outback population, it is obvious at a glance that, even at the end of the decade, four out of every seven men must still have been doomed to bachelorhood. Actually, of course, the proportion of single men among the nomad tribe of pastoral labourers was very much higher than this. Squatters, managers, overseers, shanty keepers, and others with a relatively fixed abode and high income, naturally found it easier to attract wives from among the few marriageable girls available.

The absolute shortage of women stemmed initially from the transportation days, but it was exacerbated in the outback by other factors. The rough life of a pioneering community always makes for a population predominantly masculine in composition and outlook, but the fact that the economy was almost purely pastoral accentuated the tendency. In the older and more fertile areas of the 'nineteen counties' there were some small agricultural holdings worked by family groups. But even in the remoter parts of the settled districts, climate, land laws and distance from markets combined to make such forms of land-holding unusual at this period.[43] Beyond the boundaries of location individual small holdings, worked by family groups, were almost unknown.

As though all this were not enough, the short-sighted selfishness of all but a tiny minority of squatters was such as to make them most reluctant to employ married men. J. D. Lang, Caroline Chisholm, and other thoughtful contemporaries might agree on the need for settling in the bush 'a numerous, industrious and virtuous agricultural population', but still the squatters advertised for men and more men with 'no encumbrances'. J. C. Byrne did not exaggerate when he wrote:

> Settlers and squatters will never engage, if they can help it, men with families of children; the support of the useless mouths they do not like; so it is advisable that immigrants should have as few encumbrances as possible. The morality of the bush might and would be much improved, if woman was more frequently there, but that is out of the question, if, on first arrival, they are surrounded by a number of young children; a master will avoid them, as he would a black snake, for he 'does not wish to support, and bring up other people's children'.[44]

Squatters like Charles Campbell of Duntroon, who encouraged farming families to settle on parts of his land, were almost as rare as the Bunyip.[45]

This deprivation of female companionship had very important effects on the behaviour and outlook of bush-workers. Among the convicts, especially those incarcerated at Norfolk Island and other penal stations, sodomy had been very common,[46] as it must be wherever large numbers of men are segregated for long periods. Most contemporary writers were silent upon the subject of sodomy in the outback, but none denied its prevalence and a few hinted broadly that it was common among the old hands and tended to spread to other elements of the tribe. One of the more outspoken was Byrne who pointed out that the disproportionate numbers of males and females in the colony, though striking enough, gave little idea of the true position. From the 1841 census returns he prepared figures showing the very much more striking disproportion between single adult males and females. His figures, however, are incorrect. The true state of affairs in both 1841 and 1851 is shown on the following page:

TABLE VII

	Single Males 14 and over	Single Females 14 and over	Single Males 14 and over per Single Female 14 and over
County of Cumberland—			
1841	15,839	6,485	2.4
1851	12,504	8,875	1.4
Other Counties within the Boundaries—			
1841	20,664	2,253	9.2
1851	15,959	4,687	3.4
Squatting Districts—			
1841	6,083	160	38.0
1851	11,113	825	13.5

Though the ratio of single men to single women in the outback decreased so much during the decade, this is partly accounted for by the growth of hamlets on the inner edge of the squatting districts. In the 'farthest-out' district of Maranoa there were for instance, in 1851, 65 single males over 13 years of age and *no* single women of the same age group. There were also three married men and four married women. Of New South Wales as a whole Byrne wrote:

> It is no wonder, therefore, that in such a state of society, deep-seated vice should exist, and abominable offences be practised to an appalling extent. Religious education can have but little effect on those minds already steeped in and accustomed to vice, where the great disproportion of one sex presents an insuperable obstacle to the gratification of one of the most natural desires bestowed on man— that of taking to himself a helpmate.

We have seen how much more scarce both 'religious education' and potential 'helpmates' were in the squatting districts.

Yet though white women were scarce, Aboriginal women were not. The exact number of Aboriginal inhabitants during pioneering days will, of course, never be known, but even according to the lower estimates there must have been, in 1841, nearly as many black women as there were white men beyond the boundaries. As with sodomy, most contemporary writers thought it good to say nothing of sexual relations between pastoral workers (and their employers) and the native women, but there are enough exceptions to make it certain that Mackenzie was not exaggerating when he wrote: 'black women [were] cohabiting, with the knowledge and consent of their sable husbands, in all parts of the interior, with white hut-keepers.' The direct results of the practice were that the Aboriginal race was rapidly decimated by venereal and other diseases as the white men advanced, and that countless thousands of unwanted half-caste babies were murdered. In 1849 J. P. Townsend recorded:

> Although the gins cherish some of their children, they certainly kill many, and, almost invariably, the male half-breeds; and when children, born during the residence of the mothers with the stock-men, are put to death, there can be no doubt that these men are parties consenting to the deed. The old villanous [*sic*] gins assemble at the birth, and carry away the child, and destroy it.[47]

Syphilis also helps to account for the fact that there were relatively few half-caste people in the interior, despite the widespread miscegenation.

Many writers, either ignorant of the facts or prompted by sentimentality, have attempted the scarcely possible task of making this picture blacker by implying that the 'gins' were usually unwilling victims of the white man's lust. In fact Aboriginal custom, generally speaking, restricted a woman's sexual intercourse to that with her husband, but tolerated, under certain conditions, some casual connections with other men in his kinship group. In addition women were regarded as the husband's property, and wife-lending or wife-bartering, and even something like what we should call prostitution, were common.[48] Moreover, tribal custom had no relevance to the white invaders who were neither within nor, necessarily, outside the kinship groups, and in any case tribal *mores* broke down very rapidly under the impact of the more complex and technically advanced culture. As long as the women were paid for their services with food, tobacco, or liquor, they and their husbands were usually content. Henderson wrote in 1851: 'They will frequently offer to lend *it*, meaning the *gin* to the convict-servants, for tobacco, &c. When a gin has had intercourse with a European, and produces a half-caste child, they say, "That been patter (eaten) white bread".'

Bad feeling or murder resulted when the white men ill-used or cheated the 'gins', as they very often did. There is every reason to think that Niel Black only stated the bare truth in his journal when he wrote:

> I may here state that even one instance of Natives attacking a Home Station has never yet been known in the Colony, and Several of the men on this establishment are now very ill with the Native pox which Shows how they Acted with the Blacks. Notwithstanding the bad name they had here, I am told it is no uncommon thing for these rascals to sleep all night with a Lubra (Native Female) and if she poxes him or in any way offends him perhaps Shoot her before 12 next day. I am certain it is a thing which has frequently occurred.[49]

As might be expected, sodomy became far less common where, as in most outback areas, there was a sufficient supply of gins. Byrne writes:

> . . . their *gins* (wives), or daughters, are taken from them; and the diseases of the white man, extended without remorse, destroy and daily diminish the race of Aborigines as the squatter advances. Sel-

dom, indeed, . . . is the face of a white woman seen. . . . This further promotes vice, and where black *gins* are unobtainable, there is alas! too much reason to believe, that the sin for which God destroyed 'the doomed cities' prevails amongst the servants of squatters. . . . The lessons imbibed in the chain gangs and penal settlements are diffused without control or hindrance, by the expirees of the party; and if there is any free man or immigrant among the number, *his feelings* are soon laughed away, and he is taught to regard without horror the most appalling crimes.

No doubt most of the few white women to be found on the stations were faithful to their marriage vows, but some were not, as the following passage shows. Mrs Johnston was the cook at Ballangeich, before she left to work on a neighbouring station. Her employer wrote in a letter to Niel Black:

> I have been told since that Mrs Johnston's only object on going would have been to make a little money *on her own bottom* for such a whore I never heard of. I am told my Station during her stay was a complete whore's shop, your men used to come to the tree on the Run and my fellows went to fight them while the lady was at the command of the highest bidder. They nearly knocked down the Pigs' house among them that was a favourite resort of hers and her motto was 'Ready aye Ready' and the cuckold rascal [her husband] was quite agreeable as long as it paid and let him go idle.[50]

It may be suggested that one important, though indirect, result of the absence of good women was to generate the cult of mateship in its more restricted and personal sense. The other conditions of outback life, plus convict tradition, as we have seen, are sufficient to account for the extraordinarily close class solidarity, and the strong tendency to mutual aid, displayed by outback workers. But these factors do not account for the tradition that a man should have his own special 'mate' with whom he shared money, goods, and even secret aspirations, and for whom, even when in the wrong, he was prepared to make almost any sacrifice. Casual cohabitation with Aboriginal women, or with a Mrs Johnston, might allay what St Paul called the pricks of the flesh, but could never, as a rule, begin to provide that close psychic companionship which men seek in a wife. Perhaps, as the habit of freedom and independence increased his self-respect, the typical bushman, blessedly ignorant of psychological theory, appeased this spiritual hunger by a sublimated homosexual relationship with a mate, or a number of mates, of his own sex. And probably, for the majority of men, the quite unconscious sublimation would not have occurred if there had been no *gins* and no Mrs Johnstons.

On the conscious level bushmen naturally denied this 'soft' side of their nature by protesting, perhaps too much, their masculinity. Furphy and Lawson, the two greatest Australian writers up to the time of World War I, both had a profound intuitive understanding of this ambivalence in the bushman's soul. The work of both men derives much of its power from the contrast between the uncompromising and taciturn masculine hardness on the surface and the unavowed, almost feminine, love beneath it. But in Lawson the 'softness' is nearer the surface and at times teeters over into a sentimental bathos, embarrassing to the modern reader though not, perhaps, to Lawson's contemporaries.[51]

In the 1840's most observers noticed only the rugged exterior. Describing an encampment of bullock-drivers at a waterhole, Mundy wrote of them as follows:

> . . . strange, wild-looking, sunburnt race, strong, rough, and taciturn, they appear as though they had never lived in crowds, and had lost the desire and even the power to converse. So deeply embrowned were the faces, naked breasts, and arms of these men, and so shaggy the crops of hair and beard, that a stranger had to look twice to be certain they were not Aborigines.

Another observer thought that the cedar-sawyers on the North Coast of New South Wales lived in a way 'compared with which the life of the *lumberers*, or wood-cutters in Canada, is civilization itself'.[52]

The absence of women also helped to establish firmly the old bush tradition of 'work and burst'. Like so many more outback customs, this was originally no more than a continuance of the convicts' habit of submerging their troubles, whenever opportunity offered, beneath a sea of raw rum. The appalling monotony and loneliness of up-country life would alone have been enough to encourage the bushman on holiday to engage in a 'spree'. The fact that he usually had no wife or children dependent on his earnings made it easier still for him to spend them in the nearest grog shanty or in the inns of a country township or, best of all,

in 'the big smoke',[53] where prostitutes 'swarmed' in the streets.[54]
And the universal system of paying wages, at the end of a term
of work, by cheque, made it much easier for the publican, who
obligingly cashed the cheque, to plunder the man who had
earned it.

Moreover most bush-workers seem to have felt that there was
little point in saving money, as they believed that the land laws
made it almost impossibly difficult for a poor man to become a
landowner, even in a small way. The two most acute contemporary
observers of up-country life, Sidney and Harris, shared the
popular belief, and both thought that bad land legislation was
the principal cause of the already proverbial thriftlessness of the
pastoral proletariat.[55] On the other hand most wealthy squatters
agreed with Niel Black, who wrote of the bush-workers:

> With Three or Six Months Wages (the usual term) in their pockets
> they gird their cangaroo Skin Knapsacks upon their backs contain-
> ing their whole stock on hand say a blanket, shirts and stockings.
> Thus equipt they journey often 150 miles to the next Grog Shop
> where they have 'a bright flare up' for a few days. . . . Yet if they
> did not go regularly to the Grog Shop we should have no labour at
> all; they would save and have properties of their own.[56]

Professor Shann concurred with this view, writing in his
Economic History of Australia, that most of the pastoral employees
were 'expirees too weak in initiative [to work for] wages till they
could buy "blocks"'. It is difficult to see why. Before the Gold
Rush, as he correctly states, shepherds and hut-keepers were rarely
paid more than £25 a year plus rations. More highly skilled
bush-workers such as shearers and stockmen were of course paid
somewhat more, but like the shepherds they too had to pay, often
at inflated prices, for 'all clothing and extras' issued from the
squatter's store. Even the most highly paid and virtuously ab-
stemious worker could hardly have had more than £25 cash left
to show for his year's work. From 1831, when land was normally
sold in minimum 640 acre lots at a minimum price of 5s. an acre,
the shepherd who saved every penny of his wages would have
been able to buy his own 'block' after seven years, for most of
which time he would presumably have required sufficient 'initiative' to go naked. Perhaps another seven years' self-denial would
have provided sufficient initial working capital for stock and

implements. And from 1842 onwards, when the minimum price of land was raised to £1 an acre, the quantum of initiative would have been increased accordingly. Of course there were more ways of achieving a competence than by buying blocks of land. Wages were often paid, at least partly, in cattle and sheep, and a poor man who gathered enough stock might become a legitimate squatter if fortune favoured him. Nevertheless, the working men's view of their situation seems to have been at least as realistic as Professor Shann's.[57]

Whatever the prime cause of outback drunkenness, there is no doubt that a traditional pattern of behaviour, so stereotyped that it can best be described as a ritual, grew up very early among up-country workmen. Sidney's description of it is as apt as any, but more concise than most:

> After starving for ten or twenty months on salt beef and damper, and tea without milk, often without sugar, the bushman goes down to Sydney to spend, like an ass, in a month's revelry, money he has worked for like a horse, or say a bullock. The people of Sydney who furnish information for Parliamentary petitions, debates, and Acts of Parliament, know no more about our interests, pursuits, wants, and wishes, than the people of London.

Sidney here points also to the isolation, both physical and spiritual, of outback life. Perhaps he exaggerates somewhat, but the mere physical difficulties of communication with the capital were alone sufficient to induce in outback workers an awareness of themselves as a distinct community.[58]

For working men, before the Gold Rush, the normal means of travelling was by foot or by bullock dray. Either was about as slow and wearisome as the other. Hood tried to bring the facts home to English readers when he wrote:

> My Australian son's dray has just started from this place [Sydney] with his stores for one year; and provided none of the bullocks are lost, and no mishap befalls it it will reach Connobolas [near Orange] in twenty days. This may appear a long time for goods of such a nature to be on the road, but it is a short space indeed, compared with that occupied by some of my acquaintances in carrying home their stores. One, in particular, has just sent his purchases off by sea to Maitland, where his drays are to meet them, and after a journey of at least two months, under the most favourable circumstances,

he hopes to arrive with them in the county of New England. Others whom I am acquainted with pass three months and upwards in conveying stock and stores to their stations in the new country to the southward, called Corner Inlet.

Journeys of this order were, in important respects, much more like long ocean voyages under sail than like travelling at home in Britain. Contemporaries were often struck by the strong resemblance between the life of bushmen and that of seamen, and indeed, between the lonely monotony of the bush and that of the ocean.[59] And as we have seen, the pastoral workers were constantly travelling, if not from the bush to Sydney and back again, then from one station to another in search of more congenial work, or merely for a change of scene. This constant moving about, itself largely a result of the extreme isolation of bush life, helped in the psychological conquest of that isolation. Men came to know and to trust each other much more fully than city dwellers do and, in reaction to the dividing distances, they developed a strong sense of community. Griffith records that he knew of several instances of loans of two or three pounds being made to old hands, but never of a case in which the money was not repaid.

Contemporaries noted also that bush-workers had a passion for reading and versifying. Next to a glass of rum, the loan of a book was the greatest favour one could bestow on a bushman.[60] In view of the complete absence of ready-made forms of amusement, this is scarcely surprising. In 1851, according to census returns, 36·9 per cent of the inhabitants in outback districts were illiterate, but one does not have to be able to read to enjoy reading. At a certain out-station one day in the early 'forties, a man arrived 'with a joyful countenance' and a copy of *Nicholas Nickleby*. In the hut that night another man began reading to a company consisting mainly of old hands who, however, 'advised that the reading should be stopped, until the men of two or three stations near us, had been invited' to share in the feast. By the light of 'a piece of twisted rag stuck into a pint tin of melted fat' the book was read on successive nights to a full hut, and if the reader 'could have read till daylight' the audience would not have tired.[61]

More often, because of the absence of either books or readers, the nights must have been passed in singing and story-telling.

Harris describes several such evenings in bush huts, and it is interesting to notice that the stories told were usually not nostalgic reminiscences of the old life in Britain but 'some tale of the olden time, when but few white men were in the colony', or stories of bushrangers, new runs, or the feats of working bullocks.[62] Thus these men, without consciously planning to do so, acclimatized themselves in the new land.

It is not surprising that this remote and vagabond existence should have given rise to a distinctive school of balladry, just as did the life of deep-water sailormen a hundred years and more ago. It was natural for shearers on the spree in a grog shanty at the end of the season, for stockmen watching the cattle at night, or for bullock-drivers met by chance at a favourite camping place, to improve the occasion by singing, and sometimes making, ballads. Even the solitary shepherd was accustomed to relieve the monotony of his existence by playing tunes to himself. Mundy wrote:

> [he sits] all day 'sub tegmine gum-tree', playing on the Jew's harp or accordion; or sleeps supine, while his dog does his master's duty with one eye open. The importation and sale of the above instruments—substitutes for the ancient shepherd's reed—are immense; five hundred accordions and fifty gross of the harps of Judah are considered small investments by one vessel. A shepherd has been known to walk two hundred miles from a distant station of the interior, to purchase one of them at the nearest township.

Among bushmen in the early days, stockmen and bullock-drivers enjoyed a certain pre-eminence, not only as the most highly skilled workers, but as composers and singers of ballads. One who had often met bullock-drivers on the road wrote:

> This bullock-driving cannot be a very pleasant life, although there is a certain smack of romance in camping out at night with a mob of oxen bellowing around, and the companion drivers on watch attending to the fires—where the damper is cooking and the iron kettle boiling for to-morrow's breakfast—or only leaving their warm occupation for the warmer one of driving in 'strays', with song and shout loud enough to make the deserters scamper. These bullock-songs are uncouth snatches generally improvised by the drivers themselves, but not destitute of a wild runic poetry, as the following verses from one of them will show:

Olle! Heigh ho!
Blow your horns, blow,
Blow the Southern Cross down if you will;
But on you must go,
Where the fresh gullies flow,
And the thirsty crane wets his red bill.

Olle! Heigh-ho!
Drink, boys, as we go,
Pass the brandy—let each take his fill:
On, 'Strawberry', on,
Run, 'Blossom', come run,
There is light enough left for us still.

Olle! Heigh-ho!
'Blossom', gee-woh,
There is water spread out for us here,
Fill horns while you may,
There is no one to pay,
But Mine Host up above, for such cheer![63]

One feels unhappily certain that this song was composed by an extraordinarily genteel bullock-driver, or that it has been edited out of recognition by Fowler, the writer who recorded it. The latter alternative is possibly the more likely. He goes on to say that he was particularly struck by the sentiment of the last line which he considered not really objectionable: 'Strange that the boisterous fellow who, in these Australian solitudes, first thundered out the song after his loitering cattle, should have thought of Mine Host at all!' This feeling, if not its expression, at least rings true. In 1936 I was one of a party of four, driving an old truck through the Musgrave Ranges in the extreme north of South Australia, when we came to a lonely station one evening. One of my companions gushed considerably over the beauty of the mountain sky-line, silhouetted against the sunset. An elderly stockman answered drily: 'Yes. The Old Bloke makes a good job of them up this way.' The same egalitarian and familiar, yet not essentially sacrilegious, attitude to the Deity is embodied in the popular Australian invocation often uttered during a fall of rain: 'Send 'er down, Hughie!'

There is, however, surviving from the pre-Gold-Rush period, another bullock-drivers' song which is unquestionably genuine. 'The Old Bullock Dray', like most folk-ballads, has been added to and changed by many singers, so that it contains references to John Robertson, promoter of the Free Selection Acts, and to other post-Gold-Rush events; but there is little doubt that the body of the song belongs to the earlier period. Macalister, who drove bullock-teams on the Great South Road in the 1840's, quotes a version of the chorus of 'that early Australian song, "The Old Bullock Dray", as sung in the formative years':

> So it's roll up your blankets, and let us make a push,
> I'll take you up the country, and show you round the bush;
> I'll take you round the stations and learn you how to ride,
> And I'll show you how to muster when we cross th' Great Divide!

This chorus differs from later versions precisely in the way that one would expect. It shows with unusual directness the pride of the old hands in their newly acquired mastery of the outback environment and what one might call the ballad's didactic function of assisting acclimatization. Implicit in it too are the basic elements of that outlook which later came to be thought of as 'typically Australian': a comradely independence based on group solidarity and relative economic plenty, a rough and ready capacity for 'stringy-bark and green-hide' improvisation, a light-hearted intolerance of respectable or conventional manners, a reckless improvidence, and a conviction that the working bushman was the 'true Australian', whose privilege it was to despise 'new chums' and city folk. We have seen that this ethos sprang mainly from convict, working-class, Irish and native-born Australian sources, but that these streams coalesced 'beyond the Great Divide' where remoteness and the peculiar geographical, economic and social conditions transmuted them into something new which yet included them all. In the next chapter we shall seek to estimate the influence of the Gold Rush on the outlook of 'the nomad tribe'.

CHAPTER IV

1 W. C. Wentworth, *Statistical, Historical and Political Description of New South Wales*, etc., London 1819, p. 64.

2 T. M. Perry, 'The Spread of Rural Settlement in New South Wales, etc.', *Historical Studies: Australia and New Zealand*, vol. 6, No. 24, pp. 383-4; and M. H. Ellis, *Lachlan Macquarie*, etc., Sydney 1947, p. 489.

3 All figures include districts which later became part of Queensland, but exclude the districts of Port Phillip and the penal stations of Norfolk Island and Moreton Bay. The figures for 1841 exclude the 2,130 persons on board colonial vessels at sea, and those for 1851 include the 'reputed County of Stanley' with other counties within the boundaries of location.

4 *Historical Records of Australia*, Series 1, vol. 13, pp. 136, 166-7; T. B. Wilson, *Narrative of a Voyage Round the World*, etc., London 1835, p. 336.

5 James Collier, *The Pastoral Age in Australia*, London 1911, p. 106; and cp. 'An Eight Years' Resident' (Ebenezer Thorne), *The Queen of the Colonies*, London 1876, pp. 290-1.

6 *The Emigrant Family*, etc., 3 vols., London 1849, vol. 1, pp. 121-4.

7 A. Marjoribanks, *Travels in New South Wales*, etc., London 1847, pp. 57-8; G. C. Mundy, *Our Antipodes*, etc., 3rd ed., London 1855, p. 221; and H. De Castella, *Les Squatters Australiens*, Paris 1861, pp. 137-8.

8 F. Lancelott, *Australia As It Is: Its Settlements*, etc., 2 vols., London 1852, vol. 2, pp. 115-17; John Henderson, *Excursions and Adventures in New South Wales*, 2 vols., London 1851, vol. 1, pp. 124-7; and Charles Griffith, *Present State and Prospects of the Port Phillip District*, etc., Dublin 1845, p. 77.

9 J. C. Hamilton, *Pioneering Days in Early Victoria*, Melbourne n.d. (1913), p. 75; and James Butchart, *Letter*, 10 December 1843 (Public Library of Victoria, MS.).

10 H. W. Haygarth, *Recollections of Bush Life*, etc., London 1848, pp. 92-3.

11 *Voice from the Far Interior*, pp. 18, 20, 24, 35; and cp. J. O. Balfour, *A Sketch of New South Wales*, London 1845, pp. 72-6; J. J. Knight, *In the Early Days*, etc., Brisbane 1895, pp. 179-81; and Niel Black, *Letters* to T. S. Gladstone, 10 December 1840, 30 November 1846, 21 November 1850 (Public Library of Victoria, MSS.).

12 D. L. Waugh, *Three Years' Practical Experience of a Settler*, 4th ed., Edinburgh 1838, pp. 32-3; G. F. Moore, *Diary of Ten Years' Eventful Life*, etc., London 1884, p. 119; R. Howitt, *Impressions of Australia Felix*, etc., London 1845, pp. 260-3; 'An Emigrant Mechanic', (Alexander Harris), *Settlers and Convicts*, ed. C. M. H. Clark, Melbourne 1953 (first published 1847), pp. 22-3; and Niel Black, *Letter* to T. S. Gladstone, 10 December 1840 (Public Library of Victoria, MS.):

'They . . . return into the bush indifferent whether they are employed or not as they live comfortably at the expense of the settler. At each station they meet a brother who will freely share with them and "Master must find more".'

13   Quoted Edward Curr, *An Account of the Colony of Van Diemen's Land*, etc., London 1824, p. 161.

14   *Letter* to T. S. Gladstone, 10 December 1840 (Public Library of Victoria, MS.).

15   See A. Harris, *Settlers and Convicts*, p. 1.

16   H. W. Haygarth, *op. cit.*, p. 45 ff.; and A. Joyce, *A Homestead History*, ed. G. F. James, 2nd ed., Melbourne 1949, p. 112.

17   A. Marjoribanks, *op. cit.*, p. 35 ff.; and J. Stephens, *A Voice from Australia*, etc., London 1848, p. 15.

18   *Australia As She Is and As She May Be*, London 1840, p. 19; and cp. 'James Macarthur' (Edward Edwards), *New South Wales*, etc., London 1837, p. 43.

19   Nehemiah Bartley, *Australian Pioneers and Reminiscences*, Brisbane 1896, p. 191 ff.

20   H. S. Russell, *The Genesis of Queensland*, etc., Sydney 1888, p. 166.

21   *Settlers and Convicts*, p. 176.

22   W. Westgarth, *Victoria: Late Australia Felix*, etc., Edinburgh 1853, p. 89.

23   F. Gerstaecker, *Narrative of a Journey*, etc., 3 vols., London 1853, vol. 3, p. 5 ff.

24   A. Harris, *Guide to Port Stephens*, etc., London 1849, p. 75. Harris's statement that 'every door is without bolt or lock' should be taken literally. See John Henderson, *op. cit.*, vol. 1, p. 204.

25   F. Lancelott, *op. cit.*, vol. 2, p. 112.

26   F. Gerstaecker, *op. cit.*, vol. 3, p. 12.

27   G. F. Young, *Under the Coolibah Tree*, London 1953, pp. 152-3.

28   J. P. Townsend, *Rambles and Observations*, etc., London 1849, p. 52.

29   James F. O'Connell, *A Residence of Eleven Years*, etc., Boston 1836, pp. 49-53.

30   J. P. Townsend, *op. cit.*, p. 208.

31   George Chanson, *The Sydney Songster, No. 1: A Collection of New, Original, Local and Comic Songs*, etc., Sydney n.d. (1866), Song No. 8.

32   *Settlers and Convicts*, p. 67 (my italics).

33   A. Harris, *Emigrant Family*, vol. 1, pp. 38-9.

34   F. K. Crowley, 'Working Class Conditions in Australia 1788-1851', Ph.D. thesis, Melbourne University, 7 November 1949, p. 110; and cp. Eris O'Brien, *The Foundation of Australia, 1786-1800*, etc., London 1937, pp. 64-5.

35 *Historical and Statistical Account of New South Wales*, etc., 2 vols., London 1834, vol. 2, p. 248.

36 George Boxall, *Story of the Australian Bushrangers*, London 1899, p. 49.

37 *Report, House of Commons Select Committee on Transportation, 1812*, Appendix No. 1, p. 23, Hunter's evidence; and cp. David Collins, *Account of the English Colony in New South Wales*, etc., 2 vols., London 1802, vol. 2, pp. 130, 197-8, 276-7.

38 Rev. David Mackenzie, *The Emigrant's Guide*, etc., London 1845, pp. 30, 51.

39 W. Kelly, *Life in Victoria*, etc., 2 vols., London 1859, vol. 1, pp. 105-10; and cp. B. A. Heywood, *A Vacation Tour to the Antipodes*, etc., London 1863, p. 34.

40 Rev. D. Mackenzie, *op. cit.*, pp. 48-63; 'A Bushman' (John Sidney), *A Voice from the Far Interior of Australia*, London 1847, pp. 21-3; G. C. Mundy, *op. cit.*, p. 165; and see *Sydney Morning Herald*, 18 May 1844, 29 May 1844; T. H. Braim, *A History of New South Wales*, etc., London 1846, vol. 2, pp. 164-6; W. W. Burton, *The State of Religion and Education in New South Wales*, London 1840, *passim*; E. W. Landor, *The Bushman: or, Life in a New Country*, London 1847, ch. 9; J. O. Balfour, *A Sketch of New South Wales*, London 1845, p. 114; and J. Backhouse, *A Narrative of a Visit to the Australian Colonies*, London 1843, pp. 454, 500 and *passim*.

41 A. Harris, *Testimony to the Truth*, etc., London 1852, p. 78 ff.

42 'A Bushman', *op. cit.*, p. 23; J. P. Townsend, *op. cit.*, p. 140; E. W. Landor, *op. cit.*, pp. 113-14; G. Mackaness (ed.), *The Correspondence of John Cotton*, etc., Sydney 1953, pt 3, p. 44.

43 *The Atlas*, 14 June 1845, 3 June 1848. (Quoted S. H. Roberts, *History of Australian Land Settlement*, Melbourne 1924, p. 108.)

44 *Twelve Years' Wanderings*, etc., 2 vols., London 1844, vol. 1, pp. 213-14; and *ibid.*, vol. 2, pp. 280-1; John Hood, *Australia and the East*, etc., London 1843, p. 225; C. Griffith, *Present State and Prospects of the Port Phillip District*, etc., Dublin 1845, p. 73; and R. Howitt, *Impressions of Australia Felix*, London 1845, pp. 212-13.

45 *Sydney Morning Herald*, 31 May 1844 and 1 June 1844.

46 *Report, House of Commons Select Committee on Transportation, 1837*, pp. 44-5, 66-9; and cp. W. Ullathorne, *The Catholic Mission to Australasia*, 2nd ed., Liverpool 1837, pp. 30-1, 40; and F. K. Crowley, *op. cit.*, p. 37 ff.

47 *Op. cit.*, pp. 93-4; and cp. *Report, House of Commons Select Committee on Transportation, 1837*, pp. 42-4; Rev. D. Mackenzie, *op. cit.*, p. 210; G. C. Mundy, *op. cit.*, pp. 164-5; F. Eldershaw, *Australia As It Really Is*, etc., London 1854, p. 87; James F. O'Connell, *op. cit.*, p. 83; and G. F. Davidson, *Trade and Travel in the Far East*, etc., London 1846, p. 158.

48   E. M. Curr, *The Australian Race*, etc., 2 vols., Melbourne 1886, pp. 106-40; H. Basedow, *The Australian Aboriginal*, Adelaide 1925, pp. 218-24; A. P. Elkin, *The Australian Aborigines*, etc., 4th ed., Sydney 1948, pp. 101-24.

49   23 March 1840. '*Native* pox'. The irony was presumably unconscious. cp. 'Spanish pox', 'the French disease', 'un cap anglais', etc. There were, of course, exceptions to this rule of outback behaviour. See, e.g. H. Melville, *The Present State of Australia*, etc., London 1851, p. 105: '. . . yet there are many settlers that are as much attached to the black-women as others are to those possessing fair skins: and are equally fond of their half-caste children as if they were pure white.'

50   Capt. John Eddington to Niel Black 11 June 1847 (Black Papers, Public Library of Victoria); and cp. *Report, House of Commons Select Committee on Transportation, 1837*, pp. 39-41.

51   cp., e.g., two stories of children lost in the bush: 'Tom Collins' (Joseph Furphy), *Such is Life*, Sydney 1948, pp. 233-49; and Henry Lawson, *Prose Works of*, 2 vols., Sydney 1935, vol. 2, pp. 130-48.

52   C. Hodgkinson, *Australia from Port Macquarie to Moreton Bay*, etc., London 1845, pp. 10-11.

53   This slang synonym for the city had already been taken over from the Aborigines in the 1840's. (See H. W. Haygarth, *op. cit.*, p. 6.)

54   J. Pitts Johnson, *Plain Truths Told by a Traveller*, etc., London 1840, p. 48 ff.; and cp. 'A Bushman', *op. cit.*, p. 28.

55   J. Sidney, *op. cit.*, pp. 12, 21, 40 ff.; and A. Harris, *Settlers and Convicts*, pp. 86, 224-6.

56   *Journal*, 23 March 1840 (Public Library of Victoria, MS.).

57   There is need for much detailed research on the matter of sale in minimum square mile lots, and its effects. My statements are based largely upon *Historical Records of Australia*, Series I, vol. 16, pp. 850-1; Samuel Sidney, *Three Colonies of Australia*, London 1852, p. 293; E. W. Landor, *op. cit.*, p. 255; J. C. Byrne, *op. cit.*, vol. 2, Appendix, pp. 376-99; T. A. Coghlan, *Labour and Industry in Australia*, etc., 4 vols., London 1918, vol. 1, pt 2, ch. 5, and pt 3, ch. 4; S. H. Roberts, *History of Australian Land Settlement*, Melbourne 1924, pp. 94-109; B. Fitzpatrick, *British Imperialism and Australia 1783-1833*, London 1939, p. 320 ff.; B. Fitzpatrick, *The British Empire in Australia*, Melbourne 1941, pp. 144-7; K. Buckley, 'Gipps and the Graziers of New South Wales', *Historical Studies: Australia and New Zealand*, May 1955 and May 1956.

58   J. P. Townsend, *op. cit.*, pp. 23-4; and D. L. Waugh, *op. cit.*, p. 33.

59   e.g. 'A Bushman', *op. cit.*, p. 11; H. W. Haygarth, *op. cit.*, p. 135; and
     R. Henty, *Australiana, or My Early Life*, London 1886, p. 156.

60   'A Bushman', *op. cit.*, p. 23; and cp. R. Howitt, *op. cit.*, pp. 254-7; and
     G. C. Mundy, *op. cit.*, p. 225.

61   James Demarr, *Adventures in Australia Fifty Years Ago*, etc., London
     1893, p. 119.

62   *Emigrant Family*, vol. 1, pp. 121-4; *Settlers and Convicts*, pp. 197-8.

63   Frank Fowler, *Southern Lights and Shadows*, etc., London 1859, p.
     107 ff.

THE GOLD RUSH

*With my swag all on my shoulder, black billy in my
   hand,
I travelled the bush of Australia like a true-born
   native man.*

BETWEEN 1851 and 1861 the population of all Australia nearly
trebled, growing from 405,356 to 1,145,585. It goes without saying
that such a vast influx of immigrants had very important effects
on Australian life; yet in some ways the influence of the newcomers
has been both exaggerated and misunderstood. Shann speaks of
the new arrivals 'swamping the old colonists', and Portus writes:
'the most significant results of the gold discoveries are to be found
... in the change in the quality of the population.'[1] Such statements
are perhaps broadly true, but, in conjunction with what has been
said above, the following tables suggest that they apply justly to
Victoria rather than to New South Wales or Australia generally,
to city rather than to country-dwellers, and to political and
economic rather than to social life. We shall find too that the
Gold Rush had even less revolutionary effects on the Australian
legend.

TABLE VIII[2]

Increase of Total Population in Mainland Eastern Australia

	1841	1851	Per cent Increase	1861	Per cent Increase
N.S.W.	116,988	187,243	60	380,919 (350,860)	103 (87)
Vic.	11,738	87,345	645	540,322	520

TABLE IX

Increase of Native Born Population

	1841	% of Total	1851	% of Total	1861	% of Total
N.S.W.	28,657	24·5	81,391	43·5	174,808 (164,992)	45·9 (47·0)
Vic.	792	6·7	20,470	23·4	157,911	29·2

TABLE X³

Group Comp rising Native-Born, Convict and Emancipist Population

	1841	% of Total	1851	% of Total	1861	% of Total
N.S.W.	73,367	62·7	110,713	59·1	194,000 (183,000)	50·9 (52·1)
Vic.	2,456	20·9	20,470+	?	157,911+	?

From Table VIII it is clear that although the *rate* of increase in the population rose in the mother colony during the Gold Rush decade, it was, when compared with the very high 'normal' rate of the previous ten years, by no means to be likened to a flood with a resulting 'swamping' of the already firmly rooted social *mores*. In Victoria, according to the official figures, the *rate* of increase in the population actually fell during the golden decade, but this is of little significance beside the tremendous absolute increase in numbers. In round figures it may be said that while the population of New South Wales doubled, that of Victoria increased six times. From Tables VIII and IX, however, it can be seen that the rate of increase of the native-born population, even in Victoria, was significantly higher than that of the population as a whole; while Table X shows that this former rate was higher still, if to the native-born be added the ex-convict population. If we consider these two categories of people as a single group forming the leaven of 'Australianism', it is clear that they always comprised more than half the population of the mother colony, tor at the next census in 1871 the 308,673 native-born alone made up 61·2% of the people. By the same year 49·0% of Victorians had been born in Australia.

When Portus writes:

Before the Gold era, Australia was regarded in the main as a kind of outlandish suburb of Britain at best; at worst as a place of exile for those Britons who had to live there. After that time there is apparent in Australia the consciousness of a distinct national identity.

he seems, in the context, to be suggesting that an important effect of the Gold Rush was to accelerate, if not to cause, the growth of a distinctively Australian national feeling. It is broadly true that *Britons* regarded Australia in the way he describes before the gold discoveries, but surely most of them continued to regard Australia in much the same light for long afterwards. If his words are meant to apply to *Australian* attitudes, they seem to obscure rather than to clarify the picture.

We have seen above that Australian working people, at least, developed a distinctive national feeling before 1851. The great flood of new immigrants hastened the granting of responsible government and democratic institutions,[4] but there is *prima facie* reason to think that it actually delayed the growth of national awareness. Radical politicians, like Higinbotham in Victoria, often appealed to nationalist sentiment, but this emerging *political* nationalism, like that of Wentworth or J. D. Lang in the earlier period, differed in important ways from the deeply-felt but largely un-intellectualized *social* attitudes of the lower orders. Nevertheless, the leaven (or virus) of pre-Gold-Rush 'Australianism' was not 'swamped', but rather temporarily and superficially overlaid. This early nationalist feeling of ordinary people continued to exert much influence, up-country more than in the cities. It emerged stronger than ever in the last decades of the nineteenth century, when it tended to coalesce with, and colour deeply, middle-class political and literary nationalism. More than any other single group in the community its carriers were the semi-nomadic pastoral workers. In the broad context of the population changes outlined above, what was the effect of the gold discoveries on these people?

First, it can be said with certainty that they influenced the newcomers a great deal more than they were influenced by them. That this should be so was inherent in the situation. Though the total number of new immigrants was, in Victoria, so overwhelming, their arrival was spread over ten years and each gold-seeker, on landing, found himself a single individual, or one of a small party, in a strange land inhabited by people many of whose ways of acting and thinking were new to him. In such circumstances there are two normal human reactions, not mutually exclusive. One is to seek shelter in a community grouping of one's compatriots: the other is to merge oneself in the general body of citizens by learning their strange ways as quickly as possible. In Australia during the Gold Rush the Chinese were the only foreigners whose numbers made the first course really feasible, just as the great differences between their culture and that of the colonists made it almost inevitable. For British immigrants, the second course was natural and easy. There was no language barrier, and the differences in outlook between the newcomers and the old colonists were, after all, relatively slight. Yet just because of these facts, the distinction between a new chum and an old hand was usually painfully clear.

There is no evidence that the old colonists, excepting perhaps a tiny minority of the more cultivated, were ever embarrassed by this difference. On the contrary, they considered themselves ineffably superior to the newcomers, and the more uncultivated they were, the more sure they felt of their moral ascendancy. W. Craig records an amusing story of an old hand at the diggings who was robbed by a newly arrived Scotsman:

> . . . [a] 'chuckle-headed, porridge-eating, lime-juicing son of a sea-cook' (as he fumingly designated McInnes). . . . If he had been thus tricked by an 'old hand' he would not have grieved so much over it. As he confessed later on, McInnes's apparent simplicity had, as in our case, completely deceived him. He considered that a reflection had been cast on his discernment and 'professional' skill, and he took the affair much more to heart than did the rightful owners of the property.

Generally speaking this 'moral' ascendancy seems to have been taken for granted by the immigrants who, indeed, strengthened it by paying to the colonists the supreme compliment of imitation. As one level-headed observer wrote:

It was and is a constant source of ambition among 'new chums', especially the younger ones, to be taken for 'old hands' in the colony, and they endeavour to gain this point by all manner of expedients, by encouraging the growth of their beards and moustaches to a prodigious length, as well as by affecting a colonial style of dress, and wearing dirty, battered cabbage-tree hats; but their efforts to appear 'colonial' are not always so harmless, and, as swearing is an unusually common habit among the colonists, new arrivals often endeavour, and most successfully too, to become proficient in this easily acquired art, and soon add the stock of oaths peculiar to the colony (and *very* peculiar some of them are) to the 'home' vocabulary. But with all these attempts, it is very seldom indeed that they can impose upon a colonist of even a few years' standing. The old-country greenness is sure to sprout out somewhere; perhaps, though a man's dress may be quite *à la* bush in every other respect, a neatly-made, thin-soled pair of boots—such as no old colonist would dream of wearing in the bush—may betray the fact that their cockney owner has never been accustomed to rougher walking than London pavements, or macadamized roads . . . [5]

The very fact that the search for gold drew the immigrants 'up the country'[6] for a long or short period was itself a potent factor in 'colonizing' them. Robert Caldwell records that in the early days of the gold fever, 'three years were required to make an old chum, who was expected in that time to cultivate a moustache, and to wear a dirty, cabbage-tree hat.' On the goldfields the first arrivals from overseas met a higher proportion of old hands than they would have done in or near the capital cities, for it was inevitable that the congenitally vagabond and adventurous pastoral workers should have been among the first diggers to arrive at every new field.[7] By the time later immigrants came, their predecessors had already been strongly influenced by the indigenous outlook.

A diarist gives an interesting picture of the great prestige enjoyed by the old hands who had been on the fields from the beginning:

A curious meeting sometimes takes place around the Evening camp-fire. The new chum sits on the logs about the fire listening to the tales of crime and adventure of some 'old hand' or convict. Some of these men have now great quantities of Gold and now that they are independent, boast of their former bad deeds. The greater the criminal the more he is respected amongst his own class. A murderer, stands first, then comes the housebreaker, and thence declines into the petty thief whom they denominate as tinpot men, frying pan men, cockatoos, etc. . . . [8]

Moreover the business of alluvial gold-digging itself evoked just those 'practical' qualities and skills which had for long been recognized as typically 'Australian'. Here is the record of a digger on his way to the diggings in 1852:

> [I] began to find out the difference between having servants to minister to my requirements, and having everything to do for myself; and I practically experienced the disadvantage, now I was entirely thrown upon my resources, of not having been educated to use my hands in a variety of ways. . . . I could not harness a horse, cook a beef-steak properly, nor make a damper; the latter a most important accomplishment in Australia, and more especially at a time when the price of bread at the diggings was six shillings a loaf.

Like other new chums, this man quickly learnt from old colonists these and many other arts of bushmanship, such as how to light a fire in wet weather by stripping bark from that 'side of a stringybark tree least exposed to the rain'.[9] Obviously the prestige of the old colonial hands sprang from their mastery of these skills as well as from the less tangible aura of romance which surrounded them.

Digging in the early days was also, like pastoral labour, essentially a nomadic occupation. B. A. Heywood wrote in 1863:

> Gold-diggers are a very migratory class. If they hear of the discovery of a new gold-field, they will frequently leave their old diggings and rush to the new one, often to return deeply disappointed but without having learnt wisdom. Let a new 'rush' be proclaimed and they are off again. Gold-digging appears to be a never-satisfying employment with the mass of the people who frequent diggings. They will give up good opportunities for a mere chance at a distance.

Mateship, and that curiously unconventional yet powerful collectivist morality noticed above, were two other important elements of the pastoral workers' ethos which were taken over by the diggers. It is true that life on the fields lacked the loneliness of station work, but on the other hand alluvial mining could be performed effectively only by teams of at least two or three men. On some 'wet' claims, in the beds of diverted creeks, as many as ten to fourteen men had to work together. As company mining developed, diggers showed a very strong disinclination to work for wages, and sought instead to continue working claims in small co-operative groups of half a dozen or more.[10] The customary arrangement by which one digger acted as tent-keeper and cook, while the other members of his band worked the claim, reminds one of the system of hut-keepers and shepherds at out-stations. The fact that members of these teams were universally known as 'mates' suggests the influence of the pre-existing tradition.[11] On the Californian fields, at the same time, the term used was 'partners', a word connoting, basically, a business relationship.

This group solidarity was strongly reinforced by the intensely unpopular practice of licence-hunting, for which the government was responsible. Parties of diggers might quarrel with each other over claim boundaries and other matters but, when a licence-hunt began, the cry of 'Joe! Joe!' re-echoed through the gullies as all made common cause against the police. This colloquial name for policemen reflected the diggers' opinion of Charles Joseph La Trobe, Lieutenant-Governor of Victoria, but it may have originated as a pun on 'Yo Ho!' An eye-witness reported the following. Before gold was discovered south of the Murray, at the Ophir (N.S.W.) diggings in 1851 when the police approached: 'The signal was "Yo Ho!" From man to man it would pass along the creek, at the rate of ten miles in five minutes.'[12]

In words that recall Griffith's remarks about the loyalty of old hands to each other ten years earlier, the Goldfields Commission which enquired into the causes of the Eureka rising reported:

> Evasion became a practised and skilful art among a considerable number among whom an *esprit de corps* was ever the strongest sense of honour . . . diggers without licences . . . were left quietly at work in the pits, while those who had complied with the law betook themselves to flight as if the guilty parties, with all the police at their heels.

Of one such occasion it is recorded:

> The orders of the officers could not be heard, from the loud and continuous roars of 'Joe! Joe! Joe!'—'Damn the b——y Government!—the beaks, the traps, commissioners, and all—the robbers, the bushrangers', and every other vile epithet that could be remembered, almost into their ears.

In this particular hunt the diversionary tactics of the licence-holders were so masterly that the Commissioner finally had to move away 'sullenly with his forces', without having caught a single victim. The chronicler of the incident, though a 'respectable upholder of law and order' who approved of the licence fee at least in principle, was so infected by the universal demonstration of mateship that he confesses:

> [I was] unable to repress an emotion of gratification at the result of the chase, or an impulse of hero-worship as I sought the sole actor in the successful diversion to offer my congratulations.[13]

The force of collective public opinion is demonstrated also by the fact that it, rather than state power, was responsible for maintaining order—of a sort—on the goldfields. Almost all contemporary observers agreed that this was so, but perhaps the most striking, because unconscious, testimony is supplied by one who was himself engaged in administering 'official' law and order. When this Goldfields Commissioner went to arbitrate between two parties disputing possession of a claim, 'a large crowd of men, numbering a thousand or more, immediately gathered together' to see justice done. The Commissioner heard evidence from both sides in the proper form, but he remarks: 'it was not difficult to tell by a sort of popular feeling generally, if one *really* was in the wrong.'[14]

On newly discovered or remote fields this 'sort of popular feeling' kept order, if not law, and punished wrongdoers, without the assistance of government officials. Soon after Hargraves's initial discovery in 1851 a man who had robbed his mates was 'thrashed away from the creek with saplings' by the indignant diggers,[15] and this pattern of behaviour in which the whole body of assembled miners acted as judge, jury and executioner, spread later to the Western Australian fields[16] and still persists. In January 1937, for instance, I attended a 'roll-up', called spontaneously on the Wauchope Creek wolfram field in the Northern Territory. By levying themselves, the miners paid two of their number (at better than the then prevailing wage rate) to 'clean up' the camp site, and thus were able to negative a police order that it should be moved to a more hygienic but less convenient place two or three miles away.

One remarkable feature of these 'roll-ups' was that the extreme penalty they imposed was simply a sufficiently rough expulsion from the field. Because of the diggers' nomadic habits, expulsion from one goldfield usually amounted to exclusion from all fields, for 'wherever the culprit went he found out that someone knew him and "put'him away" '.[17] Though in some cases hanging was called for by a turbulent minority, the collective good sense of the majority was such that Europeans were very rarely, if ever, done to death.

The reasons for the comparative orderliness of the Australian, as compared with the Californian, goldfields have been much canvassed.

Writing in 1851, Mundy pointed to the comparative nearness of the fields to the settled centres of government 'already firmly established', the relative homogeneity of the diggers' 'racial' stock, the virtual absence of a warlike aboriginal race, and 'the love of order inherent in Englishmen'. To these may be added the influence of those 'rude notions of honour' supported by 'a kind of public opinion amongst themselves', which Griffith had considered in 1845 to be one of the leading characteristics of the 'nomad tribe' of pastoral workers.

The diggings were also a forcing-ground for two other traits already noted as being typical of the outback Australian way of life: adaptability and egalitarian independence. A digger's need for the first quality is implicitly clear in what has been said above. When Read was travelling to the Turon diggings in 1851, some aspiring gold-seekers were unable to adapt themselves to the experience of being catapulted out of the coach when it rolled over an embankment in the dark beyond Emu Plains. They forswore digging then and there, and returned to Sydney, but others went on to the fields. It is hard to imagine how any body of men could exhibit a more aggressively 'independent' attitude than the pastoral workers of whom squatters complained in the 1840's, but contemporaries thought that the diggers managed to do so. Polehampton both describes and explains digger egalitarianism:

The population of Victoria, as I have said before, presents a marked contrast to that of England and Europe generally. As a rule, every man there is, may be, or expects soon to be, his own master; and the consciousness of this causes a spirit of independence to pervade the mass, collectively and individually; this feeling being more especially prevalent on the diggings. Here are no conventionalities; no touching of hats. Men meet on apparently equal terms; and he who enjoyed the standing of a gentleman in England becomes aware, on the diggings, that his wonted position in society is no longer recognised; and the man, who in former days might have pulled your boots off, or served you respectfully behind a counter, shakes hands with you, and very likely hails you by a nickname, or by no name at all.

This attitude differs from that of the pastoral workers not in kind but, so to speak, in quantity. To the minimum security of rations and wages was added the real chance of acquiring riches, and this chance was greater for those who had been accustomed to, say, road-mending, either in Australia or in Britain, than it was for a 'swell' unused to manual labour. Hence the levelling tendencies in society were even stronger than before the gold discoveries. Moreover, the obliteration of class barriers, inseparable from life on the actual diggings, and the constant coming and going between the fields and the colonial capitals, both tended to spread the egalitarian outlook more rapidly outward from the 'nomad tribe' and upward through the middle classes.

There is evidence to show that the less admirable 'outback' habits also were adopted, and even accentuated, by the diggers. Converts to a faith are prone to be more fanatical than those who are born to it. Gambling, profanity and drunkenness tend to flourish in any frontier society where there are few women but, as we have seen, these vices were indulged in the more readily because they were properly regarded as characteristic of the old colonial hands. C. R. Read wrote:

> Such dreadful and horribly disgusting language may be heard expressed by children on the diggings, that I do not imagine could be surpassed by the most hardened adults on Norfolk Island, and this does not rest with boys alone, but little girls from *eight* to *ten* years of age. . . .

Although some observers were impressed with the outward decorum of the diggings on the Sabbath, a diarist recorded the following even on that day: 'lots of gambling going on . . . fellows tossing for nothing less than a £8 note [*sic*] and perhaps £100 changing hands every toss among the bystanders'.[18] There is no necessary inconsistency here. To-day the streets of Kalgoorlie present an orderly appearance on Sundays, while 'the biggest two-up school in the world' operates raucously but unobtrusively not far away, and even in Newgate prison, a hundred and thirty years ago, the ancestral form of what has been called the Australian national game was played in 'schools' in 'out-of-sight corners of the prison yard'.[19]

Drunkenness could not, in the nature of things, have been *more* rife on the diggings than it had been in the days of the 'Rum Corps'. This Homeric age of Australian drinking had already become legendary in the 1840's at which time there was an 'old song', probably English rather than Australian, two lines of which went:

> There's rum and brandy, as I've heard 'em say,
> In that blessed island called Bot'ny Bay.[20]

Fearing the conjunction of old hands, rum and gold, the authorities prohibited the sale of alcoholic drinks on the fields. The result was that sly-grog tents, in which more than usually adulterated liquor was sold, sprang up like mushrooms. Two historians of Victoria who visited the fields at the time, thought that on the whole prohibition did moderate the tide of drunkenness,[21] but others thought that it created more evils than it cured.[22] However this may be, there can be no doubt at all that the sudden changes in fortune, inseparable from the life of a digger, helped to accentuate the already firmly established outback tradition of 'work and burst'. Inns on the tracks to the diggings were the scenes of almost continuous revelry, and 'many of the bad old type of landlords, who had graduated in the art of "lambing down a shepherd", put the capstone to their fortunes' in the first few years after gold was discovered. Of Melbourne itself, where the most successful diggers repaired for their sprees, the following is recorded:

> [bar-counters were] washed down with expensive wines as a preliminary ceremony to ordering 'free drinks for the crowd', and with an imbecile idea of ostentation the poor fool has excited the plaudits of his followers by sweeping all the glasses off the counter with his whip to make the bill worth paying.[23]

Long before gold was found Griffith had noticed that the old hands seemed to regard robbing people not of their own class as a 'spoiling of the Egyptians', while they despised a man who robbed his mates. This ambivalent attitude partly explains the contradictory reports about the honesty of diggers. A new chum like Craig, who lived on uneasily familiar terms with a party of thoroughly vicious Vandemonians, was protected by one of the worst of them.[24] On the other hand William Howitt and his gentlemanly party, armed with pistols, bowie-knives and vice-regal letters, though they kept all low fellows at a distance, had the most trifling articles stolen 'from their very heels'.[25] It is also noteworthy that most of the criminals were ex-convicts from Van Diemen's Land,[26] many of whom must have come straight from servitude to the diggings without any intermediate experience of up-country life. Read, who spent some months on the Turon diggings in their first year when a very high proportion of the diggers must still have been New South Wales old hands, wrote:

> there was a great deal better feeling existing, than I subsequently observed in Victoria; no one scarcely remained to take care of their tents during the day . . . [and] . . . at night no one ever thought of taking their mining tools away from their claim, and I scarcely ever heard of any being stolen, and no one ever made any hesitation of lending another a crowbar or anything they wanted, no matter whether stranger or not, it was sure of being returned.

In so far as gold brought more people to the bush and led to the growth of country towns, it may be said to have brought the bushmen into closer touch with organized religion, but this was a long-term process. At first the effect of the discoveries was to accentuate the cynical up-country attitude to the clergy.[27] One digger, who had been killed in the fighting at Eureka, was attended to his grave by a public procession of mourners among whom no clergyman was to be seen. In traditional up-country style, the body was carried 'between sheets of bark by way of a coffin'.[28]

A convincing witness to the diggers' majority opinion that most clergymen were canting hypocrites was Charles Thatcher, the immensely popular goldfields entertainer. A witty and well-educated man of middle-class upbringing, he came in 1853 from Brighton, England, to dig for gold in Victoria, but soon found he could earn a more congenial living by composing and singing topical songs to his own accompaniment. Well over two hundred of these survive in booklet or broadside form, and there are many more in the Victorian Public Library's collection of his manuscript material. On 7 April 1854 the *Argus* published a despatch from its Bendigo correspondent who declared that Thatcher's songs were 'all humorous, abounding in local allusions as a matter of course; and if circulated in England, would give a much better idea of life at the goldfields than most of the elaborately written works upon them do'. Half a century later Thatcher's song books were still among the favourite stock-in-trade of outback travelling hawkers, and many of his verses were passed on from singer to singer to become genuine folk-songs.[29] His work demonstrates what has been said above about the chameleon-like rapidity with which new chums tended to take on the colour of their surroundings. Within two years of his arrival he had produced many songs like the following:

The Bond Street Swell

(A new original song, written and sung by Chas. R. Thatcher, with unbounded applause.)

Tune: 'Nice Young Man'

I'll sing you now just a little song,
    For you must understand,
'Tis of a fine young gentleman
    That left his native land—
That bid his ma and pa farewell,
    And started brave and bold,
In a ship of fourteen hundred tons,
    To come and dig for gold.

His dress was spicy as could be;
    His fingers hung with rings—
White waistcoats, black silk pantaloons,
    And other stylish things.
His berth was in the cuddy,
    Which is on deck, you know,
And all the intermediates,
    He noted 'deuced low'

When the vessel left the London Docks,
    Most jovial did he seem;
But on the Downs, a change came o'er
    The spirit of his dream:

His ruddy cheeks turned very pale,
    His countenance looked rum;
And with a mournful sigh, said he,
    'I wish I'd never come.'

The ship at length cast anchor,
    And he was glad once more;
Six large trunks he then packed up
    And started for the shore—
His traps filled quite a whale boat,
    So of course I needn't say,
That for the freight thereof, he had
    A tidy sum to pay.

He came to town and then put up
    At the Criterion Hotel,—
If you've been there, you know the place
    And the charges pretty well.
He played at billiards half the day,
    And smoked and lounged about;
Until the hundred pounds he'd brought,
    Had precious near run out.

With five pounds in his pocket,
    He went to Bendigo;
But when he saw the diggin's,
    They filled his heart with woe—
'What! Must I venture down a hole,
    And throw up filthy clay?
If my mother could but see me now,
    Whatever would she say?'

He went and bought a shovel,
    And a pick and dish as well,
But to every ten minutes' work,
    He took an hour's spell.
The skin from his fair white hands
    In blisters peeled away—
And thus he worked, and sunk about
    Twelve inches every day.

When off the bottom just a foot,
    He got quite out of heart,
And threw his pick down in a rage
    And off he did depart;
But when he'd left his hole, and gone,
    A cove named Sydney Bob
Stepped into it and soon took out
    A pretty handsome 'lob'.

With five shillings in his pocket,
    He started in disgust,
And then he went upon the roads,
    As many a young swell must.
And if through the Black Forest
    You ever chance to stray,
You may see him do the Gov'ment stroke
    At eight bob every day.[30]

The colloquial expression 'Government Stroke' probably began as a description of the way in which 'Government men' worked. In Victoria at this time it would seem to have been a jibe levelled by colonial workmen at those whom they called 'broken-down swells', rather than the reverse, which it has become since. The then distinctively Australian custom of taking ten minutes or a quarter of an hour for 'smoke-ohs' in mid-morning and afternoon was also firmly established in Victoria in the early 1850's,[31] but both phrases may well have originated in New South Wales before the gold discoveries.

Obviously the 'practical' working-class values typified by 'Sydney Bob' were *de rigueur* on the diggin's', and it behoved the gently nurtured new chum to adopt them as rapidly as possible. Thatcher underlines this theme again and again, most interestingly perhaps in the script[32] accompanying his diorama illustrating goldfields life. He is describing typical figures on their way to the diggings:

> Then comes a wonderful contrast. Two diggers one an old hand in a stained blue shirt moleskin trousers leather belt & tin pannikin a butcher's knife heavy lace ups Cabbage tree-hat, swag slung across his back horse collar fashion & surmounting it a pick and shovel & an American axe.

But apparently the old hand's prestige had become so great that Thatcher felt diffident about drawing attention to its convict origins. The above passage is crossed out in the manuscript and, with some historical verisimilitude, the 'old hand' becomes a 'real old digger'.

> Then comes a real old digger who has been to Melbourne on the spree with his pile courted a new arrival one day married her the next and who leaves her in Melbourne while he goes up again to try his luck. The other a new arrival in a suit of broadcloth carrying a knapsack to which is attached a Railway wrapper an oilskin coat the inevitable double-barrelled gun as if gold was a thing to be shot at & brought down while the pockets of his coat contain a Cigar case powder flask a compass, sandwich box & other useless trifles the usual treasures of a new chum—

Thatcher also devotes many songs to what was perhaps the most prominent feature of the diggers' ethos: their hatred for the police. Practically every contemporary writer stresses this feature of gold-fields life, and even the most conservative[33] tacitly agree that members of the force, by their venality, arrogance, brutality and incompetence, did much to earn the contempt in which they were held. In the diary of a Bendigo store-keeper we read:

> Robberies as daring and cruel as those of the highwayman are hourly committed by the representatives of the Government. The whole system is bad . . . the commissioners and all the staff of government officers are miserably underpaid but then every opportunity is afforded them of obtaining money by means of legal plunder.

He goes on to explain that fines for licence-evasion and sly-grog selling were divided between the constable who apprehended the offender, the sergeant of his staff and the Gold Commissioners. The consequence was, he says, that to augment their incomes, the commissioners and their underlings privily encouraged sly-grog selling, and made the simple purchasing of a licence 'as difficult a matter as to get a letter from the Melbourne P.O. . . .'[34]

Read, an unusually conscientious commissioner, himself confirms the general accuracy of this picture, as indeed does the report of the Commission which enquired into the causes of Eureka.[35] In 1853 E. P. S. Sturt, Superintendent of Victorian Police, was asked by a Select Committee of the Legislative Council his opinion of the 'discharged soldiers and pensioners', who made up a large portion of the force. He replied: 'As a body they appear to me to be the most drunken set of men I ever met with; and totally unfit to be put to any useful purposes of police.'[36] Even the gentlemanly, not to say genteel, new chum, William Howitt, who was kindly received by La Trobe, denounces 'Mr Mackaye, the inspector of police' at the Ovens field, as 'a low drunken sot', and refers to the 'Russian sort of way' in which the police carried out their functions. He wrote, nearly two years before the fighting at Eureka, that police behaviour on the diggings was 'creating a spirit that will break out one of these days energetically'.[37]

Australian policemen had long been noted for bad behaviour when gold was first discovered in 1851. There was a long if not honourable tradition, which still exists, of unusually intense enmity between them and the populace, but this subject will be dealt with in the next chapter. Here it is sufficient to note that, as in so many other matters concerning the popular outlook, the Gold Rush did not so much change as intensify the existing tradition. Contemporaries believed that this was partly because to the basic stuff of police force personnel—particularly vicious and venal old convicts despised by their fellows—Gold Rush conditions added an upper stratum of:

> . . . the worst class of colonists—young men who have been accustomed to no business habits at home, whose sole capital on coming to the Colony was a letter of introduction to the Governor, or some other party who had interest to appoint them.[38]

Thus, from the point of view of the 'old Australians', the police force was composed mainly of renegades from their own ranks, and of their natural enemies: the new chum 'swells'.

The following anecdote illustrates how naturally the old hands' hatred of policemen was passed on to many new chums. When gold was first discovered at Ballarat, an old Sydney-side ex-convict named Jack was working as shepherd and handyman on a station near by. For many months he remained at work, held back from the rush by the tongue of his wife who feared that the sly-grog sellers on the field would immediately receive any gold he might find. In the end he left, fell in with three old mates from New South Wales, and rapidly dug £200 worth of gold. With this he took his wife and two bush-bred daughters to Melbourne, where the girls at once found fiancés. At the double wedding Jack provided a gargantuan breakfast, of which many guests ate and drank to the point of regurgitation. Dressed in his new suit the proud father opened proceedings by 'givin' on 'em a song', the chorus of which was borne by the whole party, the girls included, who were the most proficient, for they ' 'ad 'eard father sing it before, many a time'. The chorus was something like the following:

> Oh, the traps, the dirty traps;
>   Kick the traps whene'er you're able;
> At the traps, the nasty traps;
>   Kick the traps right under the table.

Soon afterwards the host and some of the guests composed themselves to sleep in the same place while dancing continued until daylight.[39]

A great many of Thatcher's songs also jeer at the police and the military. A stanza from one of them combines a jibe at the new type of imported policeman with one at the clergy:

> Lord Fuzzleby's nephew, who went,
>   And spent every summer at Nice,
> Says, 'now boys, you'd better move on'—
>   In short, he is in the police.
> And the Reverend Frederick Spout,
>   Who in the Church very high stood;
> And split hairs in divinity once,
>   Gets his living by splitting up wood.[40]

We have seen that in most ways the bushmen's ethos was not changed by the Gold Rush. However, racist passions, always felt for the Aborigines, were accentuated. Before 1851 the colonial contempt for new chums had sprung mainly from a feeling of nationalism, which was in turn closely associated with a lower-class *esprit de corps*. Even an Englishman might be rapidly forgiven his unfortunate heritage provided he did not give himself the airs of a 'swell'.

It is true that the skilled workers in Sydney objected as early as 1843 to the proposed importation of Indian coolies, but at this time their objections were economic rather than 'racial'. They objected to the resumption of transportation, and even to free immigration from Britain, on much the same grounds,[41] but there is little evidence of general popular enmity towards the few Maoris and other coloured people who worked and drank with the Currency men in the ships and streets of early Sydney.[42]

The first Australian bushranger was a Negro nicknamed 'Caesar' who 'subsisted in the woods by plundering the farms and huts at the outskirts of the towns'. He was described by the Judge-Advocate as 'incorrigibly stubborn', and as reputedly 'the hardest working convict in the country'. So popular was he with his fellows that, when captured in June 1789, Phillip reprieved him from the gallows because his execution 'was not expected to have the proper or intended effect'.[43] Another Negro named Billy Blue, after whom Blue's Point was named, was for many years the Sydney Harbour ferryman. He was so well liked that a broadside was printed in his honour.[44] A further remarkable piece of evidence of the relative lack of race prejudice in early Australia is provided in Harris's novel, *The Emigrant Family* (1849). Its central figure, Martin Beck, is a Negro and a station overseer.[45] That, in a work of fiction, a coloured man could occupy such a responsible post without causing marked surprise or resentment is sufficiently remarkable. Much more so is the fact that, although Martin Beck is the villain of the book, neither the author nor his characters betray any feeling that the Negro's villainy may be a function of his race.

It is not argued that Australians prior to 1851 were a peculiarly enlightened people. Their treatment of the Aboriginal race makes a rather wry joke of any such suggestion. But, with the exception of these unfortunates, there were so few foreigners of any one race that they were, as a rule, objects of interest rather than of embarrassment or fear. Moreover, in Britain and in Europe generally, nationalism and its accompanying delusions of racial grandeur were much less marked in the eighteenth century than they became in the nineteenth. It is possible that the remoteness and isolation of Australia fostered a relative prolongation of this aspect of the age of enlightenment.

With the influx of gold diggers all this was changed. Possibly the higher proportion of middle-class people among the newcomers had something to do with the rapid growth of race prejudice but nearly all, save a few enlightened or personally interested individuals, shared in the new pastime of Chinese-baiting. The fact that most of the Celestials were accustomed to work for wretchedly low wages, and were indentured to capitalists among their compatriots, or to squatters whose workmen had left for the diggings, meant that they were a potential threat to the living standard of colonial workmen and provided a rational basis for complaint. The sudden arrival of forty thousand foreigners,[46] differing so completely from the colonists in culture that even in the long term view their assimilation was doubtful, gave good grounds for worry. Much later they were accused, with some justice, of bringing smallpox and leprosy to Australia. But from these reasonable arguments most people proceeded headlong to indiscriminate abuse and, in many cases, to vicious action.

Although the Chinese usually kept to themselves and ventured only to work in areas already dug over and deserted by European diggers,[47] they were accused of encroaching on the white men's claims. It seems probable that these accusations, in the first instance, were made by Europeans who were wont to 'jump' Chinese claims which showed any sign of richness.[48] Another favourite complaint was that they fouled the creek waters, but on diggings where there were no Chinese, muddied water was accepted without question as an inevitable by-product of cradling operations.[49] Old hands were no doubt second to none in attributing to the Chinese monstrous and unnatural vices.[50] Passions rose so high that riots broke out on the diggings. The most disgraceful took place at the Buckland field in Victoria in 1857, and at Lambing Flat in New South Wales in 1861. Wholesale assault, robbery and arson were committed on the unresisting Chinamen, and on their property. Several were either murdered outright or died as a result of ill-treatment and exposure. Miners cut off their victims' pigtails, in some cases with the scalp adhering thereto,[51] and proudly displayed them as trophies. Although thoughtful colonists were ashamed of these proceedings, juries usually refused, even when confronted with the most incriminating evidence, to convict their perpetrators.[52] Children were encouraged by 'patriotic' parents to revile and stone Chinamen, who were usually too intimidated to protest. Anti-Chinese ballads, composed by Thatcher and others, were widely sung, especially on the diggings and in the back-country. Most popular was a parody of 'Rule Britannia' which Henry Lawson often heard, as a lad, on the New South Wales diggings: 'Irreverent echo of the old Lambing Flat trouble, from a camp across the gully:

> "Rule Britannia! Britannia rule the waves!
> No more Chinamen will enter New South Wales!" '[53]

From this time the mateship of the pastoral workers rigidly excluded Asians from the nomad tribe, though other coloured people were sometimes accepted. The rules of the Australian Workers' Union, in Spence's day, denied membership to 'Chinese, Japanese, Kanakas, or Afghans, or coloured aliens other than Maoris, American negroes, and children of mixed parentage born in Australia'. There seems also to have been less anti-Semitic prejudice among the bushmen than among many of their social 'superiors'.[54] An anonymous Kelly Gang folk-ballad shows this 'racism' at its most disgusting. It describes an incident at the Royal Hotel, Jerilderie:

> They mustered up the servants and locked them in a room,
> Saying, 'Do as we command you, or death will be your doom,'
> The Chinaman cook 'no savvied,' his face was full of fear,
> But Ned soon made him savvy with a straight left to the ear.

A stanza from a traditional version of A. B. Paterson's *Bushman's Song* shows the sentiment in its most excusable, or at least most rational, form—as a function of trade union militancy:

> I asked a bloke for shearing down on the Marthaguy.
> 'We shear non-union here,' he said. 'I call it scab,' said I.
> I looked along the shearing-board before I chanced to go,
> Saw eight or ten dashed Chinamen all shearing in a row.

Chorus:

> It was shift, boys, shift, there was not the slightest doubt
> It was time to make a shift with leprosy about.
> So I saddled up my horses and whistled to my dog,
> And I left that scabby station at the old jig-jog.[55]

Next to the Chinese, the foreign diggers who made most impression on bush life were the Americans. Although less numerous than the Germans, many of them came from California, and their 'frontier' culture was so like that of the colonists as to be much more readily assimilable. A clerical observer wrote:

At first, it must be confessed, [they] made themselves very obnoxious to the peacably disposed portion of the people, in spouting republicanism, and exciting to rebellion against the British Government; . . . The era of responsible government, and the advent of manhood suffrage, must have reconciled the Yankees to the country, however, as they were never afterwards heard of as meddling with politics.

On the licence-hunted goldfields some 'spouting of republicanism' must have commended the Americans to circles other than those approved by the Rev. Morison. American diggers certainly exerted at the goldfields an influence quite disproportionate to their numbers. Both the first and the worst anti-Chinese demonstrations in Victoria, on the Bendigo field in 1854 and the Buckland in 1857 respectively, took place on the Fourth of July, the anniversary of the American Declaration of Independence, and Americans played a prominent part in the defence of the Eureka Stockade. The American Consulate in Melbourne successfully exerted itself to have all its nationals who had taken up arms released before the trial, all, that is, except the American Negro, John Joseph, who stood his trial with common diggers.[56] Americans derived a certain prestige too, from being citizens of another 'new country' whose land legislation furnished a striking contrast with that of most Australian colonies. Whenever the burning issue of 'unlocking the land' was discussed, all save the squatters tended to point to the United States as a country which was successfully demonstrating how to create a large body of prosperous individual smallholders.[57]

Much more influential, however, were the colourful manners and 'go-ahead' ways of the Yankees. Old Australians, for long accustomed to despise the helplessness of new chums faced with practical problems, could not but be impressed when 'Brother Jonathan' proceeded to instruct *them* in the art of bush transport. From 1853 onwards lightly built American-type buggies, carts, and even four-wheeled coaches and wagons began to rattle over up-country tracks which had previously been considered impassable to anything but the ponderous, two-wheeled, colonial bullock-dray. In 1850 on the eve of the Gold Rush, even the Royal

Mail 'coach' from Sydney to Melbourne had been, from Yass onwards, a two-wheeled cart.[58] For a time at least American modes of dress, speech and behaviour were imitated by some of the colonists. 'Rolf Boldrewood', in his *Robbery Under Arms*, reported the situation accurately in the following passage. Two native-born bush youths, the hero's brother Jim Marston, and his mate, Joe Morton, are preparing to escape police attention by disguising themselves as Americans:

> Lucky for old Jim we'd all taken a fancy at the Turon, for once in a way, to talk like Arizona Bill and his mates, just for the fun of the thing. There were so many Americans there at first, and they were such swells, with their silk sashes, bowie knives, and broad-leafed 'full-share' hats, that lots of young native fellows took a pride in copying them, and could walk and talk and guess and calculate wonderful well considering. Besides, most of the natives have a sort of slow, sleepy way of talking, so it partly came natural to this chap Joe Morton and Jim . . .

However, colourful manners and speech may be seen equally as vulgarity and boastfulness, and smartness in business may pass over into swindling. Finding that the Yankees out-Heroded Herod in these matters, even the old Australians seem to have reacted somewhat against their influence. In view of the overwhelming evidence of sharp practice towards outsiders by the old colonial hands, it is rather amusing to find them adopting a 'holier-than-thou' attitude to Americans who, for their part, considered the 'Sydney Ducks' and 'Sydney Coves' pre-eminent in villainy among all the scoundrels who flocked to the 'Barbary Coast' during the Californian Gold Rush. Gerstaecker, the sensible German writer, spent a considerable time in both countries at the period. He considered that many 'Sydney Ducks' were justly hanged by the Californian Vigilante committees, but that even greater criminals among the native Americans often used Australian and Mexican miners as scapegoats for their own deeds. Perhaps the truth is that the emigrants from each country included a very high proportion of its more unconventionally enterprising spirits.[59] The following popular song of the period reflects nicely the mingled admiration and irritation which the Yankees inspired in Colonial breasts:

I'll sing you quite a novel song, made by a colonial brick,
Of a thorough white-washed Yankee who was 'tarnation slick'—
Who thought in every movement his imitation fine,
And aped the manners of the States so truly genuine,
    Like a regular white-washed Yankee, one of the present time.

His hat was placed quite jauntily on one side of his head,
And he fumbled his big watch-seals at every word he said;
He wore knee boots with gilt-red tops to make his legs look flash,
And at his sides the ends fell down of a long silk Yankee sash,
    Like a regular etc.

He had no whiskers nor moustache, but sported a goatee,
He guessed and calculated, and used the word 'siree';
And to every true American he'd cause a cruel pang,
His conversation was delivered with such a nasal twang,
    Like a regular etc.

He lounged at billiard tables, tenpin alleys, and hotels,
And smoked cigars six inches long with other white-washed
    swells,
Or chewed his cake tobacco, and by General Jackson swore,
Expectorating on the furniture, but seldom on the floor.
    Like a regular etc.

But with all his imitations, this 'harmless' white-washed rogue,
Was nothing but an Irishman, and had an awful brogue:
Should you ask if he's a Yankee, as his manners indicate,
He'll say, though born in Ireland, he was raised in New York
    State,
    Like a regular etc.

But men from every country the Yankee customs seek,
If in California or the States they've only been a week,
By every man of common sense such conduct must be blamed,
And all these imitators of their country are ashamed.
    Like a regular etc.[60]

After the Gold Rush there was a sharp falling off in the number
of immigrants and visitors from America. The period from about
1860 till 1900 was one in which Australia, like the United States,
was busily occupying the interior, and was relatively little affected
by the outside world. As the gold fever died down there seems

to have been a reaction against the passion for copying American ways. Certain it is that the bushman's clothing and accoutrements became more drab and utilitarian while those of his American congener, the cowboy, were soaring to ever higher peaks of complicated flamboyance. A few lines from Lawson's 'A Word to Texas Jack' will give the flavour of Australian popular feeling towards Americans by the end of the century:

Texas Jack, you are amusin'. Great Lord Harry how I laughed
When I seen your rig and saddle with its bulwarks fore and aft;
. . . .
How I'd like to see a bushman use your fixins, Texas Jack—
On the remnant of a saddle he could ride to hell and back.
Why, I've heard a mother cheerin' when her kid went tossin' by,
Ridin' bareback on a bucker that had murder in his eye.

What? You've come to learn the natives how to sit a horse's back!
Learn the bloomin' cornstalk ridin'? W'at yer giv'n us, Texas Jack?
. . . .
As poet and as Yankee I will greet you, Texas Jack,
For it isn't no ill-feelin' that is gettin' up my back;
But I won't see this land crowded by each Yank and British cuss
Who takes it in his head to come a-civilizin' us.

. . . .
So when it comes to ridin' mokes, or hoistin' out the Chow,
Or stickin' up for labour's rights, we don't want showin' how.
They came to learn us cricket in the days of long ago,
An' Hanlan came from Canada to learn us how to row,
An' 'doctors' come from Frisco just to learn us how to skite,
An' pugs from all lands on earth to learn us how to fight;
An' when they go, as like as not, we find we're taken in,
They've left behind no learnin'—but they've carried off our tin.

American gold-diggers then had only a transitory influence on the ideology of the bushmen. Implicit in the above lines is that laconic sang-froid which had inspired a visitor to write in 1834:

Even among the male Australians there is a taciturnity proceeding from natural diffidence and reserve, not from any want of mental resources; this led one of their more lively countrymen to observe, 'that they could do everything but speak'.

And which could still, in 1956, lead a distinguished Australian historian to say:

'But perhaps the majority (i.e., male) Australian approach to articulation is best indicated by a generalisation: utterance is better not done at all; but, if it is done, when it is done, it were well it were done slowly and flatly and expressionlessly, to betoken that the subject, any subject, is hardly worth talking about.'[61]

One other important effect of the Gold Rush remains to be noted. There can be little doubt that the average standard of educational attainment was much higher among the newcomers than it had been among the pastoral workers prior to the discoveries. Before the advent of free public education there was necessarily a high positive correlation between literacy and wealth. Before 1851 most immigrants had been convicts or assisted migrants—paupers, in the brutal phrase of the times. The great majority of the gold-seekers had at least enough money to pay the high fares demanded for a ticket to El Dorado.

Contemporary documents abound with references to the large numbers of educated and professional men among the motley crowds that swarmed to the diggings, and it was only after the Gold Rush that observers began to remark on the high standard of outback literacy. In 1871 for instance, 'A University Man' who had carried his swag for some years, wrote:

> There is a leaven of education and information pervading the whole [working] class which is very remarkable. Books and newspapers are eagerly sought after and read by most of them, whatever their employment. This is more remarkable when you get further into the Bush than it is in the towns.[62]

As the earliest surviving version of a cattleman's ballad has it:

> When the cattle were all mustered, and the outfit ready to start,
> I saw the boys all mounted, with their swags left in the cart;
> All sorts of men I had, from France, Germany and Flanders,
> Lawyers, doctors, good and bad, in my mob of overlanders.[63]

The result was that, to an incomparably greater extent than in the early period, the nomad tribe became conscious of itself and of its distinctive ethos. The vast majority of its surviving folk-ballads were made and sung between about 1855 and 1900. Particularly in the earlier part of this period, the poetasters who gave the pastoral workers a clearer voice were often educated, middle-class immigrants who had, through force of circumstances, thrown in their lot with the nomad tribe and become, as it were, thoroughly naturalized.[64]

Apart then from this heightened self-awareness, and the new element of racial exclusiveness, the bush-workers lived and thought in much the same way after the gold discoveries as they had done before them. And this was due not only to the strength of the old-hand-outback tradition, but at least equally to the fact that the conditions of bush life, which had done so much to mould that tradition in the earlier period, were still substantially unchanged after the Gold Rush. In the more settled districts shepherds gave way to boundary riders as a result of fencing, but in Western Queensland and other frontier areas shepherding went on well into the 1880's. This change, by substituting mounted men for the old 'crawlers', intensified the bushmen's *esprit de corps*, and many redundant shepherds found more satisfying work as fencers or tank-sinkers. The minority of immigrants who remained in the outback after most of the alluvial gold had petered out were moulded in their turn by the environment.

In 1869 a very acute observer of pastoral life in the Riverina wrote: 'Our labour in the bush has been supplied from four sources; the first is most familiarly known as "old hands"; the next is the young native-born population; the third, the digging population of the neighbouring goldfields; the last, the newly arrived immigrants.'[65] He went on to deplore the fact that labourers from the last two classes either departed from the interior as soon as opportunity offered, or settled down only too quickly into the traditional pattern of behaviour long since established by the old hands and their native-born associates. The reason for this, he argued cogently, was that the conditions of outback life were substantially unchanged. In particular, even the most enterprising newcomers, like their predecessors, could 'see no prospect' of becoming their own masters and so of marrying and making homes for themselves.

The substance of this chapter is summed up, not inaptly, in one of the comparatively few goldfields ballads which passed into oral tradition. Most of the new-chum diggers must have returned to the capital cities and larger country towns. The following song bodies forth the history of those who did not:

When first I left Old England's shore
  Such yarns as we were told,
As how folks in Australia
  Could pick up lumps of gold.
So, when we got to Melbourne town,
  We were ready soon to slip
And get even with the captain—
  All hands scuttled from the ship.

Chorus:

        With my swag all on my shoulder,
          Black billy in my hand,
        I travelled the bush of Australia
          Like a true-born native man.

We steered our course for Geelong Town,
  Then north-west to Ballarat,
Where some of us got mighty thin,
  And some got sleek and fat.
Some tried their luck at Bendigo,
  And some at Fiery Creek;
I made a fortune in a day
  And spent it in a week.

For many years I wandered round,
  As each new rush broke out,
And always had of gold a pound,
  Till alluvial petered out.
'Twas then we took the bush to cruise,
  Glad to get a bite to eat;
The squatters treated us so well
  We made a regular beat.

So round the 'lighthouse' now I tramp,[66]
  Nor leave it out of sight;
I take it on my left shoulder,
  And then upon my right,
And then I take it on my back,
  And oft upon it lie.
It is the best of tucker tracks
  So I'll stay here till I die.[67]

The Gold Rush diversified the economy, and greatly strength-ened the middle class in Australia. Nearly all new Australians of the Gold Rush decade proceeded straight to the 'diggin's' for a few months or years. There they were subjected to an intensive course of 'colonization', administered by old Australians and the very conditions of bush life which had already helped to mould the outlook of the old hands. Most of the middle-class immigrants probably returned in time to the cities, where many of them became prominent in business, politics, law and education. Some remained in the bush to become, in less time, as thoroughly acclimatized as their predecessors. In politics and economics the golden decade was a watershed, but in the development of the Australian *mystique* it was not. If anything, it had the over-all effect of delaying the emergence into full consciousness of the national legend.

It strongly accentuated, if it did not cause, the growth of race prejudice among pastoral workers. On the other hand, when the old hands deserted the runs *en masse* for the 'diggin's', pas-toralists had to begin fencing their stations. In time this did away with shepherding, the most degrading of outback occupations, and so helped to enhance the *esprit de corps* of bushmen; but it did not change, in any basic way, the nature of their outlook.

CHAPTER V

1   E. G. Shann, *Economic History of Australia*, Sydney 1948 ed., p. 167; and G. V. Portus, *Cambridge History of British Empire*, vol. 7, ch. 9, pp. 270-2.

2   In all these tables the figures are taken from the official Census Returns of the Colonies of New South Wales (1841, 1851, and 1861), Victoria (1851 and 1861), and Queensland (1861). The figures shown for 1841 under 'Victoria' are of course those for the then Port Phillip District of N.S.W. For the sake of formal statistical consistency the N.S.W. figures for 1861 *include* those for the newly separated colony of Queensland; but the 1861 figures for N.S.W. proper are placed for comparison in brackets.

3   The 1861 Census in N.S.W. ceased to distinguish emancipists from other persons born in Great Britain. In Table X therefore the figure for N.S.W. in 1861 is an estimate (to the nearest 1,000), calculated on the assumption that between 1851 and 1861 the convict-emancipist population decreased at the same rate as it had done in the preceding

decade. Victorian censuses never distinguished emancipists from other persons born in Great Britain, and as the absolute number of these people in Port Phillip in 1841 was so small, it seemed futile to attempt estimates of their numbers in that colony in 1851 and 1861. Nevertheless, contemporary records make it clear that a great many ex-convicts from Van Diemen's Land and quite a number from N.S.W. emigrated to Victoria during the period. For instance, J. C. Byrne (*Twelve Years' Wanderings in the British Colonies*, 2 vols., London 1848, vol. 1, pp. 325-6), estimates that in two years, 1845 and 1846, about 4,000 ex-convicts emigrated from Van Diemen's Land to Port Phillip. And William Howitt (*Land, Labour, and Gold*, etc., 2 vols., London 1855, vol. 2, p. 8), claims Van Diemen's Land 'official sources' for his statement that 9,023 ex-convicts emigrated to Victoria in 18 months of 1852 and 1853.

4   Pakington to Fitzroy, 15 December 1852, *Votes and Proceedings Legislative Council of New South Wales 1853*, vol. 1.

5   Rev. A. Polehampton, *Kangaroo Land*, London 1862, pp. 60-1; and cp. John A. Graham, *Early Creswick—The First Century*, Melbourne 1942, p. 183.

6   W. Westgarth, *Victoria: Late Australia Felix*, etc., Edinburgh 1853, p. vii; and Mrs C. Clacy, *A Lady's Visit to the Gold Diggings of Australia*, etc., London 1853, p. 281.

7   'A Clergyman etc.' (Rev. John Morison), *Australia As It Is: or Facts and Features*, etc., London 1867, p. 161; and C. Rudston Read, *What I Heard, Saw and Did*, etc., London 1853, p. 11.

8   William Rayment, *Diary 1852-1860*, 19 October 1852 (Public Library of Victoria, MS.).

9   A. Polehampton, *op. cit.*, pp. 52-3, 66-7.

10   *Report of Gold Fields Enquiry Commission, 1855*, Minutes of Evidence, pp. 1, 28-9, 51, 72 and *passim*.

11   cp. Anon. (Mrs J. S. Calvert), *Cowanda, the Veteran's Grant*, Sydney 1859, p. 73.

12   *Cootamundra Herald*, 9 March 1907; and cp. F. Eldershaw, *Australia As It Really Is*, London 1854, pp. 250-3.

13   William Kelly, *Life in Victoria, or Victoria in 1853*, etc., 2 vols., London 1859, vol. 1, pp. 192-5. ('Trap' was thieves' slang and 'Old Australian' for 'policeman'.)

14   C. Rudston Read, *op. cit.*, pp. 158-60 (his italics); and cp. W. Westgarth, *op. cit.*, p. 243.

15   G. C. Mundy, *Our Antipodes*, etc., 3rd ed., London 1855, p. 567; and cp. J. Sherer (ed.), *The Gold Finder of Australia*, London 1853, pp. 67-8.

16   J. Marshall, *Battling for Gold*, etc., London 1903, pp. 140-7; and cp. Sir G. F. Pearce, *Carpenter to Cabinet*, etc., London 1951, pp. 27-9.

17   J. Marshall, *loc. cit.*

18   Edward Snell, *Diary, 1849-59*, 20 June 1852, p. 296 (Public Library of Victoria, MS.).

19   'James Tucker', *Adventures of Ralph Rashleigh*, ed. Colin Roderick, Sydney 1952, p. 28.

20   J. P. Townsend, *Rambles and Observations*, etc., London 1849, p. 9.

21   W. Westgarth, *op. cit.*, p. 237; and James Bonwick, *Notes of a Gold Digger and Gold Digger's Guide*, ed. E. E. Prescott, Melbourne 1942, pp. 30-1.

22   H. G. Turner, *History of Colony of Victoria*, 2 vols., London 1904, vol. 2, pp. 13-14; and T. McCombie, *History of the Colony of Victoria*, etc., London 1858, p. 220.

23   H. G. Turner, *op. cit.*, vol. 1, p. 372.

24   W. Craig, *My Adventures on the Australian Goldfields*, London 1903, ch. 7-10, esp. pp. 133, 145.

25   W. Howitt, *Land, Labour, and Gold*, etc., 2 vols., London 1855, vol. 1, pp. 55-6, 99, 146-7.

26   W. Westgarth, *op. cit.*, p. 166 ff.

27   T. McCombie, *op. cit.*, p. 217; and cp. Martin Brennan, *Reminiscences of the Gold Fields*, etc., Sydney 1907, ch. 4, 5, 7, 8.

28   A. Polehampton, *op. cit.*, pp. 224-5.

29   See 'Giles Seagram' (H. J. Driscoll), *Bushmen All*, etc., Melbourne 1908, p. 227 ff.

30   From C. R. Thatcher, *Victoria Songster*, etc., Melbourne 1855.

31   cp. W. Westgarth, *Victoria and the Australian Gold Mines in 1857*, etc., London 1857, pp. 68, 144-5; William Howitt, *op. cit.*, vol. 1, pp. 293-4; and Robert Caldwell, *The Gold Era of Victoria*, etc., London 1855, pp. 129-30.

32   Thatcher (Public Library of Victoria, MS.).

33   e.g. H. G. Turner, *op. cit.*, vol. 2, pp. 42-4; Capt. H. Butler Stoney, *Victoria: with a Description of Its Principal Cities*, etc., London 1856, pp. 103-6 ff.; and cp. G. Serle, 'The Causes of Eureka', *Historical Studies: Australia and New Zealand: Eureka Supplement*, December 1954, p. 16.

34   A. H. Shum, *Diary and Letter Book*, June-July 1853 (Public Library of Victoria, MS.); and cp. Edward Snell, *Diary, 1849-1859* (Public Library of Victoria, MS.); George Mackay, *History of Bendigo*, Melbourne 1891, pp. 9-11; and Carboni Rafaello, *The Eureka Stockade*, ed. H. V. Evatt, Sydney 1942.

35   More, perhaps, by its reticences than its statements. See pp. x-xiii, xxiii-xxiv.

36   Committee's Report, vol. 2, p. 8, *Votes and Proceedings Legislative Council of Victoria, 1852-53.*

37   William Howitt, *op. cit.*, vol. 1, pp. 51, 182-3, 236.

38 R. Caldwell, *op. cit.*, p. 107; C. M. H. Clark, *Select Documents 1851-1900*, Sydney 1955, pp. 9-13.

39 James Kirby, *Old Times in the Bush of Australia*, etc., Melbourne n.d. (1895), p. 223 ff.

40 *Victoria Songster.*

41 *Historical Records of Australia*, Series 1, vol. 22, pp. 594-6; and K. M. Dallas, 'The Origins of "White Australia"', *Australian Quarterly*, March 1955.

42 e.g. P. Cunningham, *Two Years in New South Wales*, etc., 2 vols., London (3rd ed. 1828), vol. 1, pp. 57-8.

43 David Collins, *Account of the English Colony in New South Wales*, London 1798, pp. 70-2, 382.

44 G. C. Ingleton, *True Patriots All*, Sydney 1952, pp. 151, 270.

45 cp. Martin Brennan, *op. cit.*, p. 267: 'It was my lot in the early days to be acquainted with a Negro named Tom Britt, who had by some freak of the Fates found his way to Australia from a sugar plantation in the West Indies, settled down at Goulburn, and, from his industrious habits, suavity of demeanour, and cleanly person, always found employment.' It seems not unlikely that Tom Britt was the original of Harris's character.

46 The numbers increased from about 2,000 in 1853 to about 40,000 in 1857 in Victoria alone. (Myra Willard, *History of the White Australia Policy*, Melbourne 1923, pp. 21, 28.)

47 'Petition on the Influx of the Chinese', *Votes and Proceedings, Legislative Assembly of Victoria, 1856-57*, vol. 3.

48 W. Kelly, *Life in Victoria*, etc., 2 vols., London 1859, vol. 2, pp. 275-6.

49 *ibid.* p. 304; J. A. Graham, *Early Creswick—The First Century*, Melbourne 1942, pp. 193-4; C. R. Read, *What I Heard, Saw and Did*, London 1853, p. 22; and C. Streeton, *Memoirs of a Chequered Life*, 3 vols., London 1862, vol. 2, p. 51.

50 'Report, Select Committee on Chinese Immigration', *Votes and Proceedings Legislative Council Victoria, 1856-57*, vol. 2. And cp. p. 89 above.

51 *Sydney Morning Herald*, 20 July 1861.

52 Myra Willard, *op. cit.*, p. 33.

53 Henry Lawson, *Prose Works of*, 2 vols., Sydney 1935, vol. 1, p. 210; and cp. E. Marin la Meslée, *L'Australie Nouvelle*, Paris 1883, p. 133. (It seems likely that the Frenchman mistook the parody for the original.)

54 W. G. Spence, *Australia's Awakening*, etc., Sydney 1909, pp. 55, 72; and cp. J. Le Gay Brereton, *Knocking Around*, Sydney 1930, pp. 80-5.

55 These stanzas from the version sung to me in 1952 by Mr Joseph Cashmere of Sylvania, N.S.W.

56 L. G. Churchward, 'Americans and Other Foreigners at Eureka', *Historical Studies: Australia and New Zealand: Eureka Supplement*, December 1954, pp. 43-9; and Myra Willard, *op. cit.*, pp. 20, 24-6.

57 T. McCombie, *op. cit.*, p. 311; William Howitt, *op. cit.*, vol. 1, pp. 137, 238 ff.; R. Caldwell, *op. cit.*, pp. 84-94; and F. Gerstaecker, *Narrative of a Journey Round the World*, etc., 3 vols., London 1853, vol. 2, p. 292.

58 F. Gerstaecker, *op. cit.*, vol. 2, p. 300 ff.; and see A. Joyce, *A Homestead History*, ed. G. F. James, 2nd ed., Melbourne 1949, p. 110; W. Howitt, *op. cit.*, vol. 1, p. 88; and W. Kelly, *op. cit.*, vol. 1, pp. 277-81.

59 F. Gerstaecker, *op. cit.*, vol. 3, pp. 129-32; and cp. G. C. Mundy, *op. cit.*, p. 208 and A. B. Peirce, *Knocking About*, etc., ed. Mrs. Leatherbee, Yale 1924, pp. 22-7 and *passim*. Peirce, who reached Melbourne in 1860, lived for years in the bush by selling worthless patent medicines, and by kindred activities. He was constantly meeting, according to his own account, fellow Americans engaged in similar lines of business. He was 'disgusted', however, by the hard-headedness of the natives.

60 From C. R. Thatcher, *Colonial Minstrel*, Melbourne 1864.

61 G. Bennett, *Wanderings in New South Wales*, etc., 2 vols., London 1834, vol. 1, p. 341; and Brian Fitzpatrick, *The Australian Commonwealth*, etc., Melbourne 1956, p. 28; cp. E. Marin la Meslée, *op. cit.*, p. 53.

62 'A University Man' (G. Carrington), *Colonial Adventures and Experiences*, London 1871, p. 34; and cp. B. A. Heywood, *A Vacation Tour of the Antipodes*, etc., London 1863, pp. 109-10; G. Ranken (ed.), *Windabyne, a Record of By-gone Times in Australia*, etc., London 1895, p. 264; C. Streeton, *op. cit.*, vol. 3, pp. 104, 112.

63 *Queenslanders' New Colonial Camp Fire Song Book*, Sydney 1865.

64 See, e.g., *Bulletin*, 10 March 1888, article on 'Bush Songs'; 'A University Man', *op. cit.*, pp. 104, 202-4; A. Forbes, *Voices from the Bush*, Rockhampton 1869; D. Ferguson, *Vicissitudes of Bush Life in Australia and New Zealand*, London 1891, pp. 57, 152-3.

65 D. G. Jones(?), *Bushmen, Publicans and Politics*, Deniliquin 1869.

66 The swag.

67 This version from A. B. Paterson, *Old Bush Songs*, Sydney 1905.

THE BUSHRANGERS

'Tis of those gallant heroes, God Bless them one and
  all,
And we'll sit and sing 'God Save the King,' Dunn,
  Gilbert and Ben Hall.

HIGHWAY robbery is not a uniquely Australian phenomenon. There have been 'knights of the road' in England and bandits in America and elsewhere; but in nineteenth-century Australia bushranging was so widespread, and so strongly supported by public sympathy, that it amounted to a leading national institution. It is this fact which is singular and which demands some explanation. In England the fame of Robin Hood or Dick Turpin pales before that of Drake or Nelson, and in America Sam Bass and Billy the Kid are almost entirely eclipsed by Washington and Lincoln. In Australia, however, while every child knows something of Ned Kelly, Macquarie, even to a great many adults, is just the name of a Sydney street favoured by medical specialists, and Deakin, if known at all, is the name of a transcontinental railway siding or Canberra suburb. In this respect popular taste has not changed much since the 1840's, when Mundy wrote:

> Every country has its great man—hero, poet or philosopher. Van Diemen's Land has, appropriately enough, its great bushranger and desperado to boast of. Michael Howe, without dispute, and without disparagement to other public characters who, on more reputable grounds may deserve a memoir, is the historical great man of this island.

No doubt bushrangers came to occupy such a prominent place in Australian legend partly because, in the last century, Australia took part in no great wars, and thus there were no colourful military figures to serve, as they tend to do in other countries, as symbols of nationalist sentiment. But the matter was not as simple as this.

It is not difficult to understand the reasons for the great prestige of bushrangers in the convict period. The first settlers brought with them from Britain a traditional regard for highway robbery. The romantic aura which surrounded it was never stronger than at the end of the eighteenth century when the crime itself was becoming a thing of the past, and men in all walks of life were not unaffected by the fashion. D'Arcy Wentworth, a connection of Earl Fitzwilliam, seems to have emigrated to New South Wales lest the law should view too seriously what he claimed to have been a youthful prank on the roads,[1] and when the first highway robbery in Australia occurred, David Collins, the Judge-Advocate, is said to have considered it 'one step towards refinement' and 'at least a manly method of taking property'.[2]

Much more important, however, than the gentry's views on these matters, were those of the lower orders. We have seen above, that the distinctively Australian ethos which developed before 1851, sprang primarily from convict, working-class, Irish and native-born sources, and that it was associated particularly with up-country life. In all these respects the first bushrangers were more 'Australian' than anybody else. Nearly all of them were convict 'bolters' of whom many were Irish, including Jack Dona-hoe, the most famous of them all in the early period. A few were native-born youths and the very existence of all depended upon their being more completely 'independent' of the authorities, more adaptable, resourceful, and loyal to each other, than even the most thoroughly acclimatized bush workman. Indeed, if bush-men were the 'true Australians', runaway convicts were the first of the genus. The very word 'bushranger' had become a part of the language by 1806.[3] At first it referred to the 'bolters'' capacity for living in the bush, as much as to their predatory habits, and so in the absence of any other word it was sometimes applied to the few law-abiding citizens who were also at home in the bush. As late as 1825 a newspaper referred to the English explorer, W. H. Hovell, as lacking 'all the qualities befitting a bushranger'.[4] By the 1820's the phrase 'to take to the bush' had become a cliché,[5] but the word 'bushman' did not become common until twenty years later. In this chapter we shall find much evidence that the 'old

Australian' elements of the population, and in particular the pastoral proletariat of the interior, tended to look upon the bushrangers as heroic symbols of resistance to constituted authority, to look upon them, in short, as themselves writ large.

The convict system manufactured bushrangers. In spite of all that has been said above about the ameliorating effect on the convicts of the Australian environment, it remains true that the system was a lottery in which many government men drew unlucky tickets. A good master like Patrick Leslie might inspire his men to follow him 'to hell' itself;[6] but, if contemporary chroniclers are to be believed, such employers were rather exceptional. Harris estimated: 'two-thirds of the crimes of the lower classes of the colony are the fruits of seed sown by the masters' own hands,' and Sidney roundly declared: 'bushranging by prisoners, has in almost every instance been occasioned by cruel, unjust masters.'[7] After his retirement Macquarie wrote to Bathurst on 10 October 1823:

> I have no doubt that many convicts who might have been rendered useful and good men, had they been treated with humane and reasonable control, have sunk into despondency by the unfeeling treatment of such masters; and that many of those wretched men, driven to acts of violence by harsh usage, and who, by a contrary treatment, might have been reformed, have taken themselves to the woods, where they can only subsist by plunder, and have terminated their lives at the gallows.[8]

The more conscientiously and capably an assigned servant performed his work, the greater temptation he provided to an unscrupulous master to prolong his servitude. And this was particularly true of the 1840's when the demand for labour in the interior was keen and transportation to the mainland had ceased. J. C. Byrne wrote in 1848:

> Masters, particularly of late years have been unrelenting in their treatment of convicts; getting them punished for fancied offences, in order to prolong the term of their sentence, and prevent them obtaining a ticket-of-leave. . . . When an assigned servant obtains a ticket-of-leave it is a dead loss to the master, to the amount that has to be paid a free man to replace him, no other convict being reassigned, at present, in his stead.

Most contemporaries agreed that flogging was a particularly efficacious means of producing bushrangers. In November 1836, an officer who had been stationed at the Hyde Park Barracks, Sydney, for only about fifteen months, told the Quaker missionary, Backhouse:

> . . . upwards of one thousand men had been flogged in the course of that period! He stated his opinion to be, that how much soever men may dread flagellation, when they have not been subjected to it, they are generally degraded in their own estimation, and become reckless, after its infliction. This, we have found to be a very prevailing opinion, in the Colony.

More impressive, perhaps, is the first-hand evidence of Judge Therry who wrote:

> Bushrangers, it is known, have been the terror of New South Wales. Of some hundreds of them who passed through our criminal courts, I do not remember to have met with one who had not been over and over again flogged before he took to the bush . . . the lash was used for the purpose of extorting a confession of guilt from vaguely suspected persons.

A few actual cases will show the mingling of complete despair and indomitable defiance, with which some convicts reacted to this treatment. In 1831 a bushranger named William Webber, who had outlived his chief, Jack Donahoe, was caught, tried and sentenced to death. The day before his execution he proved to Therry, that he and others had actually committed a crime for which two innocent men were suffering at Norfolk Island. Moved by this evidence of good feeling and by his youth—Webber was only twenty-five and 'in the full vigour of a robust manhood'— Therry offered to try to save him from the gallows if he would reveal particulars of other crimes. The bushranger's reply was: 'No, sir, I thank you; but I will disclose nothing. All I could gain by it would be to be sent to Norfolk Island, and *I would rather be hanged than go there. Don't trouble yourself about me; leave me to my fate.*' The italics are Therry's, not Webber's. He was hanged at the appointed time next day.

Another early bushranger named Hall, when sentenced to death in Sydney on 15 May 1839, said from the dock: 'I've been all over the country in my time without taking the life of anyone. I've been baited like a bulldog and I'm only sorry now I didn't shoot every —— tyrant in New South Wales.' To the crowd outside the gaol he said: 'I've never had anything to say against the prisoners, but I've a grudge against every —— swell in the country. I'll go to the gallows and die as comfortable as a biddy, and be glad of the chance.'[9]

It is very interesting to find that this recalcitrant spirit seems to have been largely responsible for a reform of the kind which is customarily put down to the influence of humanitarian ideas. In November 1834 a celebrated bushranger named Jenkins was publicly hanged for the murder of Dr Wardell. According to the *Sydney Herald* of 13 November 1834, 'the neighbourhood of the gaol was crowded to a degree never before observed on any similar occasion', because Jenkins's truculent behaviour in court had aroused the expectation that he would make a particularly spirited exit from the world. His traditional speech from the drop began with the words:

> Well, good bye my lads, I have not time to say much to you; I acknowledge I shot the Doctor, but it was not for gain, it was for the sake of my *fellow prisoners* because he was a tyrant, and I have one thing to recommend you as a friend, if any of you take the bush, *shoot every tyrant* you come across, and there are several now in the yard who ought to be served so.

Apparently the incident was still being talked about ten years and more later when Marjoribanks recorded a summarized version of the speech, remarking that it had created such a 'wonderful impression' on the minds of the audience, that Governor Bourke had given orders that executions were to be carried out privately in future.[10] The *New South Wales Government Gazette*, for some years following Jenkins's execution, contains no record of any official directive concerning the practice to be followed at executions, but it seems likely that in fact some such unofficial instructions were given. For example, the collective hanging of the seven murderers of Aborigines in the notorious Myall Creek massacre, which took place four years later on 18 December 1838, created a tremendous stir in the colony. Contemporary accounts imply that this ceremony was performed semi-privately.[11] On the other hand, criminals in the Port Phillip District continued to be hanged publicly in the time-honoured fashion until 1847. In that year, partly owing to Captain Lonsdale's apprehensions of violence from the multitude, the scaffold was moved inside the gaol-yard so that all but the head and shoulders of the condemned man's body would be invisible from outside, once the trap had been sprung. At the next Melbourne hanging the whole body of the criminal, after the drop, was invisible from outside.[12] This administrative practice was legalized by two acts 'to regulate the execution of criminals' which were passed by the New South Wales and Victorian Legislative Councils, and which received the Royal approval, respectively in 1854 and 1855. Yet in England a similar statute to end public hangings was not passed until 1868, and until that year crowds flocked to the spectacles. At Courvoisier's execution in London in 1840, 'as much as £2 was paid for a window', and one titled person hired for a day and a night, for himself and his friends, an hotel room with a good view of the drop. Much later 'the rich and the idle' were still paying high prices for places 'commanding a good view'.[13]

Having regard to the intense bitterness of feeling which helped to produce this Australian legal reform, and to its causes, it is not surprising that bushranging should have been endemic in Australia, but rather that it should have been conducted with so little actual bloodshed. Some brutal and cold-blooded crimes including rape and murder were committed, but generally speaking, bushrangers took pains to avoid 'unnecessary' violence. The picture given by Marjoribanks is a balanced one:

> They cannot be called a bloodthirsty set of men; indeed, I should say, that, upon the whole, they were rather the reverse. They are, of course, for the most part, reckless and determined characters; but latterly, at all events, they have seldom been in the habit of committing murder or violence upon the person, unless when resisted, as they find this their best policy. . . . I met with at least twenty individuals in that country who had been attacked by the bushrangers, and not one of them had been maltreated, as they had offered no resistance. Indeed, I was sometimes surprised how they were allowed to walk the course, even under circumstances where defence would almost, to a certainty, have been attended with success.

It paid bushrangers to avoid bloodshed because such a policy greatly increased the esteem in which they were held by wide sections of the community. It is clear that, both before and after the Gold Rush decade, the desperadoes could not have existed for long if it had not been for the almost universal sympathy and support of the bush proletariat. Governor Darling declared that the bushrangers' accomplices and receivers of their stolen goods formed a 'very numerous Class', which was the 'root and foundation' of the evil;[14] but he does not seem to have realized that this 'class', at least if sympathizers be included in it, constituted a majority of the inhabitants of the colony. Perhaps he did realize the true position, but thought it impolitic to state it in official documents. James Macarthur, a native-born grandee, had no such illusions, or reservations. More than ten years after Darling's predecessor had determined on measures for 'eradicating' bushranging completely,[15] Macarthur wrote: 'The sympathies of the numerical majority of the inhabitants are in favour of the criminals, whom they would rather screen from punishment, than deliver over to justice.'

Later still, in 1848, Haygarth wrote that the mounted police had the very greatest difficulty in:

gaining correct information of [the bushrangers'] movements. The shepherds and stock-keepers, occupying the lonely out-stations, are the best authority upon these matters, if they choose to be so; but it unfortunately happens that many of these men, who have themselves been 'in trouble', have a secret leaning towards the runaways, or at least they remain neutral, and only see what they think proper, and this renders it very difficult for the police to worm out of them any information on which they can depend. The bushrangers, on the other hand, before they have been 'out' very long, are sure to have correct informants in many quarters . . .

And later again, when after a quarter-century of responsible government Ned Kelly was hanged in November 1880, men could still talk seriously of a revolt of sympathizers.[16]

In drawing attention to the differences between the early bushrangers and those who took to the bush after the Gold Rush, some writers have minimized or overlooked entirely the more important similarities between the two generations. It is true that most of the former were ex-convicts, driven to bushranging by harsh taskmasters, and most of the latter native-born youths who chose to take to the roads partly out of a misguidedly romantic sense of adventure. It is true too that the earliest bushrangers, in both New South Wales and Van Diemen's Land, moved about relatively limited areas of country on foot; but by the last pre-Gold-Rush decade most of them were mounted, as were those of the post-Gold-Rush period.

The continuity of the tradition is exemplified in the life of John McGuire. According to his own account, McGuire was born in Kent Street, Sydney, on 28 April 1826. His mother was a Hawkesbury native, daughter of John Masterton, convict, transported for 'making pikes' in the Irish rebellion of 1798. His father was 'a native of Dublin' who 'came out to the colonies in 1818', whether as a convict or a free immigrant we are not told. At the age of nine years he ran away from home with another boy and made his way across the mountains, mainly, it seems, because of the romantic aura which the interior had even then. It was his delight to work for bullock-drivers 'to learn the ways of the bush and listen to their tales'. While still a lad he spent some years wandering with a tribe of Aborigines. At fifteen he had accumulated a herd of twenty 'weaners' as wages from friendly stockmen. He married a daughter of John Walsh, 'a Tipperary man', who owned Wheogo Station in the Weddin Mountains, and thus became a brother-in-law of Ben Hall, the celebrated bushranger.[17] It is hard to believe that in the minds of such men there was any very significant distinction between the earlier and later outlaws.

Cold-blooded murders were committed by the Clarke brothers in 1866 and by the Kellys in 1878, as well as by Lynch in 1841, but usually, in both the earlier and later periods, bushrangers took care to give some verisimilitude to the Robin Hood role which their admirers thrust upon them. They boasted, with some truth, that they robbed only from the rich (who of course were most worth the trouble), and if they did not give much actual cash to the poor, other than their accomplices and 'bush telegraphs', they dispensed to them gratis, on every possible occasion, endless quantities of other people's rum. Thus Henry Power, mentor of the youthful Ned Kelly, defended himself in the Beechworth Police Court by maintaining that he always refrained from robbing poor men who 'worked hard for their money'; and witnesses who had been present at his 'hold-ups' (including some of the victims) corroborated him.[18] Bushrangers also singled out for special attention those squatters who had the reputation of being hard or unjust taskmasters. Indeed, it is misleading to speak of two 'waves' of bushranging, separated by the Gold Rush decade. In fact many men found it easier to rob the diggers than to dig for themselves, even at the height of the Rush in the early 'fifties when gold was obtained most easily. And many at least of these Gold Rush bushrangers, like 'Melville', also conformed to the traditional pattern of 'chivalrous' behaviour established in convict days.[19]

After the Gold Rush the tone of bourgeois respectability, so much strengthened in colonial society by the rapid growth of the urban middle classes, seems to have ensured that nearly all newspapers and most writers felt constrained to deny to the outlaws possession of any 'Robin Hood' qualities. For example, even the radical, and relatively cant-free, *Bulletin* took a wholly proper attitude in 1880 to 'the annihilation of the Kellys', denying that they, or the spirit they symbolized, possessed any redeeming qualities whatever. A stanza from an unsigned *Bulletin* 'poem' on Ned Kelly's imminent apotheosis reflects faithfully the general tone of outraged propriety, protesting itself slightly too much:

> Oh, out on such 'sympathy'! Can we discover
>   *One* reason this brigand's existence to save?
> No, indeed! for, in sooth, we should rather mourn over
>   Each poor murdered man who lies stark in his grave!
>
> As he's lived, let him die! a base wretch without feeling:
>   A bushel of quicklime is all that he's worth!
> Let the grave of a felon his corpse be concealing,—
>   And blot his name off from the face of the earth![20]

Similarly, though his own book provides it in abundance, Boxall wrote that he could 'find no evidence . . . that the highwaymen robbed the rich to give to the poor'; and he went on to bolster his claim by such extraordinary statements as that a wealthy class 'did not exist in convict times, and is only just beginning to appear now'. In fact the later bushrangers, like their predecessors, were on the whole surprisingly gentlemanly ruffians. Fifty years before Boxall wrote, Marjoribanks considered the 'peculiar institution' of bushranging with a Radical Whiggish eye, comparatively unclouded by either romantic sentimentality or considerations of bourgeois propriety. His characterization was as true of the later bushrangers as it was of those he was describing:

> . . . On the two occasions above alluded to, they returned to the different parties no less than £5 14s. for their expenses on the road; and did you ever hear of people who had been robbed in this country getting back anything at all? . . . When they rob drays, they uniformly invite the drivers, who are, for the most part, convicts also, and have a fellow-feeling towards them, to take a social glass with them, of the drink which they are almost sure to find; . . . the prospect of which at once disarms all opposition; and when they rob dwelling-houses, they generally behave in the same gentlemanly manner, provided no resistance be offered. . . . They seldom attack the dwellings of the working classes, except when hard pushed, and then they are not very severe, as if they get their pipes lighted, and something to eat, they are generally satisfied, though they almost invariably seize fire-arms, when they come in their way. . . .
>
> The more polite, and the more reasonable they are in their demands, the longer do they escape, as, when those attacked are well used, they will not put themselves to much trouble to get them apprehended. . . . When violence is used they seldom escape long, as the whole country, as it were, rise up against them.

Even Morgan, notoriously the most murderous of all post-Gold-Rush banditti, whose mind was so disordered that he habitually robbed alone and had no mates, knew in his muddled way what tradition expected of a bushranger. When he visited Stitt Brothers' Wolla Wolla Station he—

> . . . compelled the proprietor to bring rum to the wool shed and treat all the shearers. He made particular enquiries as to the treatment the servants received, and instructed the servants to acquaint him if they were ill-used, as he was always to be found thereabouts.[21]

In the eyes of the bush-workers, and of a great many other colonists, bushrangers derived added prestige merely from being, so to speak, the professional opponents of the police. It may be doubted whether the police force of any English-speaking country, except Ireland, has ever been more thoroughly unpopular than were those of most Australian colonies in the last century. Even special corps like the Queensland Native Mounted Police, in sorry contrast with such bodies as the Royal Canadian Mounted, established a reputation for ferocity rather than gallantry. The popular attitude towards policemen in general was one of hatred and contempt, reflected accurately though perhaps not felicitously, in a ballad on the death of Ben Hall. The relevant verses read thus:

> Come all Australia's sons to me—
> A hero has been slain
> And cowardly butchered in his sleep
> Upon the Lachlan Plain.
>
> He never robbed a needy man—
> His records sure will show
> How staunch and loyal to his mates,
> How manly to the foe.
>
> At last he left his trusty mates—
> The cause I ne'er could hear—
> The bloodhounds of the law were told,
> And after him did steer.
>
> They found his place of ambush then,
> And cautiously they crept,
> And savagely they murdered him
> While still their victim slept.
>
> Yes, savagely they murdered him,
> Those coward Blue-coat imps
> Who only found his hiding-place
> From sneaking peelers' pimps.[22]

When founded in August 1789, the New South Wales police force consisted entirely of convicts, for between them and the military who 'had their line of duty marked out for them ... there was no description of people from whom overseers or watchmen could be provided'.[23] And until the Gold Rush and later, partly because Currency Lads were so 'utterly averse' to the idea of police service, convicts or ex-convicts made up a large, though steadily decreasing, part of the force. From the point of view of the convicts, and of a great many other Australians who were strongly influenced by their outlook, those who became policemen and overseers were not the best prisoners but the worst. By consenting to act as constables they broke, in the most flagrant possible way, the first principle of 'government men' and bush-workers; that of loyalty to one's mates. Whatever else might be added to them of spiritual grace or worldly perquisites, they forfeited utterly the respect of their fellows. Harris records very justly the loathing in which they were held, when he writes that they were men 'who have crept up from their own [the convicts'] ranks by cunning and sycophancy, and because they would do any dirty work rather than submit to bodily toil'.[24] And Collins says that from the very beginning their fellow prisoners regarded them with 'scorn . . . fear and detestation'.

It is not surprising that policemen should have been hated or despised by criminals, old hands and their friends, but this attitude was by no means confined to the less wealthy classes. Of course there were many honourable exceptions and the quality of police personnel did improve as the years passed, but throughout the nineteenth century there are constant complaints that most Australian policemen were corrupt, besotted, cowardly, brutal and inefficient. Of the early days in Tasmania one observer wrote:

> There was a force called the Field Police, who were volunteer convicts that had served a certain time, and by additional service got a ticket-of-leave or emancipation. They were hated by all classes, for they had power without principle. Very few of them, I believe, but would have sworn a man's life away for a crown. . . . [25]

In Macquarie's day Wentworth thought the Sydney police badly organized and too few in number, while to those in the country districts he considered 'it would be a farce to apply the name of police at all'.[26]

In 1826 Atkinson, formerly principal clerk in the Colonial Secretary's office, thought 'the police of the colony—still very defective' though it had recently 'received improvements'.

Four years later the police 'received further improvement' in the shape of increased powers conferred upon them by 'An Act to suppress Robbery and Housebreaking and the harbouring of Robbers and Housebreakers' (21 April 1830). This law, which came to be known as the Bushranging Act, was passed for a period of only two years, because it was felt to be a temporary measure made necessary by the alarming activities of the bushrangers. It conferred upon 'any person whatsoever' the right to arrest, without a warrant, and hale before the nearest J.P., anyone suspected of being 'a transported felon unlawfully at large'.[27] As a rule the only persons to exercise this right were police constables, and their feckless and arbitrary use of it caused untold annoyance to all colonists, except those who were themselves J.P.'s or people almost equally well-known and presumably respectable. J. C. Byrne, for instance, was arrested at the Ovens River in the Port Phillip district, to be taken back to Sydney for identification, for no better reason than that a venal mounted police corporal wanted an excuse for visiting the publican's daughter at Yass on the way back to the capital.[28] Harris records half a dozen or more similar cases which he observed personally, being 'very careful on so serious a point to state only what [he was] positive of'. One man who came free to the colony told Harris that he was 'generally arrested twice every year, under the Bushranging Act', and a native-born lad claimed to have 'passed seven weeks out of three months marching in handcuffs' by the side of constables who had formed completely groundless suspicions. The Currency people tended to suffer most because 'having been born in the colony [they] had no protective document whatever'.[29] Yet the Act was renewed, with slight modifications but with none of principle, every two years until the gold discoveries. Mr Justice Burton thought it repugnant to the laws of England, and Bourke was troubled with similar qualms, but the 'opinion of the best informed colonists', of the magistrates, and of the Legislative Council was decisive.[30]

In the late 1830's, after some years of the Act's operation, a China Seas skipper—not, one would imagine, an unduly squeamish witness—was 'frequently disgusted' by the brutal and barbarous manner in which the Sydney constabulary carried out their duties.[31] In March and April of 1844 the *Sydney Morning Herald* published a series of leading articles on the inefficiency of the force, and at about the same time Mrs Charles Meredith, a gently-nurtured English visitor, wrote bitterly in her book of the notorious corruption of the constables. A little later, according to Gerstaecker, drunken and brutal constables were stock characters on the Sydney stage, ensuring the success of any play. Perhaps the most significant commentary of all is that provided by the official *New South Wales Government Gazette*. Throughout the 1830's it published regularly each week laconic lists of constables who had resigned or been dismissed.

The character of the Victorian police during the Gold Rush decade has already been sketched. In New South Wales at that period complaints continued as before. In a trenchant sub-leader on 'Police Abuses' the editor of the *Empire* wrote on 29 June 1853:

> The sovereign majesty of the Sydney Police, owing to the former penal character of the colony, is under no constitutional restrictions. . . . They have a roving commission to go into the highways and byways to suspend the liberty of the subject in the exercise of their discriminating infallible 'suspicion' . . .

From the 1860's onwards there seems to have been a steady, if slight, improvement in police personnel, but by that time the tradition had been firmly established, the dogs had been given many opprobrious names, and they continued sometimes to merit them.

During the 1860's Victorians tended to pride themselves on their comparative freedom from bushranging, and to attribute it to their relative lack of convict ancestry and to their innate virtue. But even in Victoria the anti-authoritarian attitude was always ready to emerge whenever a bushranger embarrassed the forces of law and order. A long series of leading articles in the *Ovens and Murray River Advertiser* (Beechworth), published during 1869 and 1870, gives an indication of public feeling. On 2 January 1869, the editor wrote complacently of the Ovens district:

> On the borders of that vast nest of highwaymen, New South Wales, . . . perhaps there is no district in the colony where the law has made itself so respected. Few crimes of very great magnitude have been committed, chiefly, we may be sure, owing to the known activity, zeal, and intelligence of the constabulary stationed here . . .

On 27 February the leader evinced some doubts about the police and called for 'more frequent periodical visits from an inspector'; but on 8 May when Henry Power's depredations in the district were creating excitement, the paper expressed complete confidence that no bushranger could for long breathe the righteous air of Victoria. Power would soon be brought to book by a host of willing informers, or shot down by an enraged populace, as Morgan had been when he crossed the border. On 5 June the editor was moved to chide readers for their luke-warmness in assisting to capture Power, but he still felt that the police 'knew their business'. On 19 June and 31 August the leaders became increasingly critical of the police, and the later article drew attention, by contrast, to Power's bushmanship. Finally on 2 September the editor came to the end of his patience and heaped abuse and ridicule on the luckless constables.

By 7 December his confidence in the law-abiding principles of his fellow citizens had also been shaken:

> From the criminal members of the population, Power has doubtless received aid and assistance in return for the fruits of his crimes. But nothing could be further from the truth than . . . that the residents of the Ovens are, as a class, aiders and abettors of criminals. That Power has not been hunted down by the populace, is simply attributable to the fact that as yet he has refrained from the shedding of blood . . .

At last on 24 May 1870, a fortnight before Power's capture, the jaded editor came near to admitting the truth: that a majority of the population sympathized, more or less, with the bushranger: 'From a certain portion of the population he—or whoever else has been masquerading in his name—has received succour and information, while the police have been misled and deceived.'

Radical or nationalist journals often made constable-baiting a major theme, quite apart from bushranging and indeed long after the institution had practically expired with Ned Kelly. In 1875 the *Stockwhip* earnestly castigated the force for its corruption, nepotism, and so on.[32] In the following decade and for long afterwards the *Bulletin* employed a lighter but more stinging approach. Its method was to assume that policemen were, as a body, irredeemably venal, craven, lazy, incompetent and pettily tyrannical, and to take it for granted further that these were facts well known to all Australians, and that it was absurd to agitate for, or to expect, any improvement. Practically every week the paper loosed a shower of barbed darts—short paragraphs, sarcastic verses and cartoons—pungently illustrating this theme. One example, more reasonable in tone than most, will give the essential flavour:

> At the present moment there are 600 young Victorians applying for a possible 100 billets in the police force of the colony. Noble six hundred! Just bursting into vigorous manhood, they have no higher ambition than to loaf around in uniform and order little boys to move on out of that. Policemen are necessary evils in a civilised

community, but it makes us shudder to think about the 500 unsuccessful candidates who have started life with a determination not to do any work. We suppose they will ultimately be arrested by the 100 lucky enough to get sworn in.[33]

Dislike and distrust of policemen, at least partly merited, has sunk deeply into the national consciousness: how deeply is indicated by a series of leading articles, reports and correspondence on the subject published recently in the *Sydney Morning Herald*, the oldest surviving newspaper in Australia, and certainly one of the most responsible. One man's letter, published on 5 September 1953, read in part:

> I hate Sydney's policemen because they so clearly indicate by offensive language, aggressive manner, and threatening expression, their belief that they are not Public servants but masters of the Public. . . . I hate them because their apparent carelessness allows so many arrested persons to receive injuries falling down while in custody. . . . I've laughed as I've watched children outwit previously alerted policemen and thoughtlessly light a bonfire in the street—but I've ceased to laugh when the heels of issue boots were ground into my toes in an effort to extract my voluntary statement that I'd played a part in the firelighting. . . . The only thing I like about Sydney's policemen is their ability to live and raise a family on 50/- per week.

The last sentence in this letter was an ironic reference to a claim, made by a desperately embarrassed constable, in his evidence before a Royal Commission into the Liquor Trade.

The outback institution of stock-stealing also helps to explain why bushrangers were the culture-heroes of the folk. Writing of the 1820's and 1830's, Harris explained how the practice arose:

> At by far the greater proportion of sheep stations in the colony the practice of feloniously killing the owner's sheep goes on to a greater or less extent: and plenty of owners know it and wink at it; others do not, but would prosecute and transport the man if they could adduce proof of it. Those who connive at it reason thus: 'Well, the men must be fed and so must the dogs, or the work cannot be done; and it is a bad precedent to give them as much meat as they require, because that will lead to a universal and irresistible custom. I had better let them take it, and seem not to know anything about it.[34]

'Waltzing Matilda' commemorates the fact that the practice of sheep-stealing did grow into a 'universal and irresistible' outback custom.[35] It also preserves a folk-memory of hatred for those squatters who had men re-transported for stealing food in a land of abundance, where this crime at least should have been unnecessary. It is highly improbable that a swagman arrested for sheep-stealing, at any time in the last hundred years, should have been moved to commit suicide, but there was a time when it could have happened. In 1838 an up-country settler wrote: 'I have heard a man in court, when sentenced for life to Norfolk Island, beg to be hanged rather. He was a shepherd who had killed and eaten some of his master's sheep.'[36]

When Trollope visited his son, a squatter in western New South Wales, in the 1870's, stock-stealing was still an accepted custom. The novelist compared it with—

> smuggling, or illicit distillation, or sedition, or the seduction of women. There is little or no shame attached to it among those with whom the cattle-stealers live. . . . A man may be a cattle-stealer, and yet in his way a decent fellow.

The fact is that every honest bushman, more or less, was a thief upon occasion, at least from the point of view of the law. According to his own code, however, the theft of certain kinds of property, especially livestock or food, from government, squatters, or 'swells', was at worst a trifling peccadillo and at best a moral and praiseworthy act. As the narrator says in 'Boldrewood''s *Robbery Under Arms*:

> Most of the Nomah people looked upon fellows stealing cattle or horses, in small lots or big, just like most people look at boys stealing fruit out of an orchard, or as they used to talk of smugglers on the English coast, as I've heard father tell of. Any man might take a turn at that sort of thing, now and then, and not be such a bad chap after all. It was the duty of the police to catch him. If they caught him, well and good, it was so much the worse for him; if they didn't, that was their look-out. It wasn't anybody else's business anyhow. And a man that wasn't caught, or that got turned up at his trial, was about as good as the general run of people; and there was no reason for anyone to look shy at him.

It is not suggested that a few bush-workers turned bushranger, and that many glorified them, because they thought much or consciously about these things. Most up-country workers were interested consciously in politics only to the extent of wanting 'a place of [their] own by some clear waterside'. Thus, the passage of John Robertson's first New South Wales Free Selection Act in 1861 was celebrated in the following ballad:

> Come all you Cornstalks the victory's won,
> John Robertson's triumphed, the lean days are gone,
> No more through the bush we'll go humping the drum,
> For the Land Bill has passed and the good times have come.

Chorus:

> Then give me a hut in my own native land,
> Or a tent in the bush, near the mountains so grand.
> For the scenes of my childhood a joy are to me,
> And the dear native girl who will share it with me.

> No more through the bush with our swags need we roam,
> For to ask of the squatters to give us a home,
> Now the land is unfettered and we may reside,
> In a place of our own by the clear waterside.

> We will sow our own garden and till our own field,
> And eat of the fruits that our labour doth yield,
> And be independent, a right long denied,
> By those who have ruled us and robbed us beside.[37]

This song certainly shows how deep was the longing for land, but one notices that it was a song of Innocence and not of Experience. The vision splendid of 'a place of our own by some clear waterside' rapidly faded in the harsh sunlight of the western plains beyond the Great Divide. Selection Act after Selection Act was rendered in the main nugatory by the manoeuvres, usually within the letter but not the spirit of the law, of the squatters. 'And it came to pass,' as Professor Shann wrote, 'that demagogues dispersed the public estate and pastoralists gathered up the freehold thereof.'

Even if there had been no squatters to contend with, it is doubtful whether most free selectors could have succeeded. Lack of capital, primitive agricultural techniques, high transport costs and distance from markets combined with geographic factors to frustrate and impoverish the petty agriculturalist. It was not, especially in New South Wales and Queensland, until the late 1880's and 1890's that his occupation became a reasonably stable and prosperous one.

Those selectors who, in the teeth of droughts, fires, floods, pests and creditors, succeeded in sticking to their patches of land, seem to have left only one widely popular song, 'The Eumerella Shore', to celebrate their feat. This ballad not only illustrates what has been said above, but shows how strong were the traditional habits of the bushmen. It also exhibits that peculiar shade of sardonic humour which some have considered typically Australian. No doubt the Eumerella free-selector set out with golden hopes of becoming a prosperous farmer, but though his dreams were blighted, he managed to live happily enough by falling back on one of his old trades. Having free-selected his piece of the squatter's land, he proceeded to live on it by free-selecting some of his cattle. The song tells a story typical of a great many selectors:

> There's a happy little valley on the Eumerella shore,
> > Where I've lingered many happy hours away,
> On my little free selection I have acres by the score,
> > Where I unyoke the bullocks from the dray.

> *Chorus*:
> > To my bullocks then I say
> > No matter where you stray,
> > > You will never be impounded any more;
> > For you're running, running, running on the duffer's piece
> > > of land,
> > > Free selected on the Eumerella shore.

> When the moon has climbed the mountains and the stars are
> > shining bright,
> > Then we saddle up our horses and away,
> And we yard the squatter's cattle in the darkness of the night,
> > And we have the calves all branded by the day.

> *Chorus*:
> > Oh, my pretty little calf,
> > At the squatter you may laugh,
> > > For he'll never be your owner any more;
> > For you're running, running, running on the duffer's piece
> > > of land,
> > > Free selected on the Eumerella shore.

If we find a mob of horses when the paddock rails are down,
    Although before they're never known to stray,
Oh, quickly will we drive them to some distant inland town,
    And sell them into slav'ry far away.

Chorus:
        To Jack Robertson we'll say,
        You've been leading us astray,
        And we'll never go a-farming any more;
    For it's easier duffing cattle on the little piece of land,
        Free selected on the Eumerella shore.[38]

Bushrangers, after all, were only men who did openly, profession-
ally, and on a grand scale, what every bushman did furtively and
sporadically, or only dreamed of doing.

Fundamentally, they became folk-heroes because they were
symbols of the emergent Australian national feeling. Neither they
nor their admirers cherished any very conscious nationalist
'philosophy', but the very conditions of bushranging life ensured
that its protagonists should be the first and most thoroughly
'colonized' of all white dwellers in Australia. Distinctive national
traits were, as we have seen, bred of adaptation to the new environment. Adaptation, of necessity, proceeded faster on the frontiers of settlement than in the relatively civilized coastal areas
near Sydney. Bushrangers necessarily exemplified, in its most
extreme form, the nomad tribe's manner of life. In their case even
the tenuous link with traditional *mores* provided by the head
station was absent. They were not semi-migratory but entirely
so. They were more isolated from good women, clergymen and
other mollifying influences. Their adaptation to the new environment, in its rawest and most difficult form, was as nearly as it
could be complete. Their lives depended on its being so. Only the
Aborigines were more at home in the bush and these, when they
took service with the police as black-trackers, the bushrangers
feared and hated accordingly. Thus to the pastoral workers, to the
free-selectors, to lower-class people in general, and usually to
themselves, they appeared as 'wild colonial boys', Australians
par excellence.

We have already seen the strength of the early working-class
feeling that Australia was morally 'the prisoners' country', and the
resentment of the native-born that so much of it should be given

by government to rich newcomers with little knowledge of, or love for, the land. Of the post-Gold-Rush period Hancock writes: 'Australian nationalism took definite form in the class struggle between the landless majority and the land-monopolizing squatters.'[39] In both periods bushrangers expressed these deep-seated feelings not so much in words as by the more potent symbolism of their colourful deeds, and there is some evidence to suggest that they were often partly conscious of the role they were playing.

In the 1820's most people believed that men became bushrangers out of sheer inborn depravity, or because they were driven to desperation by the inhuman brutality of some masters and overseers. Cunningham, the most acute observer of this early period, and the most sensitive to the emerging Currency ethos, had a different explanation. He wrote:

> The vanity of being talked of, I verily believe, leads many foolish fellows to join in this kind of life—songs being often made about their exploits by their sympathising brethren; . . . It is the boast of many of them, that their names will live in the remembrance of the colony long after their exit from among us to some penal settlement, either in this world or the next; Riley, the captain of the Hunter's River banditti, vaunting that he should be long spoken of (whatever his fate might be), in fear by his enemies, and in admiration by his friends!

The fame they coveted and achieved sprang not merely from their profession, but from their use of typically 'Australian' and up-country qualities in the pursuit of it. Michael Howe, at any rate, must have been quite conscious of his symbolic role when he addressed an insolent public letter from 'the Governor of the Ranges to the Governor of the Town'. In it he offered to surrender in return for a free pardon, and demanded that a responsible official should be sent to meet him so that they might parley 'as gentleman to gentleman'.[40] The fact that his offer was accepted shows, among other things, how popular was his playing to the gallery.

Unhappily, none of the bushranging ballads to which Cunningham refers in the above passage has survived. It was not until 1830 that the death of a bushranger gave rise to a ballad which has come down to us. Born and convicted in Dublin, Donahoe, at the age of nineteen, arrived in Sydney by the transport *Ann and*

Amelia. Two years later he took to the bush and, with a companion, robbed two cars on the Windsor road. At the ensuing trial Mr Justice Stephen, with perhaps superabundant justice, sentenced each man to death twice, once for each cart they had robbed. Donahoe, however, escaped from custody and became the acknowledged captain of a gang of bushrangers which, for over two years, terrorized the country districts between Sydney and the Blue Mountains. On 1 September 1830 the gang was cornered in the Bringelly Scrub not far from Campbelltown, and in the ensuing engagement Donahoe was shot dead by one Trooper Mucklestone.[41] The ballad composed soon afterwards tells the story with reasonable fidelity to the facts. It is quoted here in full because it was certainly the most popular of all convict-bushranger ballads, and because of the light it throws on the archetypal 'nationalism' we are discussing:

Bold Jack Donahoe

In Dublin town I was brought up, in that city of great fame—
My decent friends and parents, they will tell to you the same.
It was for the sake of five hundred pounds I was sent across the main,
For seven long years in *New South Wales* to wear a convict's chain.

Chorus:

Then come, my hearties, we'll roam the mountains high!
Together we will plunder, together we will die!
We'll wander over mountains and we'll gallop over plains—
For we scorn to live in slavery, bound down in iron chains.

I'd scarce been there twelve months or more upon the Australian shore,
When I took to the highway, as I'd oft-times done before.
There was me and Jacky Underwood, and Webber and Webster, too.
These were the true associates of Bold Jack Donahoo.

Now Donahoo was taken, all for a notorious crime,
And sentenced to be hanged upon the gallows-tree so high.
But when they came to Sydney gaol he left them in a stew,
And when they came to call the roll they missed bold Donahoo.

As Donahoo made his escape, to the bush he went straightway.
The people they were all afraid to travel night or day—
For every week in the newspapers there was published something
    new
Concerning this dauntless hero, the bold Jack Donahoo!

As Donahoo was cruising, one summer's afternoon,
Little was his notion his death was near so soon,
When a sergeant of the horse police discharged his car-a-bine,
And called aloud on Donahoo to fight or to resign.

'Resign to you—you cowardly dogs! a thing I ne'er will do,
For I'll fight this night with all my might,' cried bold Jack Donahoo.
'I'd rather roam these hills and dales, like wolf or kangaroo,
Than work one hour for Government!' cried bold Jack Donahoo.

He fought six rounds with the horse police until the fatal ball,
Which pierced his heart and made him start, caused Donahoo to
    fall.
And as he closed his mournful eyes, he bade this world Adieu,
Saying, 'Convicts all, both large and small, say prayers for
      Donahoo!'[42]

First of all no man, except a Currency Lad, could be more truly Australian, in the sense established so far in this book, than a working-class Irish convict. Moreover in the list of Donahoe's 'true associates', the native-born bushranger is doubly distinguished by being placed first and called by his christian name. As befits a hero, Donahoe, in the ballad, is no 'tinpot man' or 'cockatoo', no petty thief, but a daring highwayman transported for the sake of a mere five hundred pounds. Such lines as, 'For every week in the newspapers there was published something new, Concerning this dauntless hero, the bold Jack Donahoo', give more than a hint of the spirit which came to be known among the native-born as 'flashness', and which was such an important motive for much later bushranging. Donahoe expresses contempt for the police as, the ballad-singers felt, true Australians should, and he expresses the unconquerable aversion to working for Government, which was the origin of Currency reluctance to enlist in the army or the police force. Most significant of all is the assumption that the bush is the true Australian's natural habitat. 'As Donahoo made his escape, to the bush he went straightway', for only there could he find freedom to 'wander over mountains and gallop over plains', together with his mates, in the manner beloved of the nomad tribe of pastoral workers.

In the fullness of time the convict bolter, Jack Donahoe, became the anonymous *Wild Colonial Boy*, a native-born Australian son who takes to the bush as naturally and easily as a Viking to the sea, or a politician to the Treasury Benches. Between the oldest version of the *Donahoe* ballad and the most recent ones of the *Wild Colonial Boy* there is a gradation of texts showing how the changes may have come about. In all cases virtually the same chorus is used, and under all his various aliases the Wild Colonial Boy preserves Donahoe's initials, J.D. As one old folk-singer replied when I asked him who the Wild Colonial Boy was: 'Well, some calls him Jack Duggan, and some Jim Doolan, and some Jack Dubbin, and some Jim Dowling . . . It doesn't matter. He *just was* the Wild Colonial Boy!' The hero's very anonymity is symptomatic of the collectivist ethos of the nomad tribe, whose members were ordinarily 'known by queer nicknames or . . . by no names at all'.

The 'patriotism' figured forth in this ballad had little to do with that self-conscious and often highly respectable sentiment characterized by Dr Johnson as 'the last refuge of a scoundrel'. The people who sang the song did so because it symbolized the spirit of their country and their way of life. And they felt all the more deeply about these things because their love for them was entirely un-official, and largely unformulated and unselfconscious. The chorus of the ballad is really irrelevant to the specific deeds of Donahoe and his associates. Nor does it state, in the manner of national anthems, that Australia is a grand country. It merely assumes, implicitly, that true Australians are those who ride 'together' in spirit with bushrangers. And, in the final analysis, these men are symbols of Australianism because of their intimate knowledge of, and love for, the endless plains and mountains of the interior, no less than because of their collective defiance of soldiers, police-men and other agents of 'government'. Few pastoral workers defined the law openly and habitually, but all shared the rough and errant liberty conferred on them by their mutual loyalty and their familiarity with the bush.

The exact flavour of this embryonic national feeling is given by Gerstaecker in a passage describing Riverina bushmen in 1850:

> Frequently the traveller finds in these huts, old bushmen who have lived a lifetime in the wild scrub of the country; have hunted and fought with the blacks; have been robbed by, and have sometimes robbed with, the bushranger; have fought the police, then taken to the bush and led a life that Europeans read of with incredulity. If you get them to talk—which requires a longer time than a few hours' acquaintance—you learn more in one hour of the wild life of the bush than by a year's residence with the swells.

In the two or three decades following the Gold Rush this national, up-country ethos, typified by the bushrangers or at any rate by the songs about them, was less strongly and much less directly reflected in the Colonial parliaments. In the last chapter it was suggested that the influence of the Gold Rush immigrants was felt mainly in middle-class circles and in the cities. It is generally agreed that many, if not most, of the newcomers were imbued with Chartist or other radical ideas,[43] but up to and beyond the middle of the nineteenth century British Radicalism at the legislative level, as exemplified in its attitude to the Corn Laws, was fundamentally *laissez faire* and individualist rather than collectivist in outlook. Leading Chartists were often strongly influenced by individualist ideas deriving mainly from Bentham, but the rank and file of the movement was much more often collectivist, being driven by hunger to fight for improved conditions through trade union activity.[44] Men of this kind reinforced the strongly collectivist sentiment which had long been developing in Australia, so that 'state interference' and collectivist legislation became pronounced here earlier than in Britain. Nevertheless, the strong middle-class radical element among the gold-seekers probably helped to make Australian parliamentary life more individualistic, in at least one respect, than that of Great Britain at the same period. Since the rise of the Labour Party in the 1890's, many observers have remarked on the extent to which Australian parliamentarians have become mere delegates, disciplined to vote with their party right or wrong, and pledged to support policies approved by the party machines. Before that time there was a virtual absence of parties in politics, although the beginnings of fairly fixed party groupings can be discerned in the late 1880's in New South

Wales and somewhat earlier in Victoria. With bewildering rapidity members transferred their allegiance from one leader or faction to another, whenever moved to do so by conscience or private interest. Humffray, the Welsh Chartist secretary of the Ballarat Reform League, was later elected as representative of Ballarat East by the diggers. When taken to task by his constituents in 1862, for having voted in favour of a ten years' extension of squatters' leases, he replied that he claimed—'the most unfettered freedom in the exercise of my judgement while recording my votes; as I would not, for one hour, occupy the humiliating position of a mere delegate, and vote according to order'.[45] The attitude was typical, but very far removed from the indigenous, strongly collectivist spirit of the bushmen.

One contemporary at least understood something of this disjunction between the emerging national ethos and the expression of it in politics. The first 'principal' of the Sydney University warned in 1861 that a great deal more than self-government would be required to make a handful of infant colonies into a nation. After painting a rather idealized picture of the cultural and national homogeneity of ancient Greece, he asked:

> Can we hope that Australia in a hundred years will present a counterpart to this picture? Five years ago [i.e., immediately after the granting of responsible government] we should have answered with an indignant and enthusiastic affirmative. But experience has taught us humility; we have learned that no accidental impulse can precipitate an infant community into a nation. . . . A corporate like a national body grows only from within.[46]

We can now see that a distinctively Australian national ethos had been growing from within, almost from the moment of the first unpromising landing in Sydney Cove; but that, as the professor implied, its growth was complicated, and in some ways checked, at least to outward appearance, by the immediate results of the gold discoveries.

Yet even in the 1860's the gulf between the outlook of the nomad tribe and that of the more individualistic townsmen was by no means unbridgeable. Bushrangers brought to Sydney for trial were usually given heroes' welcomes by large crowds of working people,[47] whose votes were among those to be wooed by politicians. In 1874 a New South Wales parliamentary crisis over bushranging showed that the ideology of staid middle-class people, including many who had landed in the previous decade, had already been strongly coloured by up-country, Australian values.

The two most famous, or infamous, bushrangers in New South Wales during the 1860's were Francis Christie (alias Frank Gardiner or 'The Darkie') and Ben Hall. Like Ned Kelly and most other bushrangers of the post-Gold-Rush period, both were native-born and bush-bred boys with some convict blood. After a long series of daring and successful robberies, Gardiner organized and led, in June 1862, the attack on the mail-coach at Eugowra, which remains the most celebrated of all bushranging exploits except those of the Kelly Gang. After this he retired unobtrusively to Queensland with his paramour and at Apis Creek, seventy miles north-west of Rockhampton, set up as a respectable bush publican. In 1864 he was arrested and, at the second trial, found guilty of two charges of robbery under arms and of wounding with intent to do grievous bodily harm. Chief Justice Stephen sentenced him to a total of thirty-two years' imprisonment. After one vain attempt to escape he became a model prisoner, and his sisters and friends circulated a petition for his release on the grounds of his good behaviour both at Apis Creek and in gaol, of his health being undermined by prison conditions, and so on. The petition was endorsed by two leading politicians, William Forster and William Bede Dalley, both of whom during their careers held the premiership. Dalley was the attorney who had conducted Christie's defence at both his trials. He was also the native-born son of an emancipist.

When the Governor of New South Wales, Sir Hercules Robinson, decided to pardon Christie, after he had served ten years, by exercising the Royal Prerogative, a storm broke in the Legislative Assembly. Mr Combes, member for Bathurst, in the vicinity of which many of 'Gardiner's' robberies had been committed, asked questions about the proposed pardon and was supported by Mr Buchanan, member for the associated Western Goldfields constituency. Scenting the possibility of defeating the Parkes Government, the Opposition moved to the attack.[48] The Parkes Ministry defended itself by tabling a long list of other criminals who had been released with remissions of sentence during the previous five-year period ending 31 December 1873, by pointing out that twenty-three other bushrangers were to be released with 'Gardiner' and by claiming that in any case remission of criminals' sentences was not and should not be in any sense a political matter, but one for the gubernatorial discretion. Public meetings for and against the bushrangers' release were held in Sydney and in the country. In the Assembly the argument culminated in a marathon debate extending from 3 to 11 June 1874.

Although Opposition members thundered that the Government were little better than aiders and abettors of bushranging, Parkes was fairly successful in confining the debate to the constitutional issue of whether or not it was proper for a government to advise the Governor on the matter of granting remission of criminal sentences. Few Government speakers were drawn into defending the bushrangers except in a partial and back-handed fashion, though the feeling that the 'wild colonial boys' symbolized the national spirit did gain expression. Mr Burns, for instance, a native-born Opposition speaker, complained truthfully:

> [there is] a disposition, on the part of one or two hon. members, to endeavour to excite the sympathy of Australians with regard to the criminals who were spoken of as young Australians inveigled into crime by older and more designing men; and upon different occasions one or two hon. members had made special reference to Australians, as if they were a class on whose behalf some special consideration should be shown.

In one sense the ostensible subject of the debate was unimportant. Both sides were vastly more interested in the occupancy of the Treasury Benches than in the fate of the prisoners.[49] But while both sides ostentatiously disclaimed any sympathy for the bushrangers, the truth seems to be that many members of both Government and Opposition benches felt it. Forster, Buchanan, and John (later Sir John) Robertson all took a leading part in the attack, but, as Parkes was not slow to point out, Forster while serving earlier as Colonial Secretary had endorsed the petition for Gardiner's release, and Buchanan had nine years previously moved for the release of Fordyce and Bow, two of the twenty-four men whose emancipation he was now opposing with such a display of outraged propriety. And Robertson had previously referred publicly to Ben Hall as 'the king of the bushrangers'.[50] On the last night of the debate the façade of correct feeling which had been maintained by most members wore very thin. Mr Cooper, the last speaker, began by appealing to Magna Carta and the principles of the British Constitution in support of the well-worn Government argument that the Governor—not the Government—had acted rightly, but in his peroration he threw restraint to the winds:

> What was the mover of the resolution seeking to do? He was striving to consign Gardiner to a living tomb, or to inflict on him a lingering life-in-death, to crush hope out of his soul, and people his dungeon with the phantoms of despair. Should we join in this deed? . . . There were in this House, he hoped—there were in the country, he believed—few men so infamously bold!

The House divided and the voting was twenty-six for and twenty-six against the motion. The Speaker gave his casting vote for his Chair and 'Gardiner''s freedom, after which, according to the *Sydney Morning Herald's* report:

> disorder continued for five minutes, during which time the Speaker was standing in his place, but his voice was drowned in the uproar, and his presence did not appear to be perceived by a majority of the members, so great was the clamour of many, and the excitement of all.

'Gardiner', who was exiled as a condition of his pardon, took ship from Newcastle, and lived until his death in about 1895 as proprietor of the 'Twilight' Saloon, corner of Kearney and Broadway Streets, San Francisco. According to legend he:

> felt very strongly his enforced banishment from his native land, and it was his wont to go down to the wharf at the departure of each mail-boat bound for Australia, and he was often seen mournfully weeping as the vessel put off, probably bewailing the fate which had parted him from home and country and the well-known scenes of his dramatic career. And, no doubt, with all his lapses, Gardiner had all the Australian bushman's love of his country . . .[51]

The picture of the saturnine bushranger-publican swelling the volume of the Pacific with an exile's tears is ludicrous, but that the story could be repeated seriously by his countrymen indicates how deep-seated was the folk feeling that bushrangers symbolized the national spirit.

There is some evidence that they were not unaware of this aspect of their role, and not above playing up to it. 'Gardiner', whether with his tongue in his cheek or not, spoke to Australian visitors to California of his longing to return home.[52] One of his gang, Jack Piesley, in a letter dated 'Fish River, 4 September 1861', to the *Bathurst Free Press and Mining Journal*, wrote quite irrelevantly: 'I love my native hills, I love freedom and detest cruelty to man or beast.' Bushrangers often made a display of partiality for native-born Australians, as on the occasion when Gilbert, O'Meally, 'and a young man wearing a mask' robbed the Bathurst-Carcoar Mail:

> One of those stuck up was riding a racehorse back to its owner at the Lachlan; they took the horse, and returned the saddle and bridle, observing that as the man in charge was a native, they would not suffer him to go afoot; and they presented him therefore with one of their own horses in exchange.[53]

And in November 1864 after searching the letters and papers abstracted from the Binalong Mail, Ben Hall's gang burnt them, declaring that they did so in order to 'put a stop to the —— English correspondence'.[54] But whether the outlaws took much or little trouble to make nationalist gestures, folk tradition clothed their crimes in a nationalist garb.

At this period the colonial parliaments were dominated by those whom Higinbotham characterized as 'the wealthy lower orders'—'lawyers, journalists, officials, publicans and traders of the metropolis', most of whom were not native-born Australians. Farmers and working men were very thinly represented in the legislatures. Squatters, however, were very strongly represented, constituting, at least in New South Wales from 1870 to 1890, the strongest single parliamentary pressure group.[55] Basically because of the land grievance, the pastoral proletariat felt especially exploited, as its progenitors had felt, however inarticulately. And yet, though they rarely owned a foot of it, the bush-workers felt too that they loved and understood the land in a way, and with an intimacy, that the men of power and place in the cities did not. A stanza from one of the many Ben Hall ballads contains more than a memory of the days when men used to say, 'He's one of the free objects . . . What business have they here in the prisoners' country', and of the time when Michael Howe addressed his open letter from 'the Governor of the Ranges to the Governor of the Town'.

> 'We've just stuck up the escort, and we've seen the troopers fall,
> And we've got the gold and money,' says Dunn, Gilbert and
>   Ben Hall;
> 'And next we'll go to Bathurst, and clean the banks out there,
> So if you see the "peelers" just tell them to take care,
> And next to Sydney city we mean to make a call,
> For we're going to take the country,' says Dunn, Gilbert and
>   Ben Hall.[56]

Stanzas like this also pointed to the future, when it came to pass that the outback ethos symbolized by 'Dunne, Gilbert and Ben Hall', did capture the imagination of the whole country, to the point where the sheep-stealing swagman who 'sprang into the billabong' became the culture-hero of Australian nationalism, acknowledged alike by bushman and city-dweller, radical and conservative, and recognized even by foreigners.[57]

In the 'sixties the most successful and 'noblest' bushranger of them all was Ben Hall, native-born son of emancipated Irish and English parents who had early gone 'up the country'. The man in charge of the small army of his police pursuers was a new-chum English baronet, Sir Frederick Pottinger, who finally shot himself, more, it seems, through clumsiness, than out of chagrin at his unpopularity and his failure to capture the outlaw.[58] Such facts were symptomatic of real differences between respectable and lower-class people at the period. The same Ben Hall ballad, with a deliciously double-edged irony, explicitly states the up-country feeling that the bushrangers were the true representatives of the 'legitimate' Australian spirit. It begins:

> Come! all ye lads of loyalty, and listen to my tale;
> A story of bushranging days, I will to you unveil,
> 'Tis of those gallant heroes, God bless them one and all,
> And we'll *sit* and sing 'God Save the King, Dunn, Gilbert
>   and Ben Hall.'[59]

Bushranging began as the gesture of a few desperate men, goaded beyond despair to defiance. It continued for so long because of the very widespread popular sympathy enjoyed by the criminals, and this sympathy sprang partly from the disjunction between the outlook of 'old Australians' and that of respectable, urban and middle-class people, whose numbers and influence were so greatly increased by the effects of the gold discoveries. When the above ballad was made men often felt they were striving against English 'tyranny' when, in fact, they were striving, albeit unconsciously, to grow up nationally, to become a homogeneous Australian people. When the end was achieved, even if only formally, in 1901, the Anglophobe, republican, and separatist facets of the national spirit soon weakened almost to vanishing point.

CHAPTER VI

1 *Australian Encyclopaedia*, 2 vols., Sydney 1926, vol. 2, p. 649.

2 *ibid.*, vol. 1, p. 219. (Collins's book does not substantiate the reference given in the *Encyclopaedia*.)

3 E. E. Morris, *Austral English*, etc., London 1898, p. 71.

4 *Australian Encyclopaedia*, vol. 1, p. 219.

5 James F. O'Connell, *A Residence of Eleven Years in New Holland*, etc., Boston 1836, pp. 60-1.

6 H. S. Russell, *The Genesis of Queensland*, etc., Sydney 1888, p. 171.

7 *Settlers and Convicts*, ed. C. M. H. Clark, Melbourne 1953 (first published 1847), p. 188; 'A Bushman' (J. Sidney), *Voice from the Far Interior*, London 1847, p. 20; and cp. R. Therry, *Reminiscences of Thirty Years' Residence*, etc., London 1863, pp. 47-8.

8 Quoted A. Marjoribanks, *Travels in New South Wales*, etc., London 1847, pp. 170-1.

9 G. E. Boxall, *The Story of the Australian Bushrangers*, London 1899, p. 59.

10 A. Marjoribanks, *op. cit.*, pp. 221-2; and cp. *Historical Records of Australia*, Series 1, vol. 17, p. 647.

11 See *Sydney Herald* and *Colonist* for 19 December 1838; and cp. G. C. Ingleton, *True Patriots All*, Sydney 1952, pp. 200-1.

12 'Garryowen' (Edmund Finn), *Chronicles of Early Melbourne*, etc., 2 vols., Melbourne 1888, vol. 1, pp. 394-412.

13 *Halsbury's Laws of England*, etc., 2nd ed., London 1938, ed. Viscount Hailsham, vol. 30, p. 137; and cp. L. O. Pike, *History of Crime in England*, etc., 2 vols., London 1876, vol. 2, pp. 451-2; and L. Radzinowicz, *History of English Criminal Law*, etc., London 1948, vol. 1, p. 204.

14 *Historical Records of Australia*, Series 1, vol. 12, pp. 208-10.

15 *ibid.*, vol. 11, p. 553.

16 John Sadleir, *Recollections of a Victorian Police Officer*, Melbourne 1913, p. 239; and Max Brown, *Australian Son: The Story of Ned Kelly*, Melbourne 1948, pp. 235, 239 and *passim*.

17 See McGuire's narrative, 'Early Colonial Days, etc.', *Cootamundra Herald*, 5 January 1907-22 June 1907.

18 *Ovens and Murray River Advertiser*, 14 June 1870; and cp. C. Macalister, *Old Pioneering Days in the Sunny South*, Goulburn 1907, p. 256; and A. Joyce, *A Homestead History*, ed. G. F. James, 2nd ed., Melbourne 1949, p. 162.

19 See e.g. W. Craig, *My Adventures on the Australian Goldfields*, London 1903, pp. 89-106; 'A Resident', *Social Life and Manners in Australia*, etc., London 1861, pp. 112-13; and G. H. Wathen, *The Golden Colony: or Victoria in 1854*, etc., London 1855, pp. 147-52.

20 *Bulletin*, 3 July 1880, p. 9, 10 July 1880, p. 8, and 6 November 1880, p. 8.

21 Charles White, *History of Australian Bushranging*, 2 vols., Sydney 1903, vol. 2, p. 152.

22 A. B. Paterson, *Old Bush Songs*, Sydney 1905, 1930.

23 David Collins, *Account of the English Colony in New South Wales*, etc., London 1798, pp. 77-9.

24 *Settlers and Convicts*, p. 185.

25 Rev. John Graham (ed.), *Lawrence Struilby*, etc., London 1863, pp. 57-8.

26 *Statistical, Historical and Political Description of New South Wales*, London 1819, p. 358; and cp. J. T. Bigge, *Report on State of the Colony*, etc., London 1822, pp. 106-7.

27 *Statutes of New South Wales*, 11, Geo. IV, No. 10.

28 *Twelve Years' Wanderings*, etc., 2 vols., London 1848, vol. 1, p. 166 ff.; and cp. *Sydney Herald*, 19 December 1838, Letter on 'Mounted Police'.

29 *Settlers and Convicts*, pp. 75-84; and cp. *The Currency Lad*, 29 December 1832, Letter from 'A Currency Lad'.

30 *Historical Records of Australia*, Series 1, vol. 17, pp. 520-36.

31 G. F. Davidson, *Trade and Travel in the Far East*, etc., London 1846, p. 122; and cp. *Report, House of Commons Select Committee on Transportation, 1837*, pp. 61-2, 161-2, 185.

32 13 March 1875 and 23 October 1875.

33 *Bulletin*, 8 September 1888, p. 12.

34 *Settlers and Convicts*, p. 185.

35 cp., e.g., Edward Curr, *An Account of the Colony of Van Diemen's Land*, etc., London 1824, p. 35; John Henderson, *Excursions and Adventures in New South Wales*, etc., 2 vols., London 1851, vol. 1, p. 289; and R. Therry, *op. cit.*, p. 213.

36 (David L. Waugh), *Three Years' Practical Experience*, etc., 4th ed., Edinburgh 1838, p. 37.

37 Vance Palmer and M. Sutherland, *Old Australian Bush Ballads*, Melbourne 1951.

38 A. B. Paterson, *op. cit.*

39 *Australia*, Sydney 1948 ed., p. 52 ff.

40 G. E. Boxall, *op. cit.*, p. 20.

41 M. H. Ellis, *Bulletin*, 25 February 1953, p. 25; and *Sydney Gazette*, 4 September 1830 and 7 September 1830.

42 A. B. Paterson, *op. cit.*

43 J. A. LaNauze, *Political Economy in Australia*, etc., Melbourne 1949, p. 119.

44 R. A. Gollan, 'Radical and Socialist Ideas in Eastern Australia 1850-1910', Ph. D. thesis, London 1950, p. 12 ff.

45 W. B. Withers, *History of Ballarat*, 2nd ed., Ballarat 1887, p. 167; and cp. E. E. Morris, *Memoir of George Higinbotham*, etc., London 1895, pp. 63-6 and *passim*.

46 John Woolley, *Schools of Art and Colonial Nationality: A Lecture*, etc., Sydney 1861.

47 Charles White, *op. cit.*, vol. 2, pp. 270, 310 and *passim*.

48 For details of the Gardiner 'case' and its treatment in Parliament, see *Votes and Proceedings Legislative Assembly of New South Wales, 1873-74*, vol. 2, pp. 189-245; and *Sydney Morning Herald* and *Empire* files for June 1874.

49 cp. *Illustrated Sydney News*, etc., 27 June 1874, p. 2; and A. W. Martin, 'Political Groupings in New South Wales, etc.', Ph.D. thesis, Australian National University 1955, pp. 348-53.

50 'A Clergyman etc.', (Rev. John Morison), *Australia As It Is*, etc., London 1867, p. 228; and cp. *Stockwhip*, 30 October 1875, pp. 599-600.

51 Charles Macalister, *op. cit.*, pp. 269-70.

52 *ibid.*

53 Charles White, *op. cit.*, vol. 1, p. 207 and vol. 2, p. 30.

54 G. E. Boxall, *op. cit.*, p. 243.

55 G. Greenwood (ed.), *Australia: A Social and Political History*, Sydney 1955, pp. 107-9; and A. W. Martin, *op. cit.*, pp. 31, 46, 121, 132-45 and *passim*.

56 Charles Macalister, *op. cit.*, p. 284.

57 Tom Hungerford (ed.), *Australian Signpost*, Melbourne 1956, pp. 12-20; and *Sydney Morning Herald*, Correspondence, Leading Articles and News Items, 15 May 1955 ff.

58 To many contemporaries his ineptitude seemed to amount almost to wilful blindness. Sidney J. Baker (*Sydney Morning Herald*, 19 July 1952, p. 7) asks: 'Again, who was the original Freddy and how did he come by the disability which we recall so pointedly in saying "even blind Freddy couldn't miss it"?' It seems very possible that Sir Frederick Pottinger's exploits gave rise to this still current slang expression.

59 A. B. Paterson, *op. cit.* (my italics).

THE BUSHMAN COMES OF AGE

*When the shearing's at an end we'll go fishing in a
   bend.
Then hurrah! for the Wallaby Brigade.*

It has been argued that most of the bushman's essential characteristics took shape before the Gold Rush. Nevertheless, important
changes did take place in bush life afterwards. Before the bushman could be enshrined as the national culture-hero, he had to
reach full stature in his up-country habitat. It is not necessary to
construct from documents a detailed picture of the bushman of
the last decades of the nineteenth century for comparison with
that of his prototype. The work has been done from the life, and
for all time, by Furphy, Lawson and Paterson, and the striking
ancestral likeness between their portrait and that sketched in the
preceding pages will have been apparent to the reader. In this
chapter we shall cite only a few passages from the more factual
writers of the time to underline the accuracy of the 'fictional'
characterization. Our main business will be to notice those comparatively minor aspects of the bushman's nature which were
changing during the period, rather than his underlying attitudes
which usually remained constant or became more marked.

The later bushman exhibited, perhaps even more clearly than his
fore-runners, that 'manly independence' whose obverse side was
a levelling, egalitarian collectivism, and whose sum was comprised in the concept of mateship. How little bush *mores* had
changed in these respects may be seen by comparing Harris's
description of bush hospitality in the 1830's with the following
picture of the same usages painted by an English visitor half a
century later:

A bushman's hospitality is proverbial; in fact, if it be rejected, or even if when passing an acquaintance fail to drop in to the hut, and fail either to be helped or to help himself to the food he finds hanging up in the bags from the roof (a larder intended to circumvent the ants, though not always successful), he will not improbably give his would-be host much offence.

The stockman is, notwithstanding his rough life, rather sensitive on the score of fancied slights, and this refusal, active or passive, to partake, is in his opinion but the expression on the part of the inchoate guest of superiority, a quality which the levelling colonial admits in very few mortals. If you find the stockman away from home the orthodox custom is to go in, hand out the meat and bread, put the 'billy' (a tin quart saucepan) on the fire smouldering in the big chimney, throw in a *quant. suff.* of tea and then take your fill, always remembering to rake the ashes back again over the blazing logs, and to place the viands back in their proper places.[1]

And yet there had been a change. A well known story relates how a socialist orator promised his audience that there would be strawberries and cream for all after the revolution. To a persistent interjector who reiterated that he didn't like strawberries and cream, the orator replied: 'Comrade, after the revolution everyone will *have* to like strawberries and cream.' In the early period Harris had noted that every man drinking in a tavern 'seemed to consider himself just on a level with all the rest, and so quite content either to be sociable or not, as the circumstance of the moment indicated as most proper'. By the 1880's mateship had become such a powerful institution that often one could refuse an invitation to drink only at one's peril. The same visitor quoted above thus describes outback manners in the bar of a Coonamble hotel:

Here's a 'jolly companion' coming up to ask you to 'have a booze' with him, so if you don't want to you had better make off, or he will get mightily offended. 'Eh, what you won't? Why you *adjectival substantive*, you *adverbially adjectival substantive*, you're too adverbially flash to drink with such as me, I suppose.'

If you treat the thing as a joke you will have but little trouble, if you do not, woe betide you, you will raise the wrath of a Hercules who will thirst for your blood. See there a man who is working for yonder squatter has asked him the same question, and replied to his refusal in much the same terms. Such is the eternal fitness of things in this land of approximation to a state of nature, levelling, and unconventionality.

In the same way the later bushman possessed, as his frontier descendants still do to-day, at least as such 'stringy-bark and green-hide' adaptability as had distinguished his predecessors. He was as incorrigible a wanderer, as profane a swearer, as firmly attached to the use of pseudonyms and almost as profoundly reserved in his attitude to policemen.[2] And although there were many more women in the outback townships and in the squatters' houses, there were still few to be found in the men's huts, in shearing sheds, at musterers' camps or on the roads where most of the real work of the pastoral world was carried on. For instance, at Avoca Station near Wentworth in the 1890's there were three or four female servants in the house besides the squatter's wife and children. But in the men's huts were sixteen men and one married couple, and in the 'Bachelors' Quarters' the overseer, his brother, the book-keeper and the rabbiter. The bad old tradition of 'no encumbrances' still retained considerable force right into the present century.[3] In the issue of 14 August 1889, a *Bulletin* contributor wrote that in western river townships there were two races, 'the magistracy, civil service, and Respectability (hem!) on the Hill', and the working people 'on the flat'. He went on to ask:

How is it then that the fully-developed denizens of the flat are all female? I mean the portion visible by day. The fact is that those who have husbands have them not, and those who have not 'old men' are just as well off. The men are always away, working or travelling, or perhaps on another flat or hill. Children there are by the scores . . .

There were also many more churches and itinerant clergymen in the outback than there had been in the 1840's, but the old anti-clerical bias of the bush-workers, reflected very strongly in the *Bulletin*, weakened only slowly. Some verse sent in to Paterson, and published by him in 1905 as an old bush song, expresses essentially the same attitude to organized religion as that which had prevailed among bush-workers sixty years earlier. It also shows that bushmen continued to value 'practical' virtues as highly as of yore:

My Religion

Let Romanists all at Confessional kneel,
  Let the Jew with disgust turn from it,
Let the mighty Crown Prelate in Church pander zeal,
  Let the Mussulman worship Mahomet.

From all these I differ—truly wise is my plan,
  With my doctrine, perhaps, you'll agree,
To be upright and downright and act like a man,
  That's the religion for me.

I will go to no Church and to no house of Prayer,
  To see a white shirt on a preacher.
And in no Courthouse on a book will I swear
  To injure a poor fellow-creature.

For parsons and preachers are all a mere joke,
  Their hands must be greased by a fee;
But with the poor toiler to share your last 'toke',
  That's the religion for me.

Let psalm-singing Churchmen and Lutherans sing,
  They can't deceive God with their blarney;
They might just as well dance the Highland Fling,
  Or sing the fair fame of Kate Kearney.

But let man unto man like brethren act,
  My doctrine that suits to a T,
The heart that can feel for the woes of another,
  Oh, that's the religion for me.[4]

This little song also suggests the extent to which, by the end of the last century, mateship had become for some bushmen a consciously-held substitute for religion.[5] Another piece of verse, actually written by an aged bushman in 1901, expresses the same sentiment with a depth of feeling which renders the halting lines not entirely ludicrous. Remembering the many occasions in his life when clergymen might have been present but were not, the old 'whaler', envisioning his own death and burial, admonishes his son:

I don't want the parson to pilot me thro',
  Nor suavely stretch his gloved paw for my gold;
When my Jean named ye did they sprinkle their dew?
  Eh? We won't have no parson over the wold.

Wrap him a long sheet, a winding sheet round him;
  Coffin him in—the Walerman hoary and old:
Rest at the last: ah! long rest where they'll ground him,
  Down deep in the hole where he'll lie o'er the wold.
There the dingoes howl at the dawn of the day,
  When the shivering days skulk the winter's cold;
There the crows seek shade as a rest by the way;
  But there's rest for the Walerman on the wold.[6]

It is not suggested that 'mateship' was, or ever could have been, in any serious philosophical sense, comparable with Christianity or any other world religion possessing a long historical tradition. Bushmen were, above all, 'practical' men, little given to abstract speculation. Such ideas as they held in common were practical rules of conduct, or habitual modes of thought and action, springing directly from the conditions of their life or from their traditions which, as we have seen, were themselves largely a response to the material environment. And this environment was such that a bushman was, almost axiomatically, a man who could turn his hand to most tasks.

Nevertheless, there were differences among pastoral workers. As in the earlier period, the most important broad division was between those who tended cattle and those who tended sheep. Stockmen still considered themselves the most distinguished of bushmen. Because cattle camped for the night must be sung to, or otherwise reassured that there is no cause for stampeding, stockmen were probably also more given to ballad-singing than were other bush-workers; but Brian Elliott, in his *Singing to the Cattle* (1947), goes much too far in 'ascribing the whole vigour of the [Australian] ballad tradition', to the need for pacifying these beasts.

Even among stockmen there was an élite—the overlanders who spent months in driving stock from one station or colony to another. A number of overlanding ballads attest the truth of the remark that there was 'no class of men in the colonies who fraternize more among themselves than the overlanders. There seems to be a sort of freemasonry among them.'[7] And yet though cattlemen continued to enjoy more prestige than sheepmen, the difference between the two groups was much less marked than it had been in the early days. Indeed, even the mounted overlander was more often employed, in the later years of the nineteenth century, in droving sheep than in droving cattle. The 'crawling' shepherd was still despised, perhaps even more thoroughly than he had been in the past. One stanza of a cattle-mustering song goes:

> A long-haired shepherd we chanced to meet
> With a water-bag, billy, and dog complete;
> He came too close to a knocked-up steer,
> Who up a sapling made him clear.[8]

But by the last decade of the century there were very few shepherds left in Australia. Permanent fencing of runs, at first with post-and-rails and then with wire, was well under way by 1860, but the bulk of the work was done in the two following decades. Though the movement seems to have begun in the wealthy Western District of Victoria,[9] it did not proceed quite evenly from the coast inland. In the early 1870's for instance, one could drive through north-central Victoria on tracks—

> sparely bisected by the primitive bush-fence—two or three a day, perhaps—brush, dog-leg, chock-and-log, the post-and-rail reserved for the stockyards and home enclosures.[10]

At the same period wire fencing was extending rapidly over the much more recently settled Peak Downs district of east-central Queensland. For perhaps twenty years 'the West seethed' with fencers and tank-sinkers, and with them came the mounted boundary rider whose work was at least comparable, in the skill and activity it demanded, with that required of a stockman.[11]

By increasing the carrying capacity of sheep runs and at the same time reducing the wages bill, fencing caused sheep-raising to forge ahead much faster than the cattle industry. Between 1861 and 1894 the number of cattle in New South Wales remained approximately constant at about 2,300,000. During the same period the sheep population of the colony increased from about 6,000,000 to 57,000,000.[12] The discrepancy was not so great in Queensland however. These facts help to explain the rise in the sheepmen's prestige.

In the pre-Gold-Rush era stockmen had often 'affected a rough, bullying way which generally [obtained] for them a sort of unwilling civility from the working hands'.[13] By the 1880's, though still convinced of their own superiority, cattlemen usually felt called upon to behave politely to fellow bushmen. The first stanza of 'Wallabi Joe', a song from Paterson's collection, reads:

> The saddle was hung on the stockyard rail,
> And the poor old horse stood whisking his tail,
> For there never was seen such a regular screw
> As Wallabi Joe, of Bungaroo;
> Whilst the shearers all said, as they say, of course,
> That Wallabi Joe's a fine lump of a horse;
> But the stockmen said, as they laughed aside,
> He'd barely do for a Sunday's ride.
>
> Oh! poor Wallabi Joe,
> O-oh! poor Wallabi Joe.

It is perhaps significant that shearers comprised the company from whom the stockmen took pains to hide their mirth. Certainly in the 1880's and 1890's shearers considered themselves, and were considered by many bushmen, nonpareils of the whole earth. An octogenarian station-hand resident in Sydney[14] told me that on Campbell's Duntroon Station, in the 'nineties, a 'flash shearer' glared at him fiercely, for no reason whatever, and hissed: 'I *hate* the smell of a rouseabout!' The old man is still deeply moved by the memory of the unfairness at the heart of things. He felt it was impossible to express his resentment openly. Another octogenarian bushman, Mr Joseph Cashmere of Sylvania, in New South Wales, tells the story of how in 1933 he got into conversation with a very old man in a Riverina train. The tale ends with the words, delivered with the air of one who once saw Shelley plain: 'That man was Jimmy the Ringer, the man who once put up a tally of two hundred and sixty with the blades on the Darling.'

Most of the many extant shearers' ballads not only reflect the high renown of the calling but suggest also an important reason for it. By the 1880's shearers, more even than most other bushworkers, had acquired a high degree of pride in their professional skill. This pride was not quite comparable with that of the skilled craftsman whose aim is to produce a perfectly finished article. Bush tasks demanded rather the talents of the soldier on active service whose main effort is directed to taking the objective, without too nice a concern for its condition when captured. Shearers have always been paid by piecework, at so much per hundred sheep shorn, and so the champion shearer of the shed, the ringer, was he who could shear more sheep in a day than anyone else. Most squatters attached more importance to speed than to painstakingly careful workmanship, but of course demanded both. And shearers despised a clumsy practitioner who cut or 'haggled' his beasts, almost as much as they idolized the 'gun' or champion for his record-breaking tallies. The following ballad reflects the men's attitude accurately enough:

Flash Jack from Gundagai

I've shore at Burrabogie and I've shore at Tonganmain,
I've shore at big Willandra and upon the old Coleraine,
But before the shearin' was over I've wished myself back again,
Shearin' for old Tom Patterson on the One Tree Plain.

Chorus:

All among the wool boys,
Keep your wide blades full boys,
I can do a respectable tally myself whenever I like to try,
But they know me round the back blocks as Flash Jack from Gundagai.

I've shore at big Willandra and I've shore at Tilberoo,
And once I drew my blades, my boys, upon the famed Barcoo,
At Cowan Downs and Trida, as far as Moulamein,
But I always was glad to get back again to the One Tree Plain.

I've pinked 'em with the Wolseleys and I've rushed with B-Bows, too,
And shaved 'em in the grease, my boys, with the grass seed showing through.
But I never slummed my pen, my lads, whate'er it might contain,
While shearin' for old Tom Patterson, on the One Tree Plain.

I've been whalin' up the Lachlan, and I've dossed on Cooper's Creek,
And once I rung Cudjingie shed, and blued it in a week.
But when Gabriel blows his trumpet, lads, I'll catch the morning
    train,
And I'll push for old Tom Patterson's, on the One Tree Plain.[15]

The last stanza points incidentally to the continuance of the
bad old bush tradition of 'work and burst'. There is no doubt that
most bushmen in this period continued as their predecessors had
done, and as many still do, to 'earn their money like horses and
spend it like asses'.[16] Hardly a contemporary writer fails to com-
ment on the fanatical improvidence of the pastoral workers and
the callous villainy of the shanty keepers who so efficiently 'lambed
down' their cheques. Many bush songs, of which the following is
a good sample, commemorate the custom:

> The truth is in my song so clear,
>   Without a word of gammon:
> The swagmen travel all the year
>   Waiting for the lambin'.

Chorus:

> Home, sweet home!
> Home, sweet home!
> That is what they left it for—
> Their home, sweet home!

> Now when this dirty work is done
>   To the nearest shanty steering,
> They meet a friend, their money spend,
>   Then jog along till shearing.

> Now when the shearing season comes
>   They hear the price that's going:
> New arrivals meet old chums,
>   Then they start their blowing.

> They say that they can shear each day
>   Their hundred pretty handy,
> But eighty sheep is no child's play
>   If the wool is dense and sandy.

Now when the sheds have all cut out
　　They get their bit of paper;
To the nearest pub they run
　　And cut a dash and caper.

They call for liquor plenty
　　And are happy while they're drinking,
But where to go when their money's done.
　　It's little they'd be thinking.

Sick and sore next morn they are
　　Of course, when they awaken.
To have another drink they must,
　　To keep their nerves from shakin'.

They call for one and then for two
　　In a way that's rather funny.
The landlord says, 'Now this won't do;
　　You men have got no money.'

They're very sad next morning
　　And are lounging on the sofas:
For to finish off their spree
　　They're ordered off as loafers.

They've got no friends, their money's gone,
　　And at their disappearing,
They give three cheers for the river's bend
　　And jog along till shearing.[17]

　　However, the use of the third person in this ballad, which probably dates from about 1890, gives it a certain selfconsciousness. It is as though the singer is commemorating a ritual observance rather than describing life realistically. And there is a good deal of evidence that, as the nineteenth century drew to its close, shearers, like Australians generally, began to conduct their sprees in a less phrenetic manner. Between 1871 and 1901, while the population of New South Wales, for instance, more than doubled, the quantity of spirituous beverages, on which duties or excise was levied, increased by only about a quarter.[18]

　　For long after rum had ceased to be the common medium for 'incentive payments' to workmen it continued to be the staple alcoholic drink of bushmen. In the late 1860's George Carrington worked for a few months as barman to a shanty keeper in the Carpentaria country. He records:

> [he would] get up a gallon at a time of bad rum. This he used to put in a three-gallon keg with some tobacco, vitriol, and a modicum of laudanum. The whole was filled up with water, shaken together, and allowed to stand. This vile compound would actually leave a dark stain if used in a glass, and therefore it was found expedient to use tin pannikins. This was his whole stock-in-trade, and he charged eighteen-pence for a glass, or 'nobbler' of it and men used to drink and relish it. The advantage of it was that it made them drunk very quickly, and thus no valuable time was wasted.

Accounts left by those who knew the back country well show that this shanty keeper was typical rather than exceptional.

Till the end of the century and later visitors to the outback continued to be vastly impressed by the pattern of 'work and burst'. Writing in 1883 a French observer thought that, in view of the appalling loneliness, monotony and hardship of the pastoral workers' life, their sporadic bouts of bestial drunkenness were not at all surprising. 'Ce qui étonne bien plus encore,' he wrote, 'c'est que cette vie de solitude absolue ne les rende pas fous.'[19] But those who knew the bush more intimately, or who had known it over a long period, thought that by the late 'eighties bushmen were becoming more temperate. Thus Thomas Major, who had been both an Inspector of Runs for the New South Wales Government and a squatter, contrasted the shearer of the 1860's with his successor of the 1890's. The former he described as 'an unmitigated blackguard . . . having no home, and fearing neither God nor devil' who roamed the country on foot with his swag and invariably took his cheque to the nearest grog-shanty where, 'in a brutal state of intoxication, he might be seen for days or weeks, more like a dog than a human being'. Of the latter he wrote:

> [he spends] little of his money with the shanty-keeper, but his impudence and aggressiveness have in no way abated. . . . His more sober habits enable him to go in for horse-racing; flash balls at the township are his delight; occasionally he is the owner of one or two good horses. . . . With all his faults he not infrequently marries and settles down to farming and raising children perhaps a degree less flash than himself.

Francis Adams, whose radical outlook led him to view the pastoral workers more sympathetically, wrote:

> The legend of the 'knocking down' of cheques is still current, but the actual thing is becoming rarer and rarer. . . . The shearer of to-day is a man who arrives on a horse, leading another, and with his bank-book in his pocket. . . . His visits to the township are with a view of entering his cheque to his account, or of forwarding it by post office order to his 'old woman' at the homestead hundreds of miles away. He is a member of a union with offices at the central bush townships, and his political views are of the most decisive and 'advanced' order.

One recognizes the same man, seen through different coloured spectacles. A more balanced account of him is given in C. E. W. Bean's *On the Wool Track*.

The improvement in drinking habits was an index of the bushman's increasing self-respect and of his increasing self-awareness, the beginnings of which were noted in Chapter V. It would be easy to exaggerate the change however. On the whole one is struck, as the bushmen themselves were, more by the continuity of up-country manners and traditions than by the changes in them. The historian of Australia's part in World War I writes:

> Before 1914 it was observed, even in the Far West, that the new generation of Australians managed to preserve its cheque in the country towns, and to reach Sydney or Melbourne—and lose it there. That was a step in advance, but the advance stopped there—since 1914 we have gone back if anything . . . [20]

And though swagmen are not often seen on outback roads to-day that most characteristic of all outback institutions, 'humping the drum', flourished well into the present century. In 1887 an English magazine claimed, improbably, that as many as three hundred sundowners were fed nightly at Sir Samuel Wilson's Riverina station.[21] More typical of the true state of affairs were the ten or fifteen who received free rations and shelter each night in the season at Avoca homestead near Wentworth.[22]

Strictly speaking, a sundowner was said to be distinguishable from a swagman. Both tramped from station to station, especially from the time of the approach of the shearing season, but, while the latter genuinely sought work from the squatters, the former did not. Instead he was careful to arrive at the station store at sundown, too late to be given work, but in time to receive free rations. If one accepts this distinction between sundowners and swagmen as valid there is reason to believe that there were comparatively few of the former, in spite of a great many statements to the contrary. Squatters complained bitterly of having to provide rations gratis to travellers, whether there was work for them or not. One gentleman told Trollope that the practice cost him £300 a year, and another is said to have spent £1,000 a year in this way. Yet the antiquity and universality of the custom, and the opportunities for a revengeful swagman to fire the offending squatter's fences with impunity, were such that few graziers dared refuse rations. As Furphy wrote in his *Rigby's Romance*, the 'social system of pastoral Australia is a patriarchal despotism, tempered by Bryant and May'.

In fact, the employers' complaints were hardly justified. It is hard to see how the pastoral economy could have continued functioning successfully in the absence of this small army of itinerant labourers. A *Bulletin* correspondent, in September 1889, argued sensibly though with some partisan spirit that the system of giving free rations to travellers came into existence, and continued, because it paid the graziers, and, further, that the vast majority of the men were more anxious for work than for rations. A few weeks later in the issue of 5 October 1889 another *Bulletin* contributor argued cogently enough that, 'given the opportunity to loaf [one] can trust poor, frail, human nature to supply the loafer', but his article fails to convince that loafers predominated among the swagmen. Indeed, without intending to do so, it rather underlines the conclusion of the first correspondent that the sundowner proper was a largely mythical figure and one that Australians were determined to believe in. The only concrete case cited of men refusing work is one in which twelve 'sundowners' declined to accept jobs at rates of payment lower than those laid down by the newly formed Shearers' Union.[23] And most swagmen's songs, while they certainly stress the independence and unconventional morality of the vagabond life, also take it for granted that men go shearing in the season when work is available. Thus 'Three Little Johnny Cakes', after describing the sweets of a whaler's life, ends with the stanza:

> When the shearing time commences
> I'm in me glory then,
> Pick a shed and see the Boss
> And then secure a pen.
>
> And when the roll is called,
> And the time is drawing nigh,
> Roll me drum, rake me cheque,
> And quickly bid good-bye.

Another important development in up-country life during the later part of the last century was a very great strengthening of nationalist feeling. In part this was simply a natural concomitant of the fact that native-born people for the first time made up a rapidly increasing majority of the population. The sentiment was sharpened and made much more self-conscious by the crude 'racism' which became more and more marked from the time of the anti-Chinese agitations on the diggings. But, as in the formative period, nationalism was largely nourished also by a sufficiently chauvinist contempt for the new chum who was so obviously not at home in the bush. Of these newcomers many more seem to have been men of middle-class background than had been the case earlier. From about 1860 until 1900 the 'colonial experiencer' or 'remittance man' was just as familiar a figure in the back blocks as the swagman or sundowner. Some of them succeeded, but to judge from contemporary accounts most of them did not, perhaps partly because there was no longer much good unoccupied pastoral land to be had for the taking. Biddulph Henning, a successful pioneer squatter who left England in 1853, thought that by 1864 there was 'very little prospect' for anyone 'who had not at least £8,000 or £10,000 capital to begin with'.

Fools and failures received abundant recognition of their Englishry, but immigrants who were practical and successful seem, from that very fact, to have been accepted, if not as honorary Australians, then merely as people whose English origin was lost sight of or forgotten. Thus the well-born and well-bred Henning rapidly became a very fair bushman and successful squatter of whom his sister could write: 'Biddulph is a capital master. He never lets any of the men gain the least advantage over him and yet they all like him.' And even Furphy, arch-nationalist and democrat, falls naturally into the same way of feeling. Some of his squatters are good and some bad, but since all are more or less successful, and therefore 'practical' men, whether they are British or native-born is hardly felt to be relevant to discussion of their characters. On the other hand he pours scorn, slightly qualified with pity, on that 'descendant of Hengist', Sollicker, the plodding and oafish English boundary rider, and the 'colonial experiencer', Willoughby, the broken-down swell, is presented pitilessly as a cultivated ninny whose asininity is almost purely a function of his English birth and nurture.[24] Here as elsewhere Furphy reflects very faithfully the bush-workers' attitude. One of the many ballads on English jackaroos reads thus in Paterson's version:

> If you want a situation, I'll just tell you the plan
> To get on to a station, I am just your very man.
> Pack up the old portmanteau, and label it Paroo,
> With a name aristocratic—Jimmy Sago, Jackaroo.
>
> When you get on to the station, of small things you'll make a fuss,
> And in speaking of the station, mind, it's we, and ours, and us.
> Boast of your grand connections and your rich relations, too,
> And your own great expectations, Jimmy Sago, Jackaroo.
>
> They will send you out on horseback, the boundaries to ride;
> But run down a marsupial and rob him of his hide,
> His scalp will fetch a shilling and his hide another two,
> Which will help to fill your pockets, Jimmy Sago, Jackaroo.
> Yes, to fill your empty pockets, Jimmy Sago, Jackaroo.
>
> When the boss wants information, on the men you'll do a sneak,
> And don a paper collar on your fifteen bob a week.
> Then at the lamb-marking a boss they'll make of you.
> Now that's the way to get on, Jimmy Sago, Jackaroo.
>
> A squatter in the future I've no doubt you may be,
> But if the banks once get you, they'll put you up a tree.
> To see you humping bluey, I know, would never do,
> 'Twould mean good-bye to our new chum, Jimmy Sago, Jackaroo.
> Yes, good-bye to our new chum, Jimmy Sago, Jackaroo.

There is nothing really new in this. We have seen that, even in convict times, pastoral workers despised middle-class, English immigrants who were ill at ease in the bush. The new development is that in the later period many squatters, particularly if they were Australian-born, shared to a quite marked extent in their employees' feelings. As early as 1863 an English visitor wrote: 'the resident settlers throughout Australia feel deeply the absurd manner in which young men are sent out.' He went on to quote from the *Canterbury Press* (New Zealand) of 8 March 1862, observing that the newspaper's comments were equally applicable to Australia:

> The colonies now are not regarded generally as gaols or houses of correction, but as reformatories or penitentiaries. . . . It is the fact that no ship arrives that does not bring some one or more young men, brought up in the social rank of gentlemen, but without money, intellect, cultivation, learning, capacity for labour, good behaviour, or any features of mind or body which can enable them to retain in England the position in life their fathers filled. These men are not only useless in a colony. They become the pests of its society. . . . If the man have something in him after all, and rises in the new world, they [his English relatives] take credit for their sagacity in finding the right career for him; if he becomes a brutal, drunken, blaspheming, godless, bullock-driver, and at last dies in a ditch, then it is 'Poor John, we did all we could for him'. . . . The father has got a friend in the colony, or a friend of his has got a friend, who has got a friend who has a friend in the colony. A letter is written. . . . We have seen hundreds of such letters; and the coolness with which scapegraces are consigned to colonial families, in the assumption that they will be welcome guests, is amazingly complimentary to our Christian hospitality. . . . [25]

Of course not all gentlemen jackaroos from Britain were weaklings and wastrels. Thomas Major records the case of an Oxford man who worked on his 'frontier' run in the Gulf country in the 1860's. This Mr Todd 'had not been the recipient of high academic honours' but 'had mastered the manly art of self-defence'. When thirty shearers refused to commence work unless served with a free glass of grog a man, the Oxford jackaroo, 'with a few scientific taps, delivered in the most gentlemanly manner', knocked out the ringleader, after which shearing proceeded smoothly. Nevertheless Major also records that two men, who had been out searching for a new run, called at his homestead one morning. They had quarrelled and were barely on speaking terms:

One, it did not take me long to discover, was little better than a consummate fool. Unfortunately he was the capitalist. The other, a smart but rough young Australian bushman, was without capital, but had plenty of brains and experience. On the morning after their arrival, the latter accompanied me to the stockyard, and, seating himself on a rail, gave me an account of their trip.

'That d—— galloot,' said he, meaning his partner, 'is the biggest chuckle-headed ass God ever created. He is going back to England—a good job too; we don't want fools in this country. I can't say what England is like; if it is the same as Australia, except he has a brand put on him, and fastens a bell round his neck, he'll lose himself as sure as God made little apples . . .'

The class line between masters and men continued to be almost as sharply drawn as in convict days, except sometimes when the squatter was travelling, or for some other reason far removed from the homestead and his women-folk.[26] But even so there were many situations in which he felt nearer, as a fellow Australian, to his employees than to the green but well-connected Englishman whose manners and values were, after all, not quite his. Even the most reasonable of men must have been moved, if only sporadically, to a quite chauvinistic feeling for Australia by such importunate English guests as the Mr Mowbray described by a Victorian girl:

Father came in with his hands full of letters. One was not a pleasant epistle; it was from a Mr Mowbray: an indignant protest that my father, in answer to an appeal for help, should have forwarded him 'tickets for the Immigrants' Home'.

'I am fairly bothered about him, Alice. I have lent him considerable sums of money. As for employment, there is nothing he is fit for. I must invite him here.'

'After his letter,' I exclaimed.

'I can't leave him to starve, and what is to become of him?'

Oh, it is such a puzzling question to answer, we are so beset with this class of adventurers. Younger sons, who have fared delicately at home, and with expensive tastes and habits, are thrown remorselessly upon the resources of the colony . . . [27]

In 1883, a French diplomat who travelled widely in the outback remarked that Englishmen were unpopular throughout the Australian colonies. He thought the fault lay with the 'jeunes dandys anglais' who did not trouble to conceal their feelings of superiority from the plain-spoken and presumptively base-born 'colonials'.[28]

The 'remittance man' or 'colonial experiencer' was a vanishing species at about the turn of the century, but the attitude he did so much to strengthen lingered after him. In 1909 Bean noticed that 'for some reason they seemed just to tolerate Englishmen in the bush. They used the word almost as a mark for incapacity.' Even of a working-class immigrant who had been in the bush for many years, and who worked like a Trojan, men would say: 'He can't ride. He can graft a bit; but he's not much intelligence, oh no. He's an Englishman.'[29]

Antipathy to small farmers and selectors was another sentiment shared in the later period by both pastoral workers and their employers. The squatters' reasons for hating farmers are well known, and need not be enlarged upon here. Of itself, this mutual hostility tended to make common ground between selectors and pastoral workers. Moreover a great many selectors were, at the same time, itinerant bushmen who went shearing, horsebreaking, and so on for months at a time to help make ends meet on the farm, and when the farm failed many of these remained permanently as casual hands in the pastoral industry. And yet the bushman proper had reasons of his own for despising, rather than hating, those whom he designated 'cockies'.[30]

A major reason why the distinctive up-country ethos centred in New South Wales was that agricultural development there and in Queensland lagged so far behind that of the three southern colonies. Except for the special case of its plantation type sugar industry, Queensland's economy was more purely pastoral than that of New South Wales. Agricultural development in Western Australia was still tardier. Hence we find that Queensland is the locale of so many ballads of this period; and *Bulletin* writers and others constantly remarked that Queensland was the most 'Australian' and the most nationalistic of all the colonies. South Australia, on the other hand, was dismissed as the least 'Australian', as 'the farinaceous colony', 'the Holy Land', where loyalty to [Britain] was 'a religion'.[31] English visitors naturally noticed the reverse side of the picture, that South Australia's agricultural economy gave working men a much better chance of becoming their own masters by exercise of the thoroughly 'un-Australian' qualities of sobriety and thrift.[32] New South Wales did not grow enough wheat to feed its own citizens until the eve of Federation. Thus, except in certain favoured areas fairly near Sydney or the coast, there were relatively few real farmers (in the sense in which the word was used in South Australia) in the parent colony. Even for many years after the first Free Selection Act of 1861, small holders on the tablelands and the western slopes, the bush-ranging country, tended to pursue their calling at least partly after the manner of the free selector of the Eumerella shore. John Martineau wrote in his *Letters from Australia* (1869): 'It was notorious that the free selectors, having in general little skill in agriculture, and being far away from any market, could exist only by eating or selling the Squatters' cattle.' And in 1874 W. H. Cooper, a young member of the New South Wales Legislative Assembly, utterly wrecked a promising political career by making an injudiciously emphatic speech in which he remarked: 'He had seen a good deal of the free selection in this country, and his opinion was that for every one of the yeomen class to be found among the selectors, they would find ten whose only stock-in-trade was a bullet mould and a harness cask.'[33]

For these reasons there is not much evidence of bad feeling between the itinerant bushmen and the small holders in New South Wales and Queensland before about 1880. Indeed, as Shann has pointed out, and as the folk-songs confirm, there was rather a close community of outlook between both groups and the bush-rangers. But as genuine farmers increased in numbers, so did the cohesiveness and self-awareness of the bushmen proper. Until after Federation an honest selector was usually extremely poor and wretchedly over-worked.[34] With the best will in the world he could not afford to issue, as the squatter did, free rations to every passing swagman. Nor could he afford to pay such comparatively high wages. Yet the work he demanded of casual labourers was usually harder, though not necessarily more skilled, than that to which the men from 'farther out' were accustomed, except perhaps for shear-ing, and the small farmer, if he had any sheep, sheared them him-self. Long before the Gold Rush the old hands had found 'the pastoral life, following flocks of sheep, and riding after cattle, was a much more agreeable and preferable occupation to them than clearing land and working at farms under a scorching sun'.[35]

Thus, by about 1890 the 'cocky' had become, at least in the mythology of the migratory bushmen, a byword for meanness and stupidity. He was mocked for his very virtues: providence and a considerable capacity for back-breaking toil. The following passage gives accurately the contemporary bush-worker's attitude to the small farmer and his way of life:

> Bill Jackson . . . had been a cocky's boy as a kid, and had known what it was to be kicked out of bed at four in the morning to milk cows, and to be kicked right through the day till nine and ten o'clock at night doing this, that and everything for Mr and Mrs Cocky and all their numerous family and friends, not to mention the poddies and the pet lambs and the dogs. It wasn't much of a school for man-liness, and to Bill's credit be it said, that one day he turned round and kicked back again, and having kicked, faced the bush with no more personal or other property than he stood up in.[36]

At bottom it was the small farmer's grinding poverty which gave rise to the pastoral worker's contempt for him. Though the itinerant bushman often owned nothing but what he carried on his back, he was accustomed to eat three times a day good meat of his own or of the neighbouring squatter's. Honest selectors, on the other hand, were traditionally supposed to live almost entirely on nothing but bread (or damper) and treacle, known contemp-tuously to the bushmen as 'cocky's joy'. To the pastoralist the bushmen accorded a measure of respect, grudging or otherwise, according to the character of the man concerned. After all, the squatter's very wealth was an index of his success, of his being a 'practical' man able also to dominate the difficult environment. But to the struggling selector, the bushman's attitude was closely akin to that spirit which, at the end of World War II, moved a minister of the Crown to declare that it was not part of Labour Government policy to encourage Australian workers to become 'little capitalists'.[37] The following ballad from Paterson's collection is one of a number which go to the heart of the matter:

The Stringy-Bark Cockatoo

I'm a broken-hearted miner, who loves his cup to drain,
Which often-times has caused me to lie in frost and rain.
Roaming about the country, looking for some work to do,
I got a job of reaping off a stringy-bark cockatoo.

Chorus:
>   Oh, the stringy-bark cockatoo,
>   Oh, the stringy-bark cockatoo,
>   I got a job of reaping off a stringy-bark cockatoo.

Ten bob an acre was his price—with promise of fairish board.
He said his crops were very light, 'twas all he could afford.
He drove me out in a bullock dray, and his piggery met my view.
Oh, the pigs and geese were in the wheat of the stringy-bark
    cockatoo.

The hut was made of the surface mud, the roof of a reedy thatch,
The doors and windows open flew without a bolt or latch.
The pigs and geese were in the hut, the hen on the table flew,
And she laid an egg in the old tin plate for the stringy-bark cockatoo.

For breakfast we had pollard, boys, it tasted like cobbler's paste,
To help it down we had to eat brown bread with vinegar taste.
The tea was made of the native hops, which out on the ranges grew;
'Twas sweetened with honey bees and wax for the stringy-bark
    cockatoo.

For dinner we had goanna hash, we thought it mighty hard;
They wouldn't give us butter, so we forced down bread and lard.
Quondong duff, paddymelon pie, and wallaby Irish stew,
We used to eat while reaping for the stringy-bark cockatoo.

When we started to cut the rust and smut was just beginning to
    shed,
And all we had to sleep on was a dog and sheep-skin bed.
The bugs and fleas tormented me, they made me scratch and screw;
I lost my rest while reaping for the stringy-bark cockatoo.

At night when work was over I'd nurse the youngest child,
And when I'd say a joking word the mother would laugh and smile.
The old cocky, he grew jealous, and he thumped me black and blue,
And he drove me off without a rap—the stringy-bark cockatoo.

Finally, in proportion as the later bushmen felt themselves to
be the 'true Australians', there are hints that they felt too some
indebtedness to the Aborigines. This is not to say that the remaining
black men in the 1880's and 1890's were admitted to the ranks

of the nomad tribe, but simply that many bushmen felt themselves to be, in some sense, the heirs to important parts of Aboriginal culture. After all, no white man has ever been the equal of the Aborigines in essential bush skills, in tracking, finding water, living on bush food, and so on. And it is doubtful whether white men have ever equalled Aborigines in some purely European-derived arts, such as horse-breaking or cattle-mustering. In the early days many a lost white man, and child, owed his life to the charity of the dark people,[38] and even now they are still called upon whenever a white man is lost in the bush. If, as has been argued, the bushman's *esprit de corps* sprang largely from his adaptation to, and mastery of, the outback environment, then the Aborigine was his master and mentor.

There is, of course, overwhelming evidence that the usual overt attitude to the Aborigines continued to be almost as brutal and contemptuous at the end of the nineteenth century as it had been earlier, but underlying this attitude and qualifying it, there grew up, often in the same person, an awareness of indebtedness to the first nomads who had come to terms with the difficult land. There are some hints, in the ballads and elsewhere, that after the Aborigines had ceased to be dangerous to even the loneliest swag-man, folk-memory tended to acknowledge, perhaps to sentimental-ize, this indebtedness which, like so many other components of the up-country outlook, has since become a commonplace attitude in Australian literary work.

Hemmed in by the vertical sandstone cliffs of the Blue Moun-tains on the floor of the valley of Mangrove Creek, there live to-day descendants of earlier Australians, both black and white. The two races have inter-married and along 'the Crick' men distinguish one family from another by speaking of the white or black Smiths, Joneses or Hogans, but all alike talk respectfully at times of 'the Old People' whose paintings may still be seen on the walls of lonely caves which, tradition says, were later used by bushrangers and cattle-duffers.

The feeling is reflected faithfully in 'The Stockman's Last Bed', one of the most continually popular bush ballads of the last century, and one of the few possessing traces of genuine poetic power. Vance Palmer's version of the relevant stanza reads:

His whip it is silent, his dogs they do mourn,
His nag looks in vain for his master's return:
No friend to bemoan him, unheeded he dies,
Save Australia's dark children none knows where he lies.

The theme is treated more realistically in another bush song,
which was originally a parody of the richly sentimental Victorian
ballad, 'Ben Bolt'. The Australian ballad, 'Sam Holt', was written by
G. H. Gibson ('Ironbark') and first published in the *Bulletin* of
26 March 1881. Its sentiments were such that it immediately
became very popular, and is still remembered by old bush
singers:

Oh! don't you remember Black Alice, Sam Holt—
    Black Alice so dusky and dark—
That Warrego gin with a straw through her nose,
    And teeth like a Moreton Bay shark;
The villainous sheep-wash tobacco she smoked
    In the gunyah down there by the lake;
The grubs that she gathered, the lizards she stewed,
    And the damper you taught her to bake?

They say you've ten thousand per annum, Sam Holt,
    In England a park and a drag,
And praps you forget you were six months ago
    In Queensland a-humping your swag.
Who'd think now, to see you dinin' in state
    With lords and the devil knows who,
You were flashin' your dover[39] six short months ago
    In a lambin' camp on the Paroo?

Oh! don't you remember the moon's silver sheen
    And the Warrego sand-ridges white?
And don't you remember the big bull-dog ants
    We found in our blankets at night?
The wild trailing creepers, the bush buds, Sam Holt,
    That scattered their fragrance around,
And don't you remember the broken-down colt
    You sold me and swore he was sound?

Say, don't you remember that fiver, Sam Holt,
    You borrowed so frank and so free,
When the publican landed your £50 cheque,
    In Tambo, your very last spree?

Luck changes some natures, and yours, Sammy Holt,
   Ain't a grand one as ever I see;
And I guess I may whistle a good many times,
   'Fore you think of that fiver or me.

Oh, don't you remember the cattle you 'duffed',
   And yer luck at the Sandy Creek 'rush',
The poker you played, and the bluffs that you bluffed,
   And yer habit of holding a 'flush'?
Perhaps you've forgotten that pastin' you got
   From the 'Barks'[40] down at Callaghan's store,
When Mick Houlaghan found a fifth ace in his hand,
   And you'd raised him his pile upon four!

You weren't quite the cleanly potato, Sam Holt,
   And you hadn't the cleanest of fins;
But you lifted your pile at 'The Towers',[41] Sam Holt,
   And *that* covers most of your sins.
When's my turn a-comin'? Well, never, perhaps,
   And it's likely enough yer old mate
'll be 'humping his drum' on the Warrego banks
   To the end of the chapter of fate.

This song has been quoted at length because it not only shows
the later bushman's attitude towards the Aborigines, but also
underlines the basic elements and the continuity of his tradition.
Plainly the narrator of the ballad, and his assumed audience, set
a very high valuation on certain forms of behaviour and a very
low one on others. The greatest good is to stand by one's mates in
all circumstances, and the greatest evil is to desert them. Sam
Holt's sin is not, primarily, that he was a thief and a cheat.[42] We
have seen that all honest bushmen, more or less, were cattle-
duffers and sheep-stealers on occasion. Cheating at cards, among
mates, seems often to have been taken for granted as that part
of the game demanding the greatest skill,[43] while the mere matter
of obtaining repayment of a 'fiver' borrowed during a spree would,
normally, hardly have been worth a second thought. But Sam
Holt's individualistic proclivities were so strongly developed as
to result in the commission of the unpardonable sin, that of his
desertion from, and elevation above, that collectivist commonwealth of vagabonds composed of his sometime mates. And if
Black Alice is not exactly a full citizen of the commonwealth, she

is at any rate much closer to a state of grace than the apostate, Sam Holt, or the alien 'lords and the devil knows who' in a far country.

CHAPTER VII

1   Percy Clarke, *The 'New Chum' in Australia*, etc., London 1886, p. 221; and cp. Harris, quoted ch. 4, p. 79 above.

2   Dugald Ferguson, *Vicissitudes of Bush Life*, etc., London 1891, p. 29 ff.; A. Trollope, *Australia and New Zealand*, Melbourne 1876, pp. 69 ff., 202, 503; P. Clarke, *op. cit.*, pp. 197, 208 ff.; R. Bedford, *Naught to Thirty Three*, Sydney n.d., pp. 96-7; *Bulletin*, 19 May 1888, p. 8; and C. E. W. Bean, *Dreadnought of the Darling*, London 1911, pp. 93-4, 336-7.

3   W. K. Harris, *Outback in Australia*, etc., Newcastle (N.S.W.) 1913, p. 59.

4   *Old Bush Songs*, Sydney 1905, 1930. 'Toke' was bush slang for bread.

5   cp. C. E. W. Bean, *On the Wool Track*, Sydney 1945, p. 149.

6   *Bulletin*, 29 June 1901, Red Page. A 'whaler' was a sundowner or tramp.

7   C. Wade Browne, *Overlanding in Australia*, Melbourne 1868, p. 38 ff.

8   *Old Bush Songs*.

9   C. E. W. Bean, *On the Wool Track*, p. 35 ff.; C. M. H. Clark, *Select Documents in Australian History 1851-1900*, Sydney 1955, pp. 180-4; J. Gregson, *The Australian Agricultural Company 1824-1875*, Sydney 1907, pp. 248-9; and P. McCaughey, *Samuel McCaughey*, Sydney 1955, pp. 46-7.

10 Ada Cambridge, *Thirty Years in Australia*, London 1903, p. 96.

11 O. de Satge, *Pages from the Journal of a Queensland Squatter*, London 1901, p. 255 ff.; C. E. W. Bean, *On the Wool Track*, p. 38 ff.

12 F. Hutchinson (ed.), *New South Wales, the 'Mother Colony'*, etc., Sydney 1896, p. 89 ff.

13 'An Emigrant Mechanic' (A. Harris), *The Emigrant Family*, etc., 3 vols., London 1849, vol. 1, pp. 91-2.

14 Mr A. J. Thornton of Pennant Hills, New South Wales.

15 This version from A. B. Paterson, *op. cit.* Paterson's note explains that the 'Wolseleys' and 'B-bows' were respectively machine and hand shears, to 'pink' a sheep was to shear it so closely, but without cutting it, that the pink skin showed through the remaining wool.

16 'An Emigrant Mechanic' (A. Harris), *Settlers and Convicts*, ed. C. M. H. Clark, Melbourne 1953 (first published 1847), p. 88.

17 Sung to me in 1952 by Mr Joseph Cashmere.

18 *Statistical Register of New South Wales 1871 and 1901.*

19 D. G. Jones (?), *Bushmen, Publicans and Politics,* Deniliquin 1869, ch. 1;
   A. W. Stirling, *The Never Never Land,* etc., 2nd ed., London 1884, pp.
   192-3; C. Lumholtz, *Among Cannibals,* etc., London 1890, p. 60; D. M.
   Gane, *New South Wales and Victoria in 1885,* London 1886, p. 163;
   A. Trollope, *Australia and New Zealand,* Melbourne 1876 ed., p. 202;
   A. Nicols, *Wild Life and Adventure in the Australian Bush,* London 1887,
   pp. 108-9; and E. Marin la Meslée, *L'Australie Nouvelle,* Paris 1883,
   p. 70.

20 C. E. W. Bean, *On the Wool Track,* pp. 151-2.

21 *Bulletin,* 14 September 1889, p. 8.

22 Mrs R. F. Roberts, 'Sarona', Coleraine, Victoria (information given to
   Miss Margaret Kiddle).

23 cp. E. C. Buley, *Australian Life in Town and Country,* London 1905,
   ch. 6; and James Inglis, *Our Australian Cousins,* London 1880, p. 181.

24 'Tom Collins' (Joseph Furphy), *Such is Life,* Sydney 1948, pp. 4-48, 171,
   204 ff.

25 B. A. Heywood, *A Vacation Tour to the Antipodes,* London 1863, p.
   239 ff.

26 'Tom Collins', *op. cit.,* p. 255; and cp. C. E. W. Bean, *On the Wool Track,*
   ch. 3; and W. A. Brodribb, *Recollections of an Australian Squatter,* etc.,
   Sydney 1883, p. 7.

27 'A Resident', *Girl Life in Australia: A Description of Colonial Life,* Liverpool 1876, pp. 2-3, 40-1.

28 E. Marin la Meslée, *op. cit.,* pp. 194-5.

29 *On the Wool Track,* p. 92. ('Graft' is bush slang for 'hard work'.)

30 For a possible derivation of the term see G. F. Davidson, *Trade and
   Travel in the Far East,* etc., London 1846, p. 143.

31 e.g., *Bulletin,* 17 September 1888, p. 13, 13 July 1889, p. 5; and cp.
   P. Clarke, *op. cit.,* p. 262.

32 W. R. G. Jessop, *Flindersland and Sturtland,* etc., 2 vols., London 1862,
   vol. 2, p. 305 ff.

33 Quoted A. W. Martin, 'Political Groupings in New South Wales 1872-
   1879', Ph.D. thesis, Australian National University, 1955, p. 204.

34 E. C. Buley, *op. cit.,* ch. 4.

35 'A Clergyman, etc.' (Rev. John Morison), *Australia As It Is,* etc., London 1867, p. 221.

36 E. S. Emerson, ('Milky White'), *A Shanty Entertainment,* Melbourne
   n.d. (1904), pp. 29 ff., 81; and cp. Sir G. Pearce, *Carpenter to Cabinet,*
   etc., London 1951, pp. 14-15; G. F. Scott, *Colonial Born,* London 1900,
   pp. 3-4; *Queensland Agricultural Journal,* 1 May 1898; *Sun-Herald,* 18
   September 1955, p. 40.

37 *Commonwealth Parliamentary Debates*, vol. 185, p. 6265.

38 See, e.g., A. Crombie, *After Sixty Years*, etc., Brisbane 1927, pp. 46-7; A. W. Stirling, *op. cit.*, 2nd ed., London 1884, p. 139; 'A Clergyman, etc.', *op. cit.*, p. 52; and G. F. Moore, *Diary of Ten Years' Eventful Life*, etc., London 1884, pp. 281-2.

39 Gibson's note reads 'Taking pot-luck with a sheath knife'.

40 Gibson's note: 'back-block vernacular for "Irish" '.

41 Charters Towers goldfield, North Queensland.

42 R. M. Crawford, *Australia*, London 1952, pp. 115, 152-3.

43 Francis Adams, *The Australians*, etc., London 1893, p. 180 ff.: 'But the bushman has also his vices. . . . Gambling at the sheds is simply the tournament of sharpers. You see your opponent cheat; he sees you; and not a word is said. . . . But rarely do you see a quarrel, unless it is a deliberately "put up job" '.

APOTHEOSIS OF THE NOMAD TRIBE

I heard the air though not the undersong,
The fierceness and resolve; but all the same
They're the tradition and tradition's strong.

Swagman and bushranger die hard, die game,
Die fighting, like that wild colonial boy—
Jack Dowling, says the ballad, was his name.

FOR the Australian colonies and their staple wool trade, the period from about 1860 to 1890 was one of fairly steady economic prosperity. Until the Russo-Japanese War of 1904-5, no overseas events gave any very obvious indication that Australia might not always be secure to develop her own way of life, without much reference to other peoples, in a world ordered by the overwhelming power and prestige of her indulgent but irritating mother-country.

The great depression of the early 'nineties made men examine their past and their way of life more closely. By drawing attention to Australia's economic dependence on Britain it helped to sharpen nationalist sentiment, but the feeling of basic security from external dangers was not seriously weakened until 1914. The stream of British immigrants was easily and profitably assimilated, being too modest in volume to cause such marked economic and social changes as had taken place during the Gold Rush. The economic and political life of Western Australia was revolutionized by the influx there in the 1890's of gold-seekers, but the great majority of these came, not from overseas, but from Victoria and the other Australian colonies. Thus, socially, Western Australia was made at once more 'Australian' by her Gold Rush, not temporarily less so, as Victoria had been during the 1850's. The percentage of the total Australian population born in the United Kingdom declined during the period as follows: *1861*, 53·18%; *1871*, 40·44%; *1881*, 30·66%; *1891*, 25·86%; *1901*, 18·00%.[1] For the first time a rapidly increasing majority of Australians were people who knew no other climate, country or customs than those to which they had been born.

Thus internal and external conditions enabled Australians to pause, to look inward on themselves, to take stock as it were, and to indulge in what their predecessors in the land might have called a 'dreaming'. Men sought, partly by looking for those things which distinguished them from their British fathers and congeners, to know themselves and their country better, and at the same time they saw utopian visions of a national future in which Australia, unsullied by the wars and wrongs of the old world, would be a light to less happy lands. Thus, in words which are to-day more likely to cause a wry smile than a quickening of the pulse, a contemporary poet, A. H. Adams, apostrophized 'The Australian':

> Once more this Autumn-earth is ripe,
> Parturient of another type
>
> While with the Past old nations merge
> His foot is on the Future's verge
>
> They watch him as they huddle, pent,
> Striding a spacious continent
>
> Above the level desert's marge
> Looming in his aloofness large
>
> . . . He sees beyond your hazy fears;
> He roads the desert of the years.
>
> . . . So, towards undreamt-of destinies
> He slouches down the centuries.

When the dreaming was over the values and attitudes of the nomad tribe had been largely adopted by the whole nation. This is not to say that thenceforward all Australians behaved and thought like the pastoral workers, but rather that thenceforward most people liked to believe that they tended 'naturally' to do so.

The process by which the distinctive up-country ethos, in a rather romanticized form, passed into the keeping of the whole people was not simple, nor was it confined in time to the period discussed here. Indeed, we have attempted to underline the con-

tinuity of the influence exercised by bushmen, throughout the
nineteenth century, on city folk and new chums. Yet, as has been
often recognized, this process culminated in the period 1890-1900
and in the years immediately before and after that decade. Only
then did the powerful current come to the surface of events, to
dominate formal literature and to provide a native tradition for
the new industrial trade union movement.

The reasons are not far to seek. Underlying them all was the
newly predominant influence of the native-born, reflected in the
great popularity of such organizations as the Australian Natives'
Association, founded in Victoria in 1871. Not less important was
the fact that the physical and psychological isolation of bush life
was ending. A myth, after all, relates to past events, real or
imaginary.

In the nineteenth century the pastoral workers had formed a
semi-literate community, isolated by distance and poor communications from the cities, and from the authority of the central
governments situated there. Thus traditional customs and usages
often came to have as much or more force than the law of the
land. In the days of sail it had taken a traveller four or five months
to reach Sydney from Britain, and sometimes almost as long again
to move by bullock wagon, or on foot, from the colonial capital
to a far distant station. By 1900 the voyage had been shortened
to one of four or five weeks, and few parts of the colony could not
be reached from Sydney within four or five days by train and
coach. In 1875 there were only 437 miles of railway in New South
Wales and 265 in Queensland. Ten years later these figures had
jumped to 1,732 and 1,433 respectively. The four main colonial
railway systems were linked at Albury in 1883, Serviceton in 1887
and Wallangarra in 1888. And as early as 1890 we find Lawson
with sentimental nostalgia, but some truth, writing of up-country
ways as something which had already passed with the coming of
the locomotive:

> Them early days was ended when the railroad crossed the plain,
> But in dreams I often tramp beside the bullick-team again;
> Still we pauses at the shanty just to have a drop er cheer,
> Still I feels a kind ov pleasure when the campin' ground is near,
> Still I smells the old tarpaulin me an Jimmy used ter throw
> O'er the timber-truck for shelter in the days o' long ago.

Chorus: Then it's yoke up the bullicks, an' tramp beside 'em slow,
An' saddle up yer horses an' a-ridin' we will go,
To the bullick-drivin', cattle-drovin'
Nigger, digger, roarin', rovin'
Days o' long ago.[2]

The electric telegraph also reduced the autonomy of bush life. Sydney, Melbourne, Adelaide and Brisbane were connected by 1861, and by 1872 when the overland line to Darwin completed the link with Britain, few bush towns of any importance retained their previous isolation. The effects of these changes on bush life were strikingly symbolized, in June 1880, at Glenrowan in north-eastern Victoria. There the Kelly Gang was annihilated by a train load of police from Melbourne, summoned and directed by tele-graph. Fifteen years earlier, when 'Gardiner' 's and Ben Hall's gangs had terrorized much of New South Wales, the main western railway from Sydney had extended only thirty miles to Penrith at the foot of the Blue Mountains.

Up-country *mores* were modified also by the establishment of a relatively numerous and prosperous agricultural population in the eastern part of what had once been almost purely pastoral country. Between 1860 and 1890, despite the Selection Acts, the total area sown with wheat in Australia remained small, increasing from 1¼ million to 5½ million acres. After 1890 the industry was stimulated by improved rail and road communications, by Farrer's breeding of rust and drought-resistant wheats, and by the introduction of improved farming machinery, superphosphate manures, and scientific dry-farming techniques. The years from 1890 to 1920 were the boom period of Australian agricultural expansion, during which the acreage under wheat grew from about 5½ million to 15 million acres. In the following thirty-year period, from 1920 to 1950, acreage under wheat increased by only about another 5 million acres, from 15 to 20 millions, and much of this expansion took place in Western Australia. With closer settlement, railways and better roads, many small country towns and hamlets became smaller or even disappeared, while large towns became larger and the colonial capitals grew, relatively, almost as fast.[3] Efficient postal services, newspapers, schools of arts, trade union offices and other urbanizing influences were brought much closer to the bushman. Since the 1890's, mail-order catalogues, motor-cars, telephones, aeroplanes, moving-pictures, and wireless sets have carried the process much further.

The virtual elimination of illiteracy was another powerful factor in breaking down the distinctive ethos of the bush-worker. In 1861 24·60 per cent of the people who married in New South Wales signed the register with their marks. In 1911 this figure had dropped to 0·55. Free, compulsory and secular education was introduced in Victoria in 1872 and in New South Wales in 1880.[4] By the 1890's nearly all young men could read and write. From then on many a bushman, who in earlier days might have composed a 'bush song', wrote it down instead and sent it to the *Bulletin* or the *Worker*. And of course these songs usually differed subtly from their prototypes. They were more 'literary' and selfconscious, and instead of reflecting up-country life directly they tended to romanticize it, looking back on it as something which had passed or was passing.

However, while all these changes tended to end the conditions which had produced the old up-country ethos, they also tended to make city-dwelling and other Australians much more conscious of that ethos than they had ever been before. Universal education and better communications brought Sydney nearer to the bush, as well as the reverse. Even as they faded from the workaday world, the values and attitudes of the nomad tribe were embalmed in a national myth, thence to react powerfully, as they still do, upon thought and events. The extinct bushman of Lawson and Furphy became the national culture-hero on whose supposed characteristics many Australians tend, consciously or unconsciously, to model their attitude to life.

By 1893 the stereotype was so firmly established that it was already being satirized. In that year the 'typical' Australian's self-portrait was thus criticized, from an English, middle-class viewpoint:

> The generally accepted typical cornstalk is an artistically drawn creature of some six feet, two inches, or thereabouts, in height, picturesquely habilitated in corded pants, a red shirt, wide blue sash, a blue necktie (Australian blue, of course), a cabbage-tree hat, high boots, and stock-whip wound in graceful loops on his arm. Such an artistic creation as infallibly denotes the 'Cornstalk', as the attenu-

ated gent in the starred and striped coat does 'Uncle Sam', or the fat-paunched country squire does 'John Bull'. All I suppose are equally authentic models. But the real Cornstalk, how can he be denoted?[5]

Rejecting, thus, the stock figure, the critic sets out to find the 'real Cornstalk', but fails lamentably and dully.

By the time of federation, then, the 'noble bushman' was already firmly enshrined in both the popular and the literary imagination. What were the engines of his apotheosis? Between 1880 and 1900 the slow evolutionary process by which the up-country ethos became the core of the national outlook was vastly accelerated by two events. One was the birth and rapid growth of the industrial trade union movement, the other the somewhat belated discovery of the bushman by accredited literary men.

The new type of militant trade unionism, drawing its strength from the unskilled or semi-skilled workers rather than from the more or less skilled craftsmen, burgeoned in Britain, the United States and New Zealand at the same time as it did in Australia, during the 1880's and 1890's. This congruity in time was obviously not accidental but a result of the fact that very similar, and closely inter-connected, economic and social changes in all four countries brought about similar results in all. In Australia the new unionism drew heavily on both British writers like Alfred Wallace and Americans like Henry George and Bellamy for justification of its collectivist and socialist outlook.[6] Nevertheless, the new unionism in Australia was singular in one important respect. In Britain and the United States it drew its initial strength primarily from miners and transport workers. In Australia also these groups were important, but even more influential were the shearers and other workers in the pastoral industry of the interior. Rural workers are traditionally conservative and in most western countries they have been extremely tardy in building effective trade unions, yet in Australia it was the bush-workers who formed the most numerous group of employees in the great industrial disputes, amounting at times almost to civil war, between 1890 and 1894. It was they who bore the brunt of the battle, stood as symbols of its ideology, and renewed the struggle single-handed in 1894, when the transport workers and miners had admitted temporary defeat. The Australian Workers' Union, which sprang mainly from the Amalgamated Shearers' Union, is still easily the largest and most powerful, though no longer the most militant, trade union in the country.

After what has been said above of the nature of the bush-workers' outlook, their enthusiastic acceptance of the new union-ism should not be surprising. From the earliest times the typical Australian pastoral unit had been a large station employing, intermittently, many casual hands. Because most of the work was seasonal the employer could not generally, even had he wished earnestly to do so, have had any kind of close personal or paternalistic relationship with his workmen. As Trollope noted, the squatter seldom knew even the names of the men he employed, let alone whether they were married or single. Yet at the same time the large size of the stations and the very loneliness of the pastoral country, combined with the roving habits of its deni-zens, drove them into a peculiarly close form of association. Para-doxically, the relationship between masters and men was much closer to that existing in a large British mine or factory, than to that between employer and employee on a farm or in a small business, whether British or Australian. We have seen that these conditions very early gave rise to a strongly collectivist and 'independent' outlook, which in turn often issued in purely spon-taneous, *ad hoc* action to secure better conditions from the em-ployers. Though the bushmen had for so long thought little of politics, and perhaps even less of formal trade union organization, their whole way of living and feeling made them quite extra-ordinarily receptive to trade union ideas of the new type, when these at length did come within their ambit.

In 1886, owing to a fall in the price of wool, most pastoralists attempted to reduce the contract price for shearing from one pound per hundred sheep to seventeen and sixpence. This seems to have been the most important immediate stimulus to the formation of the Amalgamated Shearers' Union in that year, al-though for some time bushmen had been questioning the extremely hard working conditions[7] which they had once accepted as part of the established order of outback life. The spontaneity of the movement is shown by the fact that in the latter half of 1886 organizations sprang up, apparently independently, in three widely separated bush towns: Ballarat, Wagga Wagga, and Bourke.

William Guthrie Spence, who had been for four years the secretary of the Amalgamated Miners' Association of Victoria, was
elected chairman of the Ballarat group by the shearers who met
there on the evening of 12 June. By the following January (1887)
the three separate groups had merged to form the Amalgamated
Shearers' Union which, under the presidency of that 'magnificent
opportunist'[8] Spence, rapidly recruited thousands of members in
the back country.

The phenomenally rapid growth of the union probably sprang
more from the bushmen's already existing ethos than from the
organizing genius and missionary zeal of prominent leaders. Once
the idea of trade union combination was put before them, it
seemed to most bushmen merely a natural extension of the non-
political, but cherished and familiar, sentiments associated with
the concept of mateship. Spence himself wrote:

> Unionism came to the Australian bushman as a religion. It came
> bringing salvation from years of tyranny. It had in it that feeling of
> mateship which he understood already, and which always charac-
> terised the action of one 'white man' to another. Unionism extended
> the idea, so a man's character was gauged by whether he stood true
> to Union rules or 'scabbed' it on his fellows. The man who never went
> back on the Union is honored to-day as no other is honored or re-
> spected. The man who fell once may be forgiven, but he is not fully
> trusted. The lowest term of reproach is to call a man a 'scab'. . . . At
> many a country ball the girls have refused to dance with them, the
> barmaids have refused them a drink, and the waitresses a meal.

The role of leading organizers like Spence and of publicists like
William Lane was, of course, vital, but most of the real work
of building a pastoral workers' union was done by thousands of
the nameless bushmen themselves. Preserved in a forgotten song-
book[9] is a cycle of very interesting ballads which tell how the
Union was being built on the remotest stations beyond the Darling,
even before Spence called his inaugural meeting in Ballarat. One
ballad begins:

> The shearing's nearly over, but with many, much I fear,
> The price they tried to cut down has cost them very dear.
> So give your kind attention, and I'll tell you in my song
> Of squatters and those shearer boys, the way they jog along.
> The life is one of luxury, it's truly something grand
> To be a roving shearer in Australia's happy land.

In February, eighty six, I left Burke [*sic*] with a sigh,
I saddled up my 'neddy's' [*sic*], and bade the girls good-bye.
My friends and I together, for Nocoleche bound,
To meet those Paroo squatters, and fight them for the pound.
They used the 'Town and Country' to break our gallant band,
But we sent the cry of victory through Australia's happy land.[10]

Another ballad in the series seems more didactic or agitational
than narrative in purpose. Two stanzas read:

If you give me but an hearing,
I'll tell you of the shearing,
The one we just got over,
Eighteen hundred, eighty six.
The time of which I'm singing
Is about of the beginning,
How the squatters blowed they'd cut the price
To seventeen and six.

The shearer has his version,
And with truth make [*sic*] the assertion,
Our hardships they are many
That we meet with going round.
You would starve us devil doubt you,
But we've lived before without you,
Take my tip a blow we'll never cut
Per hundred less a pound.[11]

And the refrain of yet another ballad, which deals with the history
of this outback struggle in some detail, pillories the unfortunate
shearers who at Merriula Station accepted work at the pastoralists'
price of seventeen and six per hundred sheep shorn. In the eyes
of union men all 'scabs' were incompetent bunglers who 'haggled'
the beasts:

So you Merriula haglers [*sic*], it's not the likes of you
That joined the Dunlop shearers, and the men on the Paroo.

All these ballads read as though the composer-narrator did in
fact play the part in the struggle which he assigns to himself in
the hobbling doggerel. Another section of the last-quoted song
shows the naïve boastfulness, idealism and almost complete
innocence of political theory[12] which must have been typical of

the narrator and his comrades, and which yet explain vividly the mushroom-like growth of bush unionism, once the germ of the idea had been sown. In the same month that Spence was addressing his first meeting of shearers in Ballarat, others seem to have been organizing themselves, in a somewhat more direct manner, nearly a thousand miles away:

Now the fight commenced at Dunlop, then the Paroo in the bush,
The boys, too, of Yankannia they joined in the manly push.
It was out at Nocoleche shed, the latter end of June,
When Gamson came to call the roll (You might know the little coon).
When everything was quiet, and you could not hear a sound,
He told us in a crying style he could not pay the pound.

We did not hoot, but listened, for we had not much to say,
But gave him our terms in writing, boys, and then we walked away.
He then took a fortnight's practice in some very funny tricks,
And then he got two snaggers for seventeen-and-six;
But they knew to make a start, boys, that too dear they'd have to pay,
So they saddled up their Neddys [sic], and like loafers sneaked away.

   .   .   .   .   .

Said he, 'If I had gained the day I'd then cheer loud and long,'
But we showed that we were merciful, for we knew that we were strong.
I then signed his agreement, and in action put my pen,
I wrote to the Burke [sic] paper, to inform my fellow men.
For I knew the news was welcome to those living far away,
When I told of Nocoleche boys, and how we gained the day.

In the crowd someone must do it,—speak for those shearing knights—,
I'm black-balled at Nocoleche 'cause I spoke up for our rights,
But don't think his shed's a fortune, it is nothing of the kind,
One man can always live without one squatter you will find.
Other sheds start early if I'm in the living ruck,
You can bet your bottom dollar the old chap will get a cut.

   .   .   .   .   .

Now I wish you young coves fortune as years go rolling on,
You may think about the old chap when some splaw [sic] bawls out
    his song.
For I've shorn upon Manara, and in Queensland far out back,
But I never shore at Paddington, I could not shear for Mac.
So cheer up my Lachlan ringers, as you travel the Maroo,
Stand out like Dunlop shearers, and the men on the Paroo.

Thus did the bushman's ethos permeate and colour that of the trade union movement, which in turn has spread it through wide sections of the Australian community. But it may be that literature has been a more important medium of the osmotic process, both because its influence was not so much limited by class lines, and because it was exercised at a more subconscious level. Vance Palmer, in his *Legend of the Nineties*, has justly summed up the story of Australian literature before about 1880:

Faced by a strange scene and puzzling conditions, the literary mind (unless it is an extremely robust and original one) tends to return to its base and refuse the task of assimilation. What can be wrung from this raw, unfamiliar world, with its rough and ready ways? Better make a genteel escape from it, or try to translate its earthy activities into a formal literary convention.

The disjunction between formal literary activity and the actual life of Australian country people was deplored by one bush bard in 1883, but the very fact of his commenting on the semi-autonomous culture of the interior was a sign that it was ending. In a rather long piece of verse constructed something after the manner of the *Canterbury Tales*, Keighley Goodchild wrote:

Then other songs were sang [sic]: most of them bad—
'The Wild Colonial Boy', 'The Bourke-street Lad';
Ballads in praise of each bushranging gang,
'Burke's Dream', with others filled with beastly slang;
Thieves' ditties, like the famed 'Black Velvet Band'—
Such are the songs you'll hear throughout the land.
Some better things at times are heard 'tis true,
But if we bar 'The Bonnie Native Blue',
All the good songs you hear where'er you roam,
Are not colonial but come from home.
Our bards are busy with cantatas, odes, and things,
And care not what the young Australian sings.

In the sphere of 'cantatas, odes and things', before 1880, the two greatest names are Harpur and Kendall. Both were native-born and both made attempts to come to grips with the Australian environment, but neither was very successful. When they wrote of the local scene they tended to see it through the borrowed spectacles of English literary convention. Their attitude to the interior, 'Australia proper', was the very opposite of that which had long been held by the working people who lived there. Instead of glorying in its dry distances, as did the bush-workers (although often with a rather wry humour), these early verse writers felt called upon to depict it as the *Ultima Thule* of horrid desolation.[13] Their attitude is exemplified in Harpur's 'Creek of the Four Graves', or in this stanza from Kendall's 'On a Cattle Track':

> It is far to the station, and gaunt Desolation
>   Is a spectre that glooms in the way;
> Like a red smoke the air is, like a hell-light its glare is,
>   And as flame are the feet of the day.
> The wastes are like metal that forges unsettle
>   When the heat of the furnace is white;
> And the cool breeze that bloweth when an English sun
>   goeth,
>   Is unknown to the wild desert night.

But it was only rarely that they tried to depict the inland plains. Naturally enough, they wrote mainly about the mountain and coastal country which they knew. It was not their fault that the wild gorges and rain-forests accorded, far more closely than the parched distances of the interior, with conventional English contemporary ideas of the 'picturesque', or that parts of the relatively domesticated coastal plain could more readily be described in conventional English 'poetic' diction. But the result was a certain anglicizing of even these parts of the Australian landscape. Harpur's most successful poem, 'Midsummer Noon in the Australian Forest', might be more informatively entitled 'Midsummer Noon in the Pseudo-Tennysonian Forest'. The one word 'lagoon' alone strikes a rather jarring colonial note. And Kendall, in his best-known lyric, draws attention to the imperfect literary taste of the bell-birds who 'sing in September their songs of the May-time'.

In prose writing before 1880 the story is rather different. We have seen that there were a great many factual writers who caught something of the spirit of the bush life which they set out to describe. But most of these men were inspired more by practical considerations, or by the scientific temper, than by purely literary ambitions. If we set aside memoirs, travel books, emigrants' guides and other forms of non-fictional writing, prose literature failed almost as completely as did poetry to assimilate itself to what was new and characteristic of the new land. A few factual writers like Samuel Sidney, trying their hand at fiction in an Australian setting, managed to preserve traces of the more realistic approach.

Easily the best novel of this kind is Alexander Harris's *Emigrant Family*. Judged as a work of art it is perhaps inferior to Henry Kingsley's more purely literary *Geoffry Hamlyn*, but as a social document it is very much more interesting. In his *Letter from Sydney*, Wakefield had written in 1829, 'Whilst in old countries modes and manners flow downwards from the higher classes, they must, in new countries, ascend from the lowest class.' The universal validity of the statement may be queried, but hardly its appositeness to nineteenth-century Australia. Thus while Kingsley gives us a picture of well-bred English ladies and gentlemen conducting an extended but decorous picnic in the 'picturesque' Australian environment, Harris, with his sympathy for the lower orders and his keen eye for what was *new* in their manners, gives us a more penetrating picture of early Australian life, if not a better novel. It may be doubted whether all the hundreds of pages Kingsley devotes to the English minor gentry add anything essential to our knowledge of their manners in the first half of the nineteenth century, but we would give much to know more about the ways of the first generation or two of native-born Australians. To compare with Harris's characterization of the latter, Kingsley gives us in *Geoffry Hamlyn* only one page of light satire. Yet his first paragraph is enough to show that Harris's picture of the Currency Lads' taciturnity and self-assurance was not exaggerated:

> . . . one of those long-legged, slab-sided, lean, sunburnt, cabbage-tree-hatted lads, of whom Captain Brentwood kept always, say half a dozen, and the Major four or five (I should fancy, no relation to one another, and yet so exactly alike, that Captain Brentwood never called them by their right names by any chance); lads who were

employed about the stable and the paddock, always in some way with the horses; one of those representatives of the rising Australian generation, I say, looked in, and without announcing himself came up to Jim across the drawing-room, as quiet and self-possessed as if he was quite used to good society, and, putting a letter in his hand, said merely, 'Miss Alice', and relapsed into silence, amusing himself by looking round Mrs Buckley's drawing-room, the like of which he had never seen before.

Marcus Clarke, who began writing in 1867, was the first novelist to evoke, by his vivid pictures of the convict past, some historical feeling for their own country in large numbers of Australian readers, but he too had strangely little to say about the native whites and the *genius loci*. 'Rolf Boldrewood' (T. A. Browne) was the first prose-writer to strike the new note with some confidence. The first paragraph of *Robbery Under Arms* (1881) reads:

> My name's Dick Marston, Sydney-side native. I'm twenty-nine years old, six feet in my stocking soles, and thirteen stone weight. Pretty strong and active with it, so they say. I don't want to blow— not here, any road—but it takes a good man to put me on my back, or stand up to me with the gloves, or the naked mauleys. I can ride anything—anything that ever was lapped in horsehide—swim like a musk-duck, and track like a Myall blackfellow. Most things that a man can do I'm up to, and that's all about it. As I lift myself now I can feel the muscle swell on my arm like a cricket ball, in spite of the—well, in spite of everything.

Here, if anywhere in imaginative literature, is the actual birthplace of the 'noble bushman', the romanticized figure at home on horseback anywhere in the interior, and standing as a symbol of emergent nationalism. And yet, as Vance Palmer has noted, the book 'has an air of unreality in spite of the vivacity with which it is imagined'. 'Boldrewood' came to Australia as an infant of three years old, and few knew better than he the life and values of bushworkers, reflected so colourfully in such passages as the above. But he was also a gentleman squatter, a police magistrate and Gold Commissioner, and the son of an East India Company officer. T. A. Browne, the pillar of morality and respectability,

is constantly at the elbow of 'Rolf Boldrewood', the writer, deplor-
ing the irregular conduct of his characters and putting into their
mouths such improbable moralizing passages as the following
description of a squatter:

> Mr Knightley was a tall, handsome man, with a grand black beard
> that came down to his chest. He walked like a lord, and had that
> kind of manner with him that comes to people that have always been
> used to be waited on and have everything found for them in this
> world. As for his wife she was given in to be the handsomest woman
> in the whole countryside—tall and graceful with a beautiful smile,
> and soft fair hair. Everybody liked and respected her, gentle and
> simple—everybody had a good word for her. You couldn't have got
> any one to say different for a hundred pounds. There are some
> people, here and there, like this among the gentlefolk, and, say
> what you like, it does more to make coves like us look a little closer
> at things and keep away from what's wrong and bad than all the
> parson's talk twice over.

There is no doubt that most bushmen did recognize and respect
real worth, in squatters as in other men, but there is even less
doubt that they were not wont to express their feelings in such
self-consciously priggish terms as the above. Even one of Kingsley's old hands, when expressing the same feeling towards his
employer, Hamlyn, is made to say merely that he was 'one of the
right sort, and was to be taken care of'.

In poetry Adam Lindsay Gordon provided the bridge between
formal literature and folk songs and tales, just as 'Boldrewood'
did in prose. The great bulk of his work is completely within the
mid-nineteenth-century English romantic tradition and quite un-
Australian in tone and setting, but *Bush Ballads and Galloping
Rhymes*, published on the day of his suicide, 23 June 1870, contained 'The Sick Stockrider' and one or two similar poems which
had an enormous influence. There is some evidence to suggest
that these 'bush' poems of Gordon's may have themselves been
directly inspired by earlier folk-songs circulating orally in the
pastoral country.

It has become a truism that the Sydney *Bulletin* was easily the
most important single medium by which the 'bush' ethos was
popularized, both in prose and verse, but a close examination
of its files suggests that the paper's success was due more to the

pressure of the inchoate demand for 'up-country' material, than to the genius of Archibald in anticipating it. Except for a period in the sub-editor's chair from June 1881 till 1887, he was editor from the *Bulletin's* birth in January 1880 until 1903. Yet for the first fourteen months of the paper's existence there was scarcely a sign of the 'outback' writing with which its name later became almost synonymous. There was much verse of the political-satirical, comic, and contemporary drawing-room varieties, but of bush balladry not a trace. Then on 5 March 1881 (the year of publication of *Robbery Under Arms*) two 'Gems from Gordon' were printed, one consisting of three stanzas from 'The Sick Stockrider'. The following issue saw Mary Hannay Foott's 'Where the Pelican Builds Her Nest'. After these ranging shots the issue of 26 March scored a bull's-eye with a poem by 'Ironbark' (G. H. Gibson). The social values and attitudes implicit in this ballad, 'Sam Holt', were those which had been dominant among bush-workers for half a century, and so the verses immediately passed back, as it were, into folk currency. They also stimulated correspondents to send in more of the same *genre*. From this point on in the *Bulletin* columns there is a rapidly swelling volume of 'up-country' ballads, stories and correspondence. The stream remained at full flood for thirty years and did not dry up completely until the journal's ownership and format changed in 1960.

It is probably not too much to say that, as closely as the appearance of *Lyrical Ballads* in 1798 marked the beginning of the Romantic movement in England, the publication of Gibson's poem marks the beginning of the conquest of formal literature in Australia by an indigenous and 'nationalist' approach. From this point of view the significance of the poem is heightened by the fact that it represented a new development in the work of its author, just as much as it heralded a new literary fashion for others. Only three years earlier, in 1878, Gibson had published *Southerly Busters*, a selection of his verse from various journals. In this volume poems like 'The Old Hand', 'The Ancient Shepherd' and 'The Shepherd's Vengeance' show first-hand knowledge and close observation of bush life, plus considerable versifying ability, but Gibson's attitude to his subject is quite close to that of 'Lewis Carroll' in his 'The Walrus and Carpenter', or of Sir W. S. Gilbert in:

> . . . a cook, and a captain bold,
> And the mate of the *Nancy* brig,
> And a bo'sun tight, and a midshipmite,
> And the crew of the captain's gig.

The bushman is treated whimsically as a barbarous and lazy criminal.[14] There is humour in the approach certainly, but not the 'realism', admiration, and pathos (or bathos), which are essential ingredients of 'Sam Holt', as they are of the work of Lawson, Paterson, Furphy and their hosts of imitators. For long a homespun folk-hero, the bushman became from 1881 the presiding deity of formal Australian literature, not always at ease in his new, city-tailored garments. Before long the painters, too, began to be inspired by the feeling that the 'Great Beyond' was the 'real Australia'.[15]

The *Bulletin* 'discovered' and published the three greatest 'nationalist' writers of the 'nineties, as well as nearly all of their brethren. Palmer writes:

> It is hard to realize now the excitement caused by such ballads as Paterson's 'Clancy of the Overflow' or such stories as Lawson's 'The Drover's Wife'; but to the people who read them they seemed to open new vistas, and though these are landmarks that have remained they were surrounded by a rich growth of minor balladry, story-writing, gay and satirical verse—the work of such varied writers as Barcroft Boake, Harry Morant, John Farrell, Alex Montgomery, Harry Siebel, and Mannington Caffyn.

Some idea of the influence enjoyed by 'The Bushman's Bible' and by the writers associated with it, may be gained from sales figures. Paterson's first book of verse, *The Man from Snowy River and Other Verses*, was published in 1895 and reprinted in 1902, 1917 and 1924. Apparently over a hundred thousand copies of this poem were sold altogether, and this figure of course takes no account of two other books of the 'Banjo' 's verse selections, though it includes his *Collected Verse* which ran through nine editions between 1921 and 1938. In 1895 the estimated population of Australia was only 3,491,621. The *Literary Year Book* rather understated the case in its review of *The Man From Snowy River*: 'The immediate success of this book of bush ballads was without parallel in Colonial Literary annals, nor could any living English or American poet boast so wide a public, always excepting Mr

Rudyard Kipling.'[16] Lawson's first book, *Short Stories in Prose and Verse*, appeared in 1894. His immediate sales were not as vast as Paterson's, but the influence of Lawson's prose work has increased with the years, while that of Paterson's verse has tended perhaps to decline.

Of the decade 1880-90, when both men's work had been published only in journals, Randolph Bedford wrote in his autobiography: 'Then I saw my first copy of the *Bulletin*, and thereby entered a new world. . . . It was Australia; whereas all the daily papers of Sydney were English provincials.'

Even the august and remote London *Times* warned its readers of the new spirit in Australia, a spirit of nationalism dangerously tinged with republican and even communistic ideas, which emanated from the bushmen of the interior and which was persistently nourished and intensified by the *Bulletin. The Times* wrote:

> It is hard to over-estimate the extent to which this journal modifies the opinions (one might almost say the character) of its readers. Most Australian newspapers alter no-one's opinion, being read only by those who already agree with them. . . . The organ (real or supposed) of some 'ring' or clique is suspected; . . . The *Bulletin* is beyond suspicion in these matters; . . . its candour verges on the cynical, but the Australian has no objection to humour in his politics or grimness in his jests. . . .[17]

We have seen reasons for supposing that *The Times* may have exaggerated slightly the *Bulletin's* power to *mould* Australian opinion, but there is no doubt of the faithfulness with which it reflected, and helped to bring into full consciousness, the emerging national *mystique*. If one examines the declared political policies of the journal it is possible to trace almost all of them back to roots in the social attitudes of the pastoral proletariat. In the issue of 17 June 1893, the *Bulletin* formulated these policies as follows:

A Republican form of Government.
One Person one Vote.
Complete Secularization and Freedom of State Education.
Reform of the Criminal Code and Prison System.
A United Australia and Protection against the World.
Australia for the Australians—The cheap Chinaman, the cheap nigger, and the cheap European pauper to be absolutely excluded.

A State Bank, the issue of bank-notes to be a State monopoly.

The direct election of Ministers by Parliament, instead of Party Government or rather Government by Contradiction.

A new Parliamentary System,—one House to be elected by constituencies as at present; the other to be chosen by the whole country voting as one Constituency.

A Universal System of Compulsory Life Insurance.

The entire Abolition of the Private Ownership of Land.

The Referendum.

The Abolition of Titles of so-called 'nobility'.

It is not likely that any of these policies sprang simply and solely from the ideas of the bush-workers. Many derived more directly from contemporary British and American radical ideas. Some, like Protection and the Direct Election of Ministers by Parliament, were probably taken over from David Syme and the Melbourne *Age*. Nevertheless, it is certain that the *Bulletin's* policies were thoroughly consistent with the political implications of up-country ideas. The points were apparently listed in something approaching what was felt to be the order of their importance, most of the first six being concerned with principles rather than with means. The first and the fifth are logical conclusions (more logical and conclusive, as it proved, than most Australians desired) of the extreme nationalist sentiment symbolized so flamboyantly by the bushrangers, while the sixth emphasizes (scarcely too crudely for general acceptance) the 'racist' component of Australian nationalism. In the event a few poor European, as opposed to British, migrants were admitted, but until the end of World War II, in the face of quite strong popular prejudice. Asians and Africans are still excluded, if not quite so ignorantly reviled. The first point also, like the second and third (and the last three) emphasizes, in political terms, the levelling egalitarianism which was such a marked feature of life in the nomad tribe. The anti-clericalism of many pastoral workers, and of the *Bulletin*, also finds expression in the Education proposal. The fourth point translates into political language the bushman's deep-seated feeling about policemen.

It is perhaps a little far-fetched to divine the influence of up-country ideas in some of the more detailed organizational proposals. Yet the demand for a Government Bank, with its anti-individualist implications, is at least consistent with the collectivist and socialist bias of mateship, as is the Henry Georgean proposal for the abolition of private property in land and the plan for an upper house elected by the whole country voting as one constituency. Universal and compulsory life insurance meets the sundowner's assumption that every man was entitled to the basic necessities of life whether he could pay for them or not. And the proposed abolition of the party system by means of the direct election of Ministers by all members of Parliament would have seemed more feasible, not to say self-evidently right, to shearers in a strike camp than to city business-men of the period, each with their own individual interests to promote. The collectivist feeling behind the last-mentioned proposal has of course been partly put into practice within the Labour Party, by its system of electing by ballot ministries, among the members of which the party leader allots portfolios. The Commonwealth Senate is elected by each state voting as a single constituency. It has become almost a fixed rule for the Labour Party not to recommend citizens for titles, and for the anti-Labour parties to refrain from recommending the Royal bestowal of *hereditary* titles. For the rest, apart from formal republican independence and Henry George's panacea, the substance of the *Bulletin's* programme has been realized.

Behind the politics of the *Bulletin*, the aspirations of the new writers and the spirit of the new trade unionism was the concept of the 'noble bushman' whose evolution has been the subject of this book. His was the symbolic figure giving some kind of psychological cohesion to the dominant but disparate social forces of the time: Protection and Utopian idealism, industrial trade unionism and chauvinistic nationalism, Labour Party politics and federalism, secularism and belief in material 'progress'. Randolph Bedford records that, some time before the great strikes of 1890-4, he saw in Bourke:

> . . . a literary and economic enthusiast of the bush, rehearsing men in a play wherein the shearer met the squatter, and talked to him temperately but straightly. If I had known it, I was looking at the birth of that political force which has had more effect on Australian life and progress than any of the regularised parties of High Tariff and No Tariff, Low Tariff and Low Wages; which is the one party under a score of aliases. The great force behind the Australian

Labour Party, was the western bush worker; not the craft-union of the factory. The Australian Workers' Union, which is the father of the Australian Labour Party, was born in the bush.

To-day we may query Bedford's estimate of the Labour Party's achievement, but there is less to quarrel with in his account of its genesis. In the final analysis it is not so much the bushman's actual nature that matters, as the nature attributed to him by so many men of the day. The romantic notion that the bushman of the interior was the guardian of 'truly Australian' values had been foreshadowed by the first native-born white man to see the plains extending westward from the Blue Mountains summits. In 1820 the youthful W. C. Wentworth had written:

To those who are acquainted with the local situation of the colony,—who have traversed the formidable chain of mountains by which it is bounded from north to south— . . . the independence of this colony, should it be goaded into rebellion, appears neither so problematical nor remote, as might otherwise be imagined. . . . If the colonists should prudently abandon the defence of the sea-coast, and remove with their flocks and herds into the fertile country behind these impregnable passes, what would the force of England, gigantic as it is, profit her?[18]

In 1892 a poem of Lawson's bodied forth the myth in its most exaggerated form. The first stanza reads:

Ye landlords of the cities that are builded by the sea—
You toady 'Representative', you careless absentee—
I come, a scout from Borderland, to warn you of a change,
To tell you of the spirit that is roused beyond the range;
I come from where on western plains the lonely homesteads
    stand,
To tell you of the coming of the Natives of the Land!
        Of the Land we're living in,
        The Natives of the Land.
For Australian men are gathering—they are joining hand in
    hand
Don't you hear the battle cooey of the Natives of the Land?[19]

The national 'dreaming' of the 'nineties had, of course, a sufficiently humdrum issue. The Aborigines used to believe that conception was caused not by sexual intercourse, which these simple people regarded as an enjoyable pastime, but by the parents' dreaming of the child's spirit. Slight doubts began to arise with large numbers of half-caste babies. Wiser in our own conceit we tend to explain historical events largely in terms of material causation, heavily discounting the role of dreaming; and no doubt we are in the main right. The dreaming of the 'nineties resulted, not in a republic embodying such noble practices as would have stupefied the actual bushman, but in much hard political horse-trading and in federation. The discovery of silver at Broken Hill in 1883, and the vast industrial growth that sprang therefrom, has probably had more effect on Australian history than the publication of 'Sam Holt' in 1881 and of all the reams of prose and verse of which it was the prototype. Certainly the results of Broken Hill silver-lead mining are easier to measure and to demonstrate. Yet while economic and other material factors are, at least in a gross sense, the principal determinants of events, it is wrong to dismiss entirely less tangible influences. The dreams of nations, as of individuals, are important, because they not only reflect, as in a distorting mirror, the real world, but may sometimes react upon and influence it.

The tradition inherited from the nomad tribe perhaps has had less influence on what we do than on how we do it. Thus, in a very stimulating essay, Sir Keith Hancock points to the strongly egalitarian and collectivist feeling which underlies the Australian concept of 'Democracy', and argues that this sentiment was decisive in the choice of the word 'Commonwealth' for the name of the new national government in 1901. He also suggests that this particular kind of democratic sentiment, in some ways 'opposed to the notions of individualism which appeared with later democratic theory', derived ultimately from the ideas of Tudor England.[20] We have now seen some reasons for thinking that the sentiment derived more immediately from the ideas of the Australian pastoral proletariat,[21] though the name 'Commonwealth' was chosen, at the conscious level, because of its associations in English history.

Similarly, the Australian Army is organized formally in very much the same way as the British Army, or that of any other Dominion, but the way Australian soldiers behave is widely believed to be rather different. Surprisingly, that notable propagandist of Australian nationalism, 'Banjo' Paterson, on the way to the great war as a correspondent in November 1914, wrote of the two A.I.F. infantry battalions aboard his ship:

> A topsy-turvy force this, for the Brigadier, General MacLaurin, has never seen any active service, while the ranks are full of English ex-service men, wearing as many ribbons as prize bulls. These English ex-service men, by the way, volunteered to a man when the war broke out, and the Australian ranks were full of Yorkshiremen, Cockneys, and Cousin Jacks. . . . Any one of them would sooner be shot as a private in the Coldstream Guards than get a decoration in a nameless Australian force.[22]

Yet, such was the latent power of the myth that, as Paterson wrote with some understatement in his next sentence: 'By the end of the war, we ourselves had a tradition.' And though the men of the first A.I.F. may well have included at least many more Englishmen than is popularly supposed, even the English at home insisted on seeing them as noble, if regrettably undisciplined, bushmen, every one slouching six feet or more tall in his socks. No Australian has ever drawn a more highly idealized picture of the Anzacs than John Masefield's:

> . . . the finest body of young men ever brought together in modern times. For physical beauty and nobility of bearing they surpassed any men I have ever seen; they walked and looked like kings in old poems, and reminded me of a line in Shakespeare:
>> 'Baited like eagles having lately bathed.'
> . . . there was no thought of surrender in those marvellous young men; they were the flower of the world's manhood, and died as they had lived, owning no master on this earth.

And not even the *Bulletin* exaggerated more fondly the casual 'independence' of the Australian character than did some cartoons in the London *Punch* of the war and post-war years. One showed a London street in which all the very tall lamp-posts were bent over at the top, from having been leaned on by Australian soldiers. At home in Australia too the 'noble bushman' was all but universally cast in the role of 'typical digger'. 'The newspapers stated that by April 1915 there had been enrolled 12,000 shearers and station hands, members of the Australian Workers' Union, and 1,000 bank clerks.'[23] Obviously even newspaper men felt, paradoxically, that the pen was still a much more ignoble and unAustralian implement than the shears or the stockwhip.

C. E. W. Bean, the official historian of World War I, implies that in fact the diggers came from city and country in about equal proportions, but that in the earliest days of the war those who 'crowded the recruiting offices came mostly from the great cities'. Yet he goes on to proclaim that even city-bred Australians were bushmen at heart, equipped with all the bushmen's virtues and vices—though, to the eye of faith, the latter were inconsiderable. Many of the commanding officers expected that there would be great difficulty in training the rank and file in the techniques of war, but they were wrong. Bean writes:

> The bush still sets the standard of personal efficiency even in the Australian cities. The bushman is the hero of the Australian boy; the arts of bush life are his ambition; his most cherished holidays are those spent with country relatives or in camping out. He learns something of half the arts of a soldier by the time he is ten years old—to sleep comfortably in any shelter, to cook meat or bake flour, to catch a horse, to find his way across country by day or night, to ride, or, at the worst, to 'stick on'.[24]

One may doubt whether, even in 1914, most city slum-dwellers were wont to spend camping holidays in the country, but no one knew better than Bean that up-country values were not acquired mainly in such direct and material ways. He had written in 1911:

> The Australian, one hundred to two hundred years hence, will still live with the consciousness that, if he only goes far enough back over the hills and across the plains, he comes in the end to the mysterious half-desert country where men have to live the lives of strong men. And the life of that mysterious country will affect Australian imagination much as the life of the sea has affected that of the English. It will always be there to help the Australian to form his ideals; and one knows of no land where they have a more definite ideal than in Australia, or where the whole people, men, women, and even youngsters, are more consciously employed in working it out.[25]

The spirit of the 'noble bushman' still manifests itself in a great many ways. For instance the 1953 literary anthology, *Australia Writes*, contains twenty-nine prose contributions, twenty-four of which show more or less strong 'outback' influence in spirit or in setting or in both. But man and society being what they are, it is natural that the tribal myth should be most apparent in wartime. When the existence of a nation is threatened men seek comfort by recalling the old ways they have in common, because it is then easier to keep at bay their fear of the unknowable future. And the Australian tradition being what it is, it is natural that it should be particularly potent in wartime, because active military service reproduces so many of the conditions of life in the nomad tribe.

Like the bond or free pastoral workers of the pre-Gold-Rush era, the serviceman lives in a male world where women and drunkenness are available, only exceptionally, as concomitants of the occasional spree. Like the bushman the soldier is a wanderer by profession, and one whose basic material needs are assured, despite the dangers and hardships which his work involves. Comradeship and loyalty, resourcefulness and adaptability are as necessary to the one life as to the other. And just as the bushman liked, on principle, to emphasize his 'independence' from his masters, while being sometimes on good terms with the individual squatter, so the digger liked it to be thought that he cared nothing for officers as a class.

Thus the official historian writes cautiously of the soldiers of the First World War:

> The fact that a man had received a good education, dressed well, spoke English faultlessly and belonged to the 'officer' class, would merely incline them, at first sight, to laugh at him. . . . But they were seriously intent upon learning, and were readily controlled by anyone really competent to teach them. . . . At first there undoubtedly existed among them a sort of repressed resentfulness, never very serious, but yet noticeable, of the whole system of 'officers'.[26]

Unofficial writers state the case a good deal more strongly. The best novels so far written on the Australian army in World War II are probably those of Eric Lambert and Tom Hungerford. Lambert's work suggests that he stands, politically, near the extreme left of Australian opinion, while Hungerford's books imply that he is near the extreme right. Yet the work of both men shows, not indeed a 'noticeable', but a very strong, resentment 'of the whole system of "officers"'. Interestingly, some might say oddly, it is Lambert whose characters are prepared to admit that there are some good officers and to take these to their hearts accordingly, though on their own terms.[27] And none of his officers is so vile, and so thoroughly hated by the men, as Hungerford's Lefevre, the C.O. of the unit in *Sowers of the Wind.*

We have seen enough of the evolution of the Australian national tradition to say that such an unlooked for coincidence in outlook is not accidental. Stories and jokes about the Australian soldier's reluctance to salute his officers are legion, but Kingsley, in his *Geoffry Hamlyn,* noted of the bushmen a hundred years ago: 'the touching of the hat is a very rare piece of courtesy from working men in Australia. The convicts were forced to do it, and so the free men made it a point of honour not to do so.'

In Lambert's first novel there is a striking scene, which, with brilliant artistic insight, gives in a few sentences the essence of the whole matter. Old Middle East campaigners and newly-arrived reinforcements are being drilled in Palestine by:

> a reinforcement officer called Hollis, a man in his early twenties with an adolescent voice who tried to hide his nervousness behind a mixture of bullyragging and unbearable disdain. The ex-men laughed at him, flouted him, and used all the cunning of the hardened campaigners to outwit him. He hated the ex-men and singled them out for abuse.
>
> The atmosphere on this particular morning was tense with mutual hatred. The reos who had had months of him were choking with resentment and the ex-men obeyed his orders sluggishly, with a weary contempt. . . .
>
> At last, white and trembling, he gave up and faced them, his temper almost gone. For a minute he glared at them. Then he burst out:
>
> 'You look like a pack of bloody convicts. Your drill's a bloody disgrace!'
>
> Through the three platoons swept a wave of suppressed muttering. Then the lanky figure of Sullivan stepped smartly to his left front as the drill book required and said equably:
>
> 'And so are you.'
>
> Then he stepped back into the ranks.
>
> 'What did you say?' stammered Hollis thinly, his eyes looking a little alarmed.

Sullivan repeated his precise movement.
'I said: And so are you.'
Hollis was suddenly calm and subdued.
'Report to the orderly room,' he said.
He broke off the three platoons and followed Sullivan.

Since the slaughter at Gallipoli the anniversary of the Landing
has become not only a day of Australian mourning and remem-
brance for the war dead, but also the Australian national day above
all others. Solemn religious services are conducted and patriotic
orations are delivered by prominent citizens, but the rank and file
carry out also, different, unofficial ceremonies. During and after
the official performances knots of old soldiers gather in the public
streets and squares, there to assert their birthright by playing,
in the face of the law and the constables,[28] ritualistic games of
'two-up'. For most of the players, too, it seems both natural and
fitting to end the day with a serious attempt to make it the greatest
alcoholic debauch of the year. Lawson's words, written about the
bushmen of the 'nineties, would be equally true of these men who
crossed the North African Desert and the Owen Stanley Range,
or of the old hands who crossed the Blue Mountains over a century
earlier:

> There were between us the bonds of graft, of old times, of pov-
> erty, of vagabondage and sin, and in spite of all the right-thinking
> person may think, say or write, there was between us that sympathy
> which in our times and conditions is the strongest and perhaps the
> truest of all human qualities, the sympathy of drink. We were drink-
> ing mates together. We were wrong-thinking persons too, and that
> was another bond of sympathy between us.[29]

A very fine poem, written during the German offensive in the
Ardennes in 1944, bodies forth faithfully the more heroic aspects
of the 'noble bushman' tradition. It also suggests the extent to
which this tradition, originally belonging only to a section of
society, has captured the imagination of the whole Australian
people, for the author and the subject of the following elegy both
belong to old squatting families in the Victorian Western District,
traditionally held to be the most conservative and 'aristocratic
social group in Australia:

The Tomb of Lt John Learmonth A.I.F.

'At the end on Crete he took to the hills, and said he'd fight it out with only a revolver. He was a great soldier. . . . ' (One of his men in a letter.)

This is not sorrow, this is work: I build
A cairn of words over a silent man,
My friend John Learmonth whom the Germans killed.

There was no word of hero in his plan;
Verse should have been his love and peace his trade,
But history turned him to a partisan.

Far from the battle as his bones are laid
Crete will remember him. Remember well,
Mountains of Crete, tne Second Field Brigade!

Say Crete, and there is little more to tell
Of muddle tall as treachery, despair
And black defeat resounding like a bell;

But bring the magnifying focus near
And in contempt of muddle and defeat
The old heroic virtues will appear.

Australian blood where hot and icy meet
(James Hogg and Lermontov were of his kin)
Lie still and fertilize the fields of Crete.

•   •   •

Schoolboy I watched his ballading begin:
Billy and bullocky and billabong,
Our properties of childhood, all were in.

I heard the air though not the undersong,
The fierceness and resolve; but all the same
They're the tradition and tradition's strong.

Swagman and bushranger die hard, die game,
Die fighting, like that wild colonial boy—
Jack Dowling, says the ballad, was his name.

He also spun his pistol like a toy,
Turned to the hills like wolf or kangaroo,
And faced destruction with a bitter joy.

His freedom gave him nothing else to do
But set his back against his family tree
And fight the better for the fact he knew.

He was as good as dead. Because the sea
Was closed and the air dark and the land lost,
'They'll never capture me alive,' said he.

     •   •   •

That's courage chemically pure, uncrossed
With sacrifice or duty or career,
Which counts and pays in ready coin the cost

Of holding course. Armies are not its sphere
Where all's contrived to achieve its counterfeit;
It swears with discipline, it's volunteer.

I could as hardly make a moral fit
Around it as a lightning flash.
There is no moral, that's the point of it,

No moral. But I'm glad of this panache
That sparkles, as from flint, from us and steel,
True to no crown nor presidential sash.

Nor flag nor fame. Let others mourn and feel
He died for nothing; nothings have their place.
While thus the kind and civilized conceal

This spring of unsuspected inward grace
And look on death as equals, I am filled
With queer affection for the human race.[30]

CHAPTER VIII

1 C. M. H. Clark, *Select Documents in Australian History 1851-1900*, Sydney 1955, p. 667.

2 *Bulletin*, 24 May 1890, p. 13.

3 Between 1871 and 1891 the distribution of the population in New South Wales changed as follows:

	Sydney and Suburbs	*Other Towns*	*Rural*
1871	137,776 = 27·5%	97,037 = 19·3%	266,766 = 53·2%
1891	383,283 = 34·3%	346,736 = 31·0%	388,231 = 34·7%

(Figures from A. W. Martin, 'Political Groupings in N.S.W. 1872-1899, etc.', Ph.D. thesis, Australian National University, 1955, p. 25.)

4 C. M. H. Clark, *op. cit.*, p. 691.

5 'Whaks Li Kell' (Daniel Healey), *The Cornstalk: His Habits and Habitat*, Sydney 1894 (first published 1893), p. 53.

6 For the best treatment of this subject, from an Australian viewpoint, see R. A. Gollan, *Radical and Working Class Politics: A Study of Eastern Australia, 1850-1910*, Melbourne 1960.

7 Between 1875 and 1884 the average price obtained for New South Wales wool only once fell below 90% of the average price for the preceding period, 1870-4. This slight drop occurred in 1878 when the figure fell to 85%. However from 1884 on the price slumped steeply to 78% in 1885 and down to a nadir of 50% in 1894. (See T. A. Coghlan, *Wealth and Progress of New South Wales 1897-98*, Sydney 1899, p. 1070, and cp. W. G. Spence, *Australia's Awakening*, etc., Sydney 1909, ch. 7.)

8 Brian Fitzpatrick, *British Empire in Australia*, Melbourne 1941, p. 303.

9 *Tibbs' Popular Song Book*, etc., Sydney n.d. (about 1887).

10 'Nocoleche', 'Dunlop', 'Toorale', and 'Fort Bourke', were four sheep-stations west of the Darling River. They were owned by Sir Samuel McCaughey, and comprised together about 3,000,000 acres. The Paroo is a tributary which flows (rarely) into the Darling from the north-west. The *Town and Country Journal* was a weekly paper favoured, at this period, by squatters, much as the *Bulletin* was by their hands.

11 'Blowed' = boasted; 'blow' = a stroke with the shears.

12 For an opposed, but at least equally simple-minded, view of the points at issue between pastoral workers and their employers, see Robert D. Barton, *Reminiscences of an Australian Pioneer*, Sydney 1917, ch. 15, 'Unions and Strikes'.

13 cp. Bernard Smith, 'Interpretation of Australian Nature during the Nineteenth Century', B.A. thesis, Sydney University.

14 Much of the work of Brunton Stephens reflects the same attitude. See e.g., his 'Quart Pot Creek', in *Convict Once and Other Poems*, Melbourne 1885.

15 See, e.g., R. H. Croll (ed.), *Smike to Bulldog*, etc., Sydney 1946, pp. 40, 63-4; and R. H. Croll, *Tom Roberts*, etc., Melbourne 1935, pp. 34, 120-4.

16 E. Morris Miller, *Australian Literature*, 2 vols., Melbourne 1940, vol. 1, pp. 50-2, 274.

17 31 August 1903. (Quoted C. M. H. Clark, *op. cit.*, p. 806.)

18 *Statistical, Historical and Political Description*, etc., London 1819, pp. 277-8.

19 *Bulletin*, 27 August 1892, p. 20.

20 'A Veray True and Comyn Wele', *Politics in Pitcairn and Other Essays*, London 1947.

21 cp. Russel Ward, 'Collectivist Notions of a Nomad Tribe', *Historical Studies: Australia and New Zealand*, May 1955.

22 *Happy Despatches*, Sydney 1934, p. 179.

23 C. E. W. Bean, *Official History of Australia in the War of 1914-18*, 12 vols., Sydney 1936-42, vol. 1, p. 44.

24 *ibid.*, pp. 43-6.

25 *The Dreadnought of the Darling*, London 1911, pp. 317-18.

26 C. E. W. Bean, *Official History of Australia in the War*, etc., vol. 1, p. 48; and cp. vol. 6, pp. 5-6 ff.

27 e.g., Henry Gilbertson and Chips Prentice in *Twenty Thousand Thieves*, London 1952; and David Bruce in *The Veterans*, London 1954 (see especially pp. 112-14).

28 cp. W. E. Harney, *North of 23°*, etc., Sydney n.d. (1949), p. 80.

29 From Lawson's story, 'For Auld Lang Syne', published in *While the Billy Boils*, Sydney 1896. Of course Lawson uses the word 'graft' in its Australian slang sense of 'hard work'.

30 John Manifold, *Selected Verse*, New York 1945, pp. 77-9.

TWO NOBLE FRONTIERSMEN

———

*No Yankee hide e'er grew outside such beef as we can
    freeze;
No Yankee pastures make such steers as we send o'er
    the seas—
As we send o'er the seas, my boys, a thousand pounds
    they weigh—
From the far Barcoo, where they eat nardoo, a
    thousand miles away.*

HAVING traced the steps by which the ethos of the Australian pastoral workers came to have a quite disproportionate influence on that of the whole nation, we may ask *why* this happened. The simple answer may be best given in terms of the American historian F. J. Turner's 'frontier theory', the germ of which he summed up in the conclusion of an early article:

What the Mediterranean Sea was to the Greeks, breaking the bond of custom, offering new experiences, calling out new institutions and activities, that the ever retreating Great West has been to the eastern United States directly, and to the nations of Europe more remotely.[1]

Turner's new approach to American history was first clearly outlined in his paper 'The Significance of the Frontier', delivered on 12 July 1893, in Chicago, the old 'capital of the West'. For many years afterwards his teaching generated mounting enthusiasm, for two reasons. The approach was new, even revolutionary, casting much light on aspects of American history which had previously been unnoticed rather than misunderstood; and the spirit of the new gospel was at least thoroughly consistent with all the most popular and powerful beliefs of the time. Like other great historians, Turner explained the past in a significant new way, without altogether realizing the extent to which his work would also constitute for the future a picture of the mind of his own time. Before seeking to set his doctrine in perspective, however, we shall ask just what it was and what significance his ideas have for Australian as well as for American history.

Since new countries like Australia, the United States or the Latin American republics, were settled by Europeans, the natural tendency of historians—by definition students of the past—was to explain developments in terms of successive influences from Europe. Turner's achievement was to show that indigenous, and particularly 'frontier' influences, were not less important for a just understanding of American history. In so far as the American was not just a transplanted European but a different kind of man, the change could only have been brought about by influences met with in the new land. And, as we have seen in Australian history, these indigenous influences, of necessity, were most potent on the expanding frontier of settlement where they were met by the colonists in their most undiluted form. Turner puts it like this in a well-known passage:

> The wilderness masters the colonist. It finds him a European in dress, industries, tools, modes of travel, and thought. It takes him from the railroad car and puts him in the birch canoe. It strips off the garments of civilization and arrays him in the hunting shirt and the moccasin. . . . In short, at the frontier the environment is at first too strong for the man. He must accept the conditions which it furnishes, or perish, and so he fits himself into the Indian clearings and follows the Indian trails. Little by little he transforms the wilderness, but the outcome is not the old Europe, not simply the development of Germanic germs, any more than the first phenomenon was a case of reversion to the Germanic mark. The fact is, that here is a new product that is American.[2]

Charles Reade, the English novelist who never set foot in Australia, had the germ of the same idea when he wrote that the settlement of the continent and the rush for gold furnished the theme for a great epic: '. . . in the sudden return of a society far more complex, artificial and conventional than Pericles ever dreamed of, to elements more primitive than Homer had to deal with'.[3]

In Australia the frontier has not had so much lasting effect on the external forms of life, political, legal, institutional and so on, as it has had upon men's attitude to life and so, at one remove as it were, upon the way in which these institutions are made to work in practice. Most Australians no longer bake dampers or wear cabbage-tree hats, but their ethos, like the speech which clothes it, differs from that of their British congeners more than it did a hundred years ago. The same is obviously true of Americans, and it is this side of Turner's doctrine which has been least shaken by subsequent criticism.[4] As Harper says, 'The important change was perhaps not the change in political structure so much as the change in intellectual outlook.'[5] In this sense at least then, according to Turner and his followers, the two most important effects of the frontier were to promote national unity and nationalism and to promote democracy.

It is significant that, as in nineteenth-century Australia, the proportion of native-born citizens was very much higher on the American frontier than on the eastern sea-board.[6] We have seen much other evidence for believing that in Australia too the frontier was a forcing-ground for the growth of distinctive national habits and sentiments, and that these in turn made for political unity of the separate colonies. At the end of the century the Federation referenda again convincingly demonstrated the frontier's unifying national influence. The strong sentiment for Federation on the new goldfields frontier in Western Australia has often been remarked upon, and the Yes vote of these 'T'other-siders', most of whom came from Victoria where federal sentiment was strongest, was overwhelming. But the 'outback' constituencies in the north-west also returned large Yes majorities. In fact it was the outback pastoral areas which carried the day in the three doubtful colonies of New South Wales, Western Australia and Queensland. In the latter colony the bushmen seem to have voted Yes in spite of the powerful exhortations to the contrary of the popular Brisbane Worker. Provincialism and inter-state jealousies were strongest in and near the coastal capital cities.[7] Vance Palmer's assessment of the situation at the time of the first convention to discuss Federation in 1891 is hardly an overstatement:

> There was an element of paradox in the situation. In the interior there was little talk of federation but the essential unity of Australia

as a country with common interests was taken for granted: in the capital cities, federation was discussed as an important issue, but it was regarded almost as an alliance between countries foreign to one another and having rival economies.[8]

It is clear then that frontier conditions exerted a unifying, nationalist influence in Australia as in America. But what of Turner's other main effect of the frontier ethos: democracy? Though no less emotive a term than nationalism, it is even vaguer and more compendious in meaning. Though the differences between the Australian and American democratic impulses are slighter and more elusive than the similarities between them, such an omnibus word as 'democracy' must serve to obscure as many differences as it reveals. We may start by asking what 'democracy' meant to Turner:

> The most important effect of the frontier has been in the promotion of democracy here and in Europe. As has been indicated the frontier has been productive of individualism. Complex society is precipitated by the wilderness into a kind of primitive organization based on the family. The tendency is anti-social. It produces antipathy to control, and particularly to any direct control. The taxgatherer is viewed as a representative of oppression.

Here and elsewhere Turner insists that an individualist outlook was easily the most important single component of American frontier democracy, and he explains how individualism was stimulated by the material conditions of frontier life. The chief factor was free land:

> So long as free land exists, the opportunity for a competency exists, and economic power secures political power. But the democracy born of free land, strong in selfishness and individualism, . . . has its dangers as well as its benefits.[9]

Critics have pointed out that the frontier lands were not absolutely free, that in fact it was not usually the discontented eastern city workman but the small farmer's younger sons and such people who went west to improve themselves, and that to have a good chance of success they needed a modest accumulation of capital and equipment. These objections modify Turner's 'safety-valve' theory, but do not alter the fact that in most[10] areas and times up to 1890 the typical American frontiersman was a small, individual agriculturist.

Throughout the nineteenth century American land legislation facilitated the settlement of the west by small farmers. Each of the Acts of 1800, 1820 and 1841 went further than its predecessor in making it easy for poor men to become their own masters on their own soil. Finally the Homestead Act of 1862 gave 160 acres of free land to each adult, or head of a family, who could prove five years' continuous residence and cultivation.[11] Even more important was the fact that American geographical conditions favoured the farmer rather than the pastoralist. Clearing the forests of the Mississippi Valley was back-breaking work, but once the land had been prepared for the plough, soil, rainfall and relatively accessible markets made it perfectly possible for a poor man, backed by his wife and family, to achieve a competence if not riches. As Turner says,[12] the American farmer knew no real check until the 1880's when the wave of settlement reached the semi-arid area of the Great Plains beyond longitude 98°. But by then agricultural settlement had been well established also in Oregon, California and the whole western littoral. In older lands the small-scale agriculturist is known as a peasant. It is quite a long time since the European peasant has been a frontiersman in something like the American sense of the word, and so his claim now to be a promoter of democracy is dubious, but his unshakeable individualism is proverbial.

In Australia land laws and geography combined to produce in the frontiersman's mind quite a different concept of democracy. Australia is of roughly the same size and shape as the United States, but being nearer the equator and having much lower mountain chains, it is much more arid. As in the United States settlement proceeded inland from the eastern coastal plain, which, however, is much narrower in Australia. Crossing the Great Dividing Range, which corresponds roughly in height and position with the Appalachian Mountain system, Australian pioneers found the farther slopes rapidly merging into a region like the Great Plains beyond the ninety-eighth meridian in America, except that the western plains in Australia were hotter and drier, and shaded off after a few hundred miles into desert too arid for even temporary pastoral occupation. On the coast and on the slopes of the

Great Divide there is sufficient rainfall to sustain a rather sparse agricultural population, but even to-day the vast bulk of Australia's habitable land is fit only for pasturing sheep and beef-cattle. We have seen that in the nineteenth century, with comparatively backward farming techniques, it was even more difficult for a small farmer to take root and survive in the Australian west.

We have seen too that the effect of these geographical controls was accentuated by government land policies and legislation. British manufacturers wanted more and ever more wool for the Yorkshire textile mills and, at least from 1828 onwards, the effect, if not always the intention, of legislation was to favour the big pastoralists at the expense of the small settler. After the granting of responsible government to the south-eastern colonies in the 'fifties, Free Selection Acts from 1861 onwards aimed ostensibly at 'unlocking the lands' to the small agriculturist; but none of these Acts was really successful, perhaps as much because of intractable geographic facts as of the machinations of the squatters. Except in South Australia and, to a lesser extent in Tasmania and Victoria, it was only in the last decade of the century that small-scale agriculture began to become a reasonably secure and profitable occupation; but by then much good arable land had passed permanently into the hands of big graziers or pastoral companies.

Thus the typical Australian frontiersman was not a small, individualist farmer, tilling his own soil with the help of his family and perhaps a hired hand or two at harvest time. Indeed he usually had no family and scorned agricultural pursuits. It is true that the squatter was a rugged individualist even to the point of displaying a 'tendency to large-scale larceny where land was concerned'[13] but pastoral runs were so large that there were few squatters and many hands, most of them employed on a casual basis. It was not impossible for an Australian pastoral worker by superior industry, thrift, sobriety, or skill at cattle-stealing, to become his own master, but for the reasons outlined above it was very much more difficult than it was for an American frontiersman.[14]

Men like James Tyson and Sir Sidney Kidman, who rose successfully from the ranks of bush-workers to become great squatters, were sufficiently rare for their names to become legendary—not however, among bush-workers, as symbols of heroic endeavour, but as by-words for meanness and presumptive dishonesty. 'Millionaire James Tyson was sixty-seven on the 10th inst.,' wrote the *Bulletin* in January 1890; 'and presented himself with a new clay pipe as a birthday gift. James is getting extravagant as he grows older.' In northern South Australia and the Northern Territory, I have heard numerous such tales about the late Sir Sidney Kidman. One, firmly and widely believed, was that Kidman would instantly dismiss any employee whom he saw lighting his pipe with a match in the evening, instead of using a brand from the camp-fire. He was held to have believed that a man so careless of his own money would be equally careless of his employer's property.

The plain fact is that the typical Australian frontiersman in the last century was a wage-worker who did not, usually, expect to become anything else.[15] The loneliness and hardships of outback life, as on the American frontier, taught him the virtues of co-operation, but his economic interests, unlike those of the American frontiersman, reinforced this tendency towards a social, collectivist outlook. By loyal combination with his fellows he might win better conditions from his employer, but the possibility of becoming his own master by individual enterprise was usually but a remote dream. So far from being 'precipitated by the wilderness into a primitive organization based on the family', he was precipitated into an equally primitive organization of 'nomad tribesmen', if one may conceive of a tribe without women and children. Thus it came about that differing frontiers in the United States and Australia produced two different kinds of frontiersmen, with mental attitudes which were very similar in some respects but very different in others.

We have seen that both frontiers promoted a national outlook, and indeed it is also true that both frontiers promoted 'democracy', but 'democracy' had a different meaning in the two countries, as Turner himself (unlike some of his disciples) recognized: 'If . . . we consider the underlying conditions and forces that create the democratic type of government . . . we shall find that under this name there have appeared a multitude of political types radically unlike in fact.'[16]

American and Australian frontiersmen both liked to think that they were the most democratic people on earth, but for the American the implicit meaning of 'democracy' tended to be freedom to make his own way to the top by his own individual efforts, and regardless of his fellows. The implicit meaning of the word for the Australian frontiersman tended to be freedom to combine with his mates for the collective good, and the discomfiture of 'those wealthy squatters'. Thus the Australian labour movement has been, and continues to be, much more collectivist in outlook as well as much stronger, relatively, than the American. And collectivist and socialist ideas are much more widely tolerated, if not accepted, in Australian society generally, than they are in America.

Thirty years ago this vital difference in the two frontier legacies was pointed out, in a very able article, by an American visitor to Australia who wrote:

> Certainly the United States owes its individualism largely to its small man's frontier; I think it is not fanciful to suggest that Australia owes much of its collectivism to the fact that its frontier was hospitable to the large man instead.[17]

In this sense then the Australian frontier had an exactly opposite effect to that of the American, which Turner correctly described as individualistic and 'antisocial'. But in another sense Australian frontiersmen were also antisocial. While being anything but individualistic within their own social group, they displayed no less 'dislike of authority', no less 'antipathy to control, and particularly to any direct control', than did their American counterparts. Though there was less actual physical violence on the Australian frontier, the nomad tribe was incorrigibly antisocial from the point of view of its employers, and from that of the government and constituted authority generally. 'Waltzing Matilda', the most popular of Australian folk-songs, epitomizes the frontiersman's attitude towards authority. Like 'the black police' and landlords in Ireland, troopers and squatters in Australia were the natural enemies of all honest bushmen, to be spoiled as opportunity offered. A quatrain from Henry Lawson gives just weight to both aspects of the democratic impulse on the Australian frontier: the strongly social sense of solidarity within the nomad tribe, and the equally strong, antisocial hostility to any control, or even patronage, from above:

They tramp in mateship side by side—
The Protestant and Roman—
They call no biped lord or sir,
And touch their hat to no-man!

There is every reason to think then that the frontier tradition has been, at least, not less influential and persistent in Australia than in America. But the really interesting puzzle is why, in the nineteenth century and particularly towards the end of it, the frontier should have possessed so much prestige. Why should so many men have paid to the relatively uncouth frontiersman the supreme compliment of imitating, often unconsciously, his manners and outlook? Turner was perhaps too much a man of his age for the question to have occurred to him, at any rate in the form in which it may occur to us. If a man in love ever asks himself why, it is only to answer in terms of the self-evident beauties of the beloved. Turner's imagination was fascinated by the frontier as was the mind of his time.

In the broadest possible terms it may be suggested that admiration for the 'simple' virtues of the barbarian or the frontiersman is a sentiment which arises naturally in highly complex, megalopolitan societies. Lovejoy and Boas cast some light on this theme in their *Documentary History of Primitivism and Related Ideas in Antiquity*. The authors distinguish between 'soft' noble savages like the inhabitants of the Hesperides and 'hard' ones like the Germans or Scythians; and their documents suggest that interest in the former tended to precede interest in the latter. Similarly, as we shall see, eighteenth-century interest in the predominantly 'soft' noble savage, of the South Seas and elsewhere, preceded nineteenth-century interest in the predominantly 'hard' noble frontiersman.

Thus Tacitus extolled, and romanticized, the 'simple' democratic virtues of the Germani[18] but in the relatively simple and rural world of mediaeval Christendom, when the population of Rome itself had fallen from upwards of a million to twenty or thirty thousand, there was little tendency to glorify either the savage or the hind, whether or not the latter dwelt in a border march.[19] On the contrary, mediaeval literature, including popular literature, was much concerned with kings and noblemen, or with the worthies of antiquity, and these were admired not for any kind of 'simplicity', but for quite opposite reasons. Aristotle, Caesar, the Knights of the Round Table and Amadis de Gaul charmed the imagination of men because they were felt to belong to worlds more civilized, complex, rich and cultivated than that of the middle ages. Even the wonders reported by Marco Polo and Sir John Mandeville were received in a kindred spirit. Cathay and the land of Prester John were more exotic, rich and strange than Norwich perhaps, but not primarily, simpler or more virtuous. Indeed Mandeville's first chapter undertakes 'to teche zou the Weye out of homely "Englond" to the rich, mighty and wondrous city of "Constantinoble"'. The symbolic figure is that of Dick Whittington, the simple country boy who becomes Lord Mayor of London.

A few hundred years later, in the much more complex mercantilist age when England was already approaching the threshold of the industrial revolution, a very different symbolic figure was created. Robinson Crusoe, the man of parts who found the good life by 'returning' to 'nature', may stand as the harbinger in England of the 'noble frontiersman' of the nineteenth century, just as his Man Friday may be considered, in some ways, as a progenitor of the 'noble savage' of the eighteenth.[20] But such changes in taste do not take place overnight. From our point of view even a book like *Robinson Crusoe* is an isolated symptom rather than a cause. In 1694 Cotton Mather was at one with most of his contemporaries in feeling that the then frontiersmen of western Massachusetts were godless barbarians *'on the Wrong side of the hedge'* where 'the Angel of the Lord becomes their enemy'.[21] And in 1777 Dr Johnson still discountenanced romantic enthusiasm by his reproof to Boswell: 'When a man is tired of London he is tired of life; for there is in London all that life can afford.' Even as late as 1820 when Fenimore Cooper started to publish, frontier life still had so little prestige that he felt it proper to write about high life in England, of which he knew nothing from personal experience. In *The Pioneers* (1823), however, he turned to the familiar backwoods and, with the character of Natty Bumppo, began to develop the portrait of 'Leatherstocking' which, under various names, formed the altogether noble and heroic archetype for the innumerable noble frontiersmen who were to crowd the pages of subsequent nineteenth-century popular novels. Indeed,

'Leatherstocking' was a not unworthy psychological successor of the 'noble savage' whose life span extended 'from about 1730 to 1830'.[22] As a result of closer acquaintance and the reports of missionaries, the noble savage had become rather ignoble by the 1820's. By 1832 he had fallen on such evil days as to be represented as a gross comic buffoon in catchpenny British street songbooks.[23]

A substitute, however, had already been born. Here is a portrait of 'Leatherstocking', under the style of 'Deerslayer':

> In stature, he stood about six feet in his moccasins, but his frame was comparatively light and slender, showing muscles, however, that promised unusual agility, if not unusual strength. His face would have had little to recommend it except youth, were it not for an expression that seldom failed to win upon those who had leisure to examine it, and to yield to the feeling of confidence it created. This expression was simply that of guileless truth, sustained by an earnestness of purpose, and a sincerity of feeling, that rendered it remarkable. At times this air of integrity seemed to be so simple as to awaken the suspicion of a want of the usual means to discriminate between artifice and truth; but few came in serious contact with the man, without losing this distrust in respect for his opinions and motives.[24]

It will be seen that the essential attributes of this early heroic frontiersman corresponded very closely with those of the obsolescent noble savage. Both were guileless, yet not gullible, sons of 'nature', whose physical and moral excellence is held up to the admiration of readers 'corrupted' by the artificialities of a sophisticated society. For comparison we may take the following typical portrait of a noble savage of the late eighteenth century, King Abba Thulle of the Pelew Islands:

> With regard to the excellent man, who ruled over these sons of Nature, he certainly, in every part of his conduct, shewed himself firm, noble, gracious, and benevolent; there was a dignity in his deportment, a gentleness in all his manners, and a warmth and sensibility about his heart, that won the love of all who approached him.—Nature had bestowed on him a contemplative mind, which he had himself improved by those reflections that good sense dictated, and observation confirmed.[25]

Frances Burney's long description of the celebrated Omai from Otaheite, the home *par excellence* of noble savages, strikes the same note: 'Indeed he appears to be a perfectly rational and intelligent man, with an understanding far superior to the common race of us *cultivated gentry*.'[26] Omai was an atypical specimen of his genus in one respect however, being a man from the middle ranks of Tahitian society. The *cultivated gentry* of the eighteenth century usually liked their noble savages to be kings or chiefs among their own people. It was in keeping with the spirit of the following century, which witnessed the dissemination of the doctrines of the Rights of Man and universal education, that the typical noble frontiersman should be an uncultivated workman.

In Australia, too, the first signs of the new attitude to frontiersmen appeared in the same decade 1820-30. *Settlers and Convicts* was not published until 1847, but the book was based directly upon experience of up-country life gained during the period 1826-41. Though written in a rather sober and factual style, the work is instinct with that kind of admiration for frontiersmen which, by the time of H. W. Haygarth's *Recollections of Bush Life in Australia* (1848), was becoming quite common among writers.

Two passages which actually compare the life of the Australian frontiersman with that of the 'noble savage' help to show the transference of emotions from one to the other which was taking place in men's minds. In 1837 James Macarthur (or the man who wrote his book) asked whether those who opposed emigration to the colonies thoroughly weighed 'the pernicious influence of poverty upon the moral character'. He then quoted a Dr Channing who urged paupers to emigrate for the following reasons:

> The want of a neat, orderly home, is among the chief evils of the poor. Crowded in filth they cease to respect one another. . . . In these respects the poor often fare worse than the uncivilised man. True, the latter has a ruder hut, but his habits and tastes lead him to live abroad. Around him is boundless, unoccupied nature, where he ranges at will, and gratifies his passion for liberty. Hardened from infancy against the elements, he lives in the bright light and pure air of heaven . . .

Most travel books about the life of the bushman written before 1850 stress the 'naturalness' and freedom of frontier life, without consciously comparing it with that of the 'noble savage'.

But in 1845 another writer made the connection even more explicitly than in the above passage. He wrote:

> The greatest drawback to the life of an Australian settler is the solitude, and the absence of the conveniences of civilization. With some persons, however, this would be more than counter-balanced by the feeling of unrestrained independence they would enjoy; and the bushman of Australia, unshackled by the customs and constraint of civilized communities, may roam through the grassy wilderness, with his horse, gun, and kangaroo-dogs, with a thousand times more freedom than the wildest chiefs of the African deserts, or American savannahs.[27]

The same transference of attitudes is apparent in the visual arts. The earliest Australian landscape drawings are embellished with groups of Aborigines, becoming more ignoble with the years, or with figures of 'cultivated gentry' who appear to have been transported from Strawberry Hill in a vain attempt to impart an air of urbanity to the exotic frontier landscape. Then in 1823 Joseph Lycett, a convict artist, first introduced a white kangaroo-hunter outdistancing a noble savage.[28]

F. J. Turner, apparently unwittingly, gives a clue to the economic reasons why the noble frontiersman should have replaced the noble savage at about this time. In listing American frontier traits he notices that 'colonial [i.e., eighteenth-century] travellers agree in remarking on the phlegmatic character of the colonists'. He goes on to ask how such people who were of course, in the terms of his thesis, at that time frontiersmen, could have acquired 'that strained nervous energy', which he saw as a later American frontier characteristic. However he is content to leave the question unanswered beyond merely noting that 'the transition appears to become marked at the close of the War of 1812, a period when interest centred upon the development of the West . . .'[29] It seems to be only a coincidence that his phrasing of the last-quoted clause shifts the focus of attention from frontier characteristics themselves to popular attitudes *towards* the frontier. Beauty may reside partly in the eye of the beholder.

The 'transition' from mercantilism to industrialism was also 'becoming marked' during the twenty years or so 'after the War of 1812'. In the eighteenth century when European expansion depended largely upon profitable contact with remote and economically backward peoples, the noble savage had fired the imagination of cultivated persons. To say this is emphatically not to suggest that many Europeans consciously regarded him as a source of wealth. Those who did probably thought him quite ignoble. Similarly industrial capitalism, giving rise in its turn to imperialism, depended not so much upon trade with primitive peoples as upon the production of raw materials and the growth of markets in 'new countries', and these were provided, to an increasing extent, not by any kind of savage, but by the European pioneer in frontier lands. Naturally this new source of wealth began to generate a legend, as his predecessor had done. From about 1820 to beyond the middle of the nineteenth century a flood of *Emigrant's Guides*, books and pamphlets poured from the London presses. Many were well-informed and truthful enough, but nearly all invested the life of the frontiersman with a more or less shining aura of romance.

Few historians or literary men would deny that there is a causal connection, however indirect and complicated, between economic changes and changes in taste.[30] Thus Mr T. S. Eliot, who proclaims that his position is both anti-romantic and anti-materialist, observes of the Romantic movement of the early nineteenth century: ' . . . any radical change in poetic form is likely to be the symptom of some very much deeper change in society and the individual.' And elsewhere he states that this, and other such changes in taste, stem from 'deeper changes' which are primarily economic in nature, 'perhaps only in the end based upon a complication in economics and machinery'. In another place still Eliot writes:

> It would be of interest to divagate from literature to politics and enquire to what extent Romanticism is incorporate in Imperialism; to enquire to what extent Romanticism has possessed the imagination of Imperialists, and to what extent it was made use of by Disraeli.[31]

If it be agreed that the Romantic temper of the nineteenth century stems, in an important measure, from the growth of industrialism and imperialism,[32] it is even more a truism that one of the strongest *motifs* of Romanticism is the desire to escape from reality to a dream world.[33] Even in William Blake's lifetime (1757-1827), to unusually sensitive spirits such as his, distant fields looked greener than the 'dark satanic mills' which were spreading over England, and so the Romantic temper came to choose subjects distant in time and space. Consciously or not, the Romantic writers and their public fled, in imagination, from the depressing problems of the 'Bleak Age', to the bucolic simplicities of the Lake District, to Xanadu or Camelot, and later on to Samarkand, Chimborazo, Cotopaxi or even Alice Springs.

Hence the rise to power in popular imagination of the noble frontiersman, around whom there clings an aura of high romance, in Turner's writings scarcely less than in those of Fenimore Cooper and his legions of successors. As mechanization and urbanization proceeded in Western Europe and along the eastern sea-board of the United States, the noble frontiersman became a kind of popular culture-hero possessed, like the Divinity, of three aspects. He provided for the Romantic imagination, first, a symbol of escape from the drabness of urban, industrial civilization, second, a symbol of compensation and justification for the evils incidental to the process of expanding imperialism, and third, a symbol for the polarization, particularly in 'new' countries like Australia and America, of patriotic nationalist sentiment. We have already noted examples of the frontiersman's first function. Practically every book on the Australian outback contrasts very favourably the 'independence', the 'freedom', and the closeness to 'Nature' of the bushman's life with the drabness and meanness of life in cities. It is the principal theme of Furphy, Lawson and Paterson, epitomized in the latter's enormously popular 'Clancy of the Overflow'.

The frontiersman's second function, which became more important with the growth of imperialism towards the end of the nineteenth century, is well exemplified in the work of Kipling and a host of lesser popular writers like G. A. Henty. The importance of juvenile literature in building the myth of the 'noble frontiersman' can scarcely be exaggerated. Writers like Ballantyne and W. H. G. Kingston in England, Edward S. Ellis in the United States, or Mary Grant Bruce in Australia have implanted in whole generations of young minds an attitude towards the frontiersman, much of which persists subconsciously in adult life, even though the conscious mind may have long disowned romantic fancies. From our viewpoint men like Kipling were concerned chiefly with popularizing the noble frontiersmen of the Empire conceived as a unit,[34] just as Paterson popularized the romantic figure of the bushman for city-dwellers in Australia. The spectacle of Kipling's soldiers and civil servants, selflessly bearing 'the white man's burden' in far places, showed beyond all doubt that empire was good for the governed.[35] It is perhaps worth noting that, in this second aspect, the frontiersman was at least as likely to be 'gentleman' as a member of the lower orders, as was only fitting for a symbol of empire. For Kipling 'the colonel's lady and Judy O'Grady were sisters under the skin', just as the squatter and the rouseabout were brothers for the conservative Paterson,[36] though not for Lawson, and only occasionally for Furphy.

This book has been principally concerned, however, with the noble frontiersman in his third aspect: as a symbol of nationalism. Most Romantic writers were, like American and Australian frontiersmen, both democratic and nationalist in outlook, and both sentiments were obviously, like the Romantic temper itself, connected with the great economic changes of the period. 'But during the nineteenth century,' wrote J. A. Hobson, 'the struggle towards nationalism . . . was a dominant factor . . . as an inner motive in the life of masses of the population.'[37] It is probable that nationalism was in part a meretricious spiritual substitute for the religious faith, which was waning so markedly, especially in the latter part of the nineteenth century.

Turner has rightly insisted that the frontier tended to promote nationalism, but it is surely not less true that the sentiment of nationalism tended to make men, including Turner, romanticize the frontier. During the last century the United States and Australia were both new countries seeking, unconsciously in part, for national self-consciousness and cohesion. Vance Palmer, in the most valuable part of his *Legend of the Nineties*, calls the process 'myth making'. He writes:

> Men cannot feel really at home in any environment until they have transformed the natural shapes around them by infusing them with myth. . . . It is the original urge towards art: it creates food without which the imagination would starve. . . . Myth-making is an important means of communication, of bringing people together, of giving isolated communities something to hold in common.

Anthropologists take it for granted that in primitive societies this activity is of crucial importance, and that it provides much of the social cement which gives them cohesion and purpose. But historians do not always seem to realize that more complex and sophisticated societies like our own have by no means entirely outgrown the process.

In this partly unconscious search for a folk-hero who should symbolize the nation, what other possible candidate for the position was there but the frontiersman? The *average* American or Australian is not the same person as the *typical* American or Australian. How could one, in the last century, apprehend a *typical* American or Australian except by reference to those traits and manners which distinguished him most sharply from his ancestors and congeners in Europe? It was commonplace for visitors to remark that the Australian coastal cities were just 'like home'. The disappointment this circumstance caused to the romantically inclined is well brought out by John Henderson:

> I confess that, notwithstanding its vast extent and population (considering that it was but fifty-six years since its foundation), I was somewhat disappointed with the appearance of Sydney. It was too like home; I had looked for something foreign and Oriental in its appearance; but I found that, excepting a few verandahs, and the lofty and stately Norfolk Island pine, it coincided much with a second or third-class town in England.

Other visitors found pleasure in the English appearance of the cities. About twenty years after Henderson's sojourn in it, Charles Allen wrote of Sydney:

> On the green plots of grass around the flat summit of the Observatory Hill boys were playing cricket, precisely as in England; and in the same rough and ready style. In fact, what with the stone houses, and the ugly unpicturesque manner in which they are built in the crooked narrow streets, you might easily fancy yourself in England.

The relatively domesticated landscape of the coastal plains near the capitals was also felt to be comparatively home-like. In 1883 a French visitor wrote:

> Après avoir atteint le point le plus élevé des montagnes que la voie ferrée est obligée de traverser entre Goulburn et Sydney, nous descendions rapidement dans la plaine. Nous entrions au milieu d'un pays coupé de fermes, de prairies et de champs en pleine culture

qui nous rappelait l'Europe. La végétation de cette partie du pays est, du reste, toute différente de celle de la contrée située de l'autre versant de la montagne; les arbres sont moins hauts, plus touffus et plus verts.[38]

And even as early as the 1840's Mundy felt that the Illawarra landscape 'more than anywhere else in this country—might recal [sic] England'.

But all agreed that the typical (i.e. most un-English) Australia, and the typical Australians, were to be found on the western plains beyond the mountains. One man observed in 1895:

Townspeople in Australia do not differ very much from their congenors [sic] at home, but the inland life and climate do certainly tend to produce a peculiar type, distinct altogether from their northern kinsmen, and this type often indicates [sic] great capacity of a certain kind.[39]

Turner has explained why the frontiersman was necessarily, in this sense, the typical representative of his countrymen, but he does not seem to have been at all conscious of the underlying forces which impelled him to see the frontiersman in this light. We have seen that he was not alone in this. It is significant that, like Paterson who did so much to popularize the idea of the noble frontiersman in Australia, he was a fervent admirer of Kipling, the apostle of the imperial frontiersman. He was a friend and admirer, not only of the democratic (with a small 'd') Woodrow Wilson, but also of Theodore Roosevelt,[40] the father of American imperialism. Roosevelt himself had written in 1889 *The Winning of the West*, a history which anticipated in some respects Turner's ideas on the importance of the frontier.[41] All four men, Paterson, Kipling, Roosevelt, and Turner, believed strongly in another romantic myth which, in Australia also, was intimately associated with the cult of the noble frontiersman: the myth of the innate superiority of European, and especially Northern European, peoples:

While the Germans, according to Turner, had given the state added solidity and strength and fostered its best ideals, the contribution of South Italians 'to American racial characteristics' he considered 'of doubtful value'. . . . Even less desirable, he thought, were the southern and eastern European Jews, the very opposite of the frontier type which Turner so much admired—'the world over, a city people. . . . The Jew is not ready to depart from the synagogue and the market place'.[42]

In Australia this particular part of our 'frontier' heritage has fortunately suffered some depreciation since World War II.

In a review, published in 1889, of Theodore Roosevelt's book, Turner wrote:

American history needs a connected and unified account of the progress of civilization across the continent. *Aside from the scientific importance of such a work, it would contribute to awakening a real national self-consciousness and patriotism.*[43]

The work of Francis Adams helps to show that Turner was not only an historian, but also a man of his own day, moved by the complex of sentiments outlined above: romanticism and nationalism stemming ultimately from the industrial revolution. He helped to explain his times, but his times help to explain him.

Adams, poet, novelist, journalist and critic, was a gifted young Englishman who spent only about five years, from 1884 to 1889, in Australia. In 1893, at the age of thirty-one, he shot himself when at the last stage of tuberculosis. His reaction to Australian city-dwellers was very much that of Matthew Arnold to the contemporary middle-class culture of Great Britain. Adams found Australian philistinism even more contemptible since, as he saw it, it did not even stand on its own clay feet, but was a shoddy copy of its vulgar British original. About Australian bushmen, however, he wrote quite differently:

The gulf between colony and colony is small and traversable compared to that great fixture that lies between the people of the Slope and of the Interior. Where the marine rainfall flags out and is lost, a new climate, and in a certain sense, a new race begin to unfold themselves. The 'fancy' stations on this side of The Great Dividing Range produce something just different enough from anything in England to make the Englishman accept the *dictum* of the Australian cockney that this is at last the typical example of 'the bush life'. People in the country districts of Illinois and Kentucky doubtless talk in the same way of 'the West'. But they are mistaken. It is not one hundred, but three and four and five hundred miles that you must go back from the sea if you would find yourself face to face with the one powerful and unique national type yet produced in the new land. . . .

Frankly I find not only all that is genuinely characteristic in Australia and the Australians springing from this heart of the land but also all that is noblest, kindliest and best. . . .

The Anglo-Saxon has perished or is absorbed in the Interior much more rapidly than on the sea-slope and in the towns. . . .

It should be recognised more fully than it is that the successful issue of the American Secession War was due to the Western States. . . . The West was the heart of the country, the genuine America, and the Interior is the heart of the genuine Australia, and, if needs be, will do as much for the nation and the race.[44]

Adams never visited America, and the above passages were published about a year before Turner delivered his celebrated paper on 'The Significance of the Frontier', on 12 July 1893. It is therefore impossible that Adams was directly inspired by Turner and it seems almost equally unlikely that Turner owed anything to Adams. Yet the basic ideas and the spirit of their writing are extraordinarily alike. Both men wrote towards the close of an historical epoch when it was possible to see something of the pattern of what had been taking place but not, perhaps, to see it from outside. Both shared fully in the assumptions of their time. They believed in the innately 'natural' virtue of nationalism, in the inevitability of 'progress',[45] and in the self-evident superiority of white men and their civilization. Since the Napoleonic Wars there had been no international clashes of comparable scope, and innumerable little wars with ignoble savages and other 'lesser breeds without the law' had convincingly demonstrated the rightness of current beliefs. Since then we have had more and more reason to question some of the shibboleths of the age which created the 'noble frontiersman' and found him good.

Native and imported critics of our literature and life now assert repeatedly that the bush tradition exerts a stultifying influence on both. At the same time other voices, more numerous but usually more inarticulate, defend the legend, most often by simply sailing on in happy ignorance of the advice proffered from the bridge.

We should allow some merit to the volunteer pilots. It is true that the bushman carries in his cultural swag delusions of racial grandeur as well as mateship, but every tradition has good and bad aspects.

Perhaps most Australians would agree that the most discreditable and dangerous component of the legend is its 'racism'. We have seen, however, that this feature was also the most recently acquired, and already the events of the last war, no less than the following wave of immigration, have gone far to slough it off. The older elements of the tradition have more to be said for them. The welfare state seems to have come to stay whether we approve or not. Our collectivist, egalitarian bias suits it admirably; indeed, may have contributed something appreciable to its genesis. And our profound suspicion of authority and pretentiousness provides some safeguard against the main danger of our time: dictatorship from either the right or the left. In spite of our levelling tendencies Sir John Monash and Sir Howard Florey, for instance, managed to rise above the common ruck as far as, or even farther than, say, Jimmy Carruthers and Sir Donald Bradman. But it is possibly harder to imagine a Hitler, a Stalin or even a Péron flourishing here than in any other country on earth, including England itself.

We have seen that the Australian tradition is as old as our history. We have seen that it perpetuates as ideals the qualities which were characteristic of, and esteemed by, those first and worst, or best, Australians who, at the advancing edge of settlement, did rather more than their share to make our country what it is. Most of us, even if we would, could not disown its influence completely. The few who labour earnestly to do so succeed chiefly in strengthening it by providing, all unwittingly, a patently bogus latter-day substitute for the pedigreed 'new-chum swells' and remittance men of the last century.

It is generally agreed that without a distinctive national tradition a people lacks cohesion, balance and confidence. It is usually assumed that in a young country like ours, inherited attitudes exert less influence than in an old one. The truth may be that, because of its relative youth, our tradition is at once too dominating and too rigid, that we tend compulsively to worship it as, so to speak, a fair though sacred cow. But nothing could be more thoroughly within the tradition than to 'give it a go'—to venture boldly on new courses of action, and so modify, and even create, traditions as the anonymous bushmen and, later, the men of the 'nineties did. Today's task might well be to develop those features of the Australian legend which still seem valid in modern conditions.

CHAPTER IX

1 F. J. Turner, *Early Writings of*, etc., ed. E. E. Edwards, University of Wisconsin 1938, p. 83.

2 *The Frontier in American History*, New York 1948 ed., p. 4.

3 Quoted Desmond Byrne, *Australian Writers*, London 1896, p. 197.

4 For trenchant criticisms of Turner's views see G. R. Taylor (ed.), *The Turner Thesis*, etc., Boston 1949.

5 'Frontier and Section', *Historical Studies: Australia and New Zealand*, May 1952, p. 14.

6 R. E. Riegel, *America Moves West*, New York 1951, p. 71.

7 F. Alexander, *Moving Frontiers*, Melbourne 1947, p. 30 ff.; and A. G. L. Shaw, *The Story of Australia*, London 1955, pp. 190-5.

8 *Legend of the Nineties*, Melbourne 1954, p. 142.

9 *The Frontier in American History*, pp. 30, 32.

10 Chief exceptions were the westward moving frontier of big plantations in the South, and the comparatively short-lived 'open range' frontier of the Great Plains from about 1870 to 1885. (See W. P. Webb, *The Great Plains*, Oxford 1931, pp. 205-7.)

11 R. E. Riegel, *op. cit.*, pp. 54-5, 203, 414, 427.

12 *op. cit.*, p. 147.

13 N. D. Harper, 'Turner the Historian: "Hypothesis or Process?" ', *University of Kansas City Review*, Autumn 1951, pp. 82-3.

14 cp. K. Buckley, 'Gipps and the Graziers of New South Wales, 1841-46', *Historical Studies: Australia and New Zealand*, May 1955, especially pp. 406-8.

15 cp. 'An Emigrant Mechanic' (A. Harris), *Settlers and Convicts*, ed. C. M. H. Clark, Melbourne 1953 (first published 1847), p. 224 ff.; 'Tom Collins' (Joseph Furphy), *Rigby's Romance*, Sydney 1946, p. 103 and *passim*; and Alan Marshall, *I Can Jump Puddles*, Melbourne 1955, p. 180.

16 *op. cit.*, p. 243.

17 Carter Goodrich, 'The Australian and American Labor Movements', *The Economic Record*, November 1928, pp. 206-7; and cp. H. G. Adam, *An Australian Looks at America*, etc., Sydney 1927; and P. Cunningham, *Two Years in New South Wales*, etc., 2 vols., London 1827, vol. 1, pp. 255-61.

18 A. O. Lovejoy and G. Boas, *Documentary History of Primitivism*, etc., Baltimore 1935, ch. 11 and pp. 364-7; H. N. Fairchild, *The Noble Savage*, etc., Columbia University 1928, p. 5 ff.

19 The Robin Hood ballads, in some important ways, obviously constitute an exception to the statement.

20 But see Mrs Aphra Behn, *Oroonoko*, London 1694. The titular hero of this novel, which ante-dates *Robinson Crusoe* by twenty-five years, has a much better claim than Man Friday to be the progenitor of the 'noble savage' of the eighteenth century.

21 Quoted F. J. Turner, *The Frontier in American History*, pp. 63-4.

22 H. N. Fairchild, *op. cit.*, p. 498.

23 Bernard Smith, 'European Vision and the South Pacific', *Journal of the Warburg and Courtauld Institutes*, vol. 13, p. 90 and *passim*; and cp. the characterization of Billy Waters, a negro thief in London, in W. T. Moncrieff, *Tom and Jerry: or Life in London*, etc., London 1826, pp. 121-3, and several songs in *Wiseheart's Merry Songster*, etc., and *Wiseheart's New Comic Songster*, etc., Dublin 1832.

24 Quoted R. H. Gabriel, *The Course of American Democratic Thought*, New York 1940, pp. 20-1.

25 George Keate, *An Account of the Pelew Islands*, etc., London 1789, pp. 261-2; and cp. the treatment of King Kamehameha of Hawaii in Archibald Campbell, *A Voyage Round the World*, etc., Edinburgh 1816, p. 126 ff.

26 Basil Willey, *The Eighteenth Century Background*, etc., London 1949, p. 14; and F. Burney, *Early Diary of, 1768-1778*, etc., ed. A. R. Ellis, 2 vols., London 1907, vol. I, pp. 331-7.

27 Clement Hodgkinson, *Australia from Port Macquarie to Moreton Bay*, etc., London 1845, pp. 144-5.

28 cp. Bernard Smith, *European Vision and the South Pacific 1768-1850*, London 1960.

29 *The Frontier in American History*, p. 37.

30 Arnold Hauser, *The Social History of Art*, 2 vols., London 1951, vol. 2, p. 695, and *passim*; and G. V. Plekhanov, *Art and Social Life*, London 1953 ed., *passim*.

31 T. S. Eliot, *The Use of Poetry and the Use of Criticism*, London 1946, p. 75; *Elizabethan Essays*, London 1934, pp. 97-8; *Selected Essays*, London 1949, p. 16; *The Sacred Wood*, London 1934, p. 32.

32 cp. Oswald Spengler, *The Decline of the West*, 2 vols., London 1928, vol. 2, p. 108: 'The Essence of Alexandrism and of our Romanticism is something which belongs to all urban men without distinction. Romanticism marks the beginning of that which Goethe, with his wide vision, called world-literature—the literature of the leading world-city.'

33 cp. T. S. Eliot, *Selected Essays*, p. 301; and William Empsom, *Seven Types of Ambiguity*, etc., London 1930, pp. 26-7.

34 Obviously there are other, and more permanently important, elements in Kipling's work, though they do not concern us here.

35 cp. J. A. Hobson, *Imperialism*, London 1948, ed., pt. 2, ch. 3.

36 Paterson, who served in the Boer War as a newspaper correspondent, was a great admirer of Kipling whom he met in England, and whose verse style strongly influenced Paterson's. (See A. B. Paterson, *Happy Despatches*, Sydney 1934, pp. v, 129-39.)

37 *Imperialism*, p. 3.

38 E. Marin la Meslée, *L'Australie Nouvelle*, Paris 1883, p. 76; and cp. James Backhouse, *A Narrative of a Visit to the Australian Colonies*, London 1843, pp. 447-9; and G. C. Mundy, *Our Antipodes*, etc., 3rd ed., London 1855, p. 434; and P. Clarke, *The 'New Chum' in Australia*, etc., London 1886, p. 26.

39 George Ranken (ed.), *Windabyne, a Record of By-gone Times in Australia*, etc., London 1895, pp. 256-7.

40 F. J. Turner, *Early Writings of*, etc., pp. 20-7, 36; and see *Letters of Theodore Roosevelt*, ed. E. E. Morison, 8 vols., Harvard 1951. Roosevelt carried on a warm personal correspondence with both Turner and Kipling.

41 F. J. Turner, *Early Writings of, loc. cit.*; and cp. ' "Now look," said Mark Hanna, prominent Republican Party organizer, when Roosevelt succeeded McKinley in September 1896, "that damned cowboy is President of the United States." ' (R. V. Harlow, *The United States*, etc., New York 1949, p. 555.)

42 E. N. Saveth, *American Historians and European Immigrants 1875-1925*, University of Columbia 1948, p. 129.

43 F. J. Turner, *Early Writings of*, p. 23 (my italics).

44 Francis Adams, *The Australians: A Social Sketch*, London 1893, pp. 144, 154, 166, 171.

45 cp. particularly, F. J. Turner, *The Significance of Sections in American History*, ed. Max Farrand, New York 1950, ch. 8.

Bibliography

No attempt has been made to give an exhaustive bibliography, which would be very much longer than the present one. For the most part, only those books and documents to which there is a direct reference in the text and footnotes have been included.

The sources have been divided as follows:

> I. *Contemporary Sources*
>> (a) Official and Semi-official Documents.
>> (b) Newspapers and Journals.
>> (c) Manuscript Material.
>> (d) Books and Pamphlets.
>
> II. *Reference and Interpretative Works*
>> (a) Articles, Theses, etc.
>> (b) Books.
>
> III. *Sources of, and Works on, Ballads*

I (a)

OFFICIAL AND SEMI-OFFICIAL DOCUMENTS

Archer, W. H. (ed.), *Statistical Register of Victoria*, etc., Melbourne, 1854.

Bigge, J. T., *Report of the Commissioner of Inquiry into the State of the Colony of New South Wales*, London, 1822.
Report, etc., on Agriculture and Trade in N.S.W., London, 1823.

Census Returns, *Votes and Proceedings, Leg. Council of N.S.W., 1841, 1851, 1861, 1871.*
V. & P. Leg. Council, Victoria, 1851, 1861, 1871.
V. & P. Leg. Council, Queensland, 1861.
Commonwealth Census, 1947.

Clark, C. M. H., *Select Documents in Australian History 1788-1850*, Sydney, 1950.
Select Documents in Australian History 1851-1900, Sydney, 1955.

Coghlan, T. A., *General Report on the Eleventh Census of N.S.W.*, Sydney, 1894.

Colonial Secretary, N.S.W., Inward Letters, Newcastle 1823, Mitchell Library Mss.; Bundles 19-21.

Government Gazette, N.S.W., 1834-1844, 1860-1870. Victoria, 1860-1870.

Gold Fields Commission, 'Report and Minutes of Evidence of the Commission Appointed to Enquire into the Gold Fields of Victoria, etc.', 29 March 1855.

Hutchinson, F. (ed.), *New South Wales: the 'Mother Colony' of the Australias*, Sydney, 1896; Published by Authority, N.S.W. Govt.

Immigration C'tee, 'Report of Select Committee on Immigration', V. & P. *Leg. Council, N.S.W., 1838.*

Parliamentary Debates, *Commonwealth Aust., 1945.*

Parliamentary Papers, V. & P., *Leg. Assembly, N.S.W., 1870-1875.*

Police, 'Report from the Select Committee on Police', V. & P., *Leg. Council, Victoria, 1852-1853.*

South Australian Company, *First Report of*, London, 1837.

Statistical Register, New South Wales, 1871, 1891.

Statutes of N.S.W., 1830-1885.

Transportation, 'House of Commons, Report of Select Committee on Transportation, 1812', *P.P., H.C.*, 1812, vol. 2.
   'House of Commons, Report of Select Committee on Transportation, 1837', *P.P., H.C.*, 1837, vol. 19.
   'House of Commons, Report of Select Committee on Transportation' 1837-38, *P.P., H.C.*, 1837-8, vol. 22.

Watson, F., *Historical Records of Australia*, Series I, vols. 1-26.

I (b)

NEWSPAPERS AND JOURNALS

Advertiser, Adelaide, 1953-1954.

Age, Melbourne, 1905, 1951-1956.

Albury Banner, Albury.

Argus, Melbourne, 1856-1860, 1953-1955.

Atlas, Sydney, 1844-1848.

Bulletin, Sydney, 1880-1956.

Canberra Times, Canberra, 1953-1956.

Colonist, Sydney, 1838.

Cootamundra Herald, Cootamundra, 1906-1913.

Currency Lad, Sydney, 1832-1833.

Daily Mirror, Sydney, 1943-1956.

Empire, Sydney, 1853, 1874.

English Journal of Education, London, 1851 (vol. 9).

Illustrated Sydney News and N.S.W. Agriculturist and Grazier, Sydney, 1874.

Lone Hand, Sydney, 1907-1914.

Maitland Mercury and Hunter River General Advertiser, Maitland, 1843 1844.

Moore's Almanack, Sydney, 1886.

N.S.W. Calendar and General Post Office Directory, Sydney, 1834.

Ovens and Murray River Advertiser, Beechworth, 1868-1870.

Port Augusta Dispatch, Port Augusta, 1900-1905.

Portland Mirror, Portland, 1885.

Punch, London.

(Melbourne) *Punch*, Melbourne, 1855-1870.

Queenslander, Brisbane, 1902.

Stockwhip (later *Stockwhip and Satirist*, then *Satirist*), Sydney, 1875-1876.

Sun-Herald, Sydney, 1955-1956.

Sydney Gazette, Sydney, 1826-1840.

Sydney Herald, Sydney, 1834-1840.

Sydney Morning Herald, Sydney, 1844, 1871-1875, 1891, 1939-1956.

Voice, Sydney, 1952-1956.

Weekly Times, Melbourne, 1928.

Worker, Brisbane.

I (c)

MANUSCRIPT MATERIAL

Black, Niel, Papers, Public Library, Victoria.

Brady, E. J., Letters to writer.

Butchart, James, Letter, 10 December 1843.

Hobler, George, Diary 1827-1871, Mitchell Library.

Hogan, Hogan Papers, 1830-1836, M.L.

Rayment, William, Diary 1852-1860, P.L.V.

Shum, A. H., Diary and Letter Book, P.L.V.

Snell, Edward, The Life and Adventures of, from 1849 to 1859, P.L.V.

I (d)

BOOKS AND PAMPHLETS

Adam, H. G., *An Australian Looks at America: Are Wages Really Higher?*, Sydney, 1927.

Adams, Francis, *The Australians: A Social Sketch*, London, 1893.

Angas, George French, *Savage Life and Scenes in Australia and New Zealand*, etc., 2 vols., London, 1847.

'Anon.' (Mrs J. S. Calvert), *Cowanda, the Veteran's Grant: an Australian Story*, Sydney, 1859.

Backhouse, James, *A Narrative of a Visit to the Australian Colonies*, London, 1843.

Balfour, J. O., *A Sketch of New South Wales*, London, 1845.

Bartley, Nehemiah, *Australian Pioneers and Reminiscences*, Brisbane, 1896.

Barton, Robert D., *Reminiscences of an Australian Pioneer*, Sydney, 1917.

Bean, C. E. W., *The Dreadnought of the Darling*, London, 1911.
On the Wool Track, Sydney, 1945.

Bedford, Randolph, *Naught to Thirty Three*, Sydney, n.d.

Behn, Mrs Aphra, *Oroonoko*, London, 1694.

Bennett, George, *Wanderings in New South Wales*, etc., 2 vols., London, 1834.

'Boldrewood, Rolf' (T. A. Browne), *Robbery Under Arms*, London, 1947.
The Squatter's Dream, London, 1890.

Bonwick, James, *Notes of a Gold Digger and Gold Digger's Guide* (ed. E. E. Prescott), Melbourne, 1942.

Braim, Rev. T. H., *A History of New South Wales*, etc., London, 1846.

Brennan, Martin, *Reminiscences of the Gold Fields and Elsewhere in N.S.W., covering a period of forty-eight years' service as an Officer of Police*, Sydney, 1907.

Brereton, J. Le Gay, *Knocking Around*, Sydney, 1930.

Brodribb, W. A., *Recollections of an Australian Squatter or Leaves from My Journal since 1835*, Sydney, 1883.

Browne, C. Wade, *Overlanding in Australia*, Melbourne, 1868.

Buley, E. C., *Australian Life in Town and Country*, London, 1905.

Burney, Frances, *Early Diary of, 1768-1778*, etc. (ed. A. R. Ellis), 2 vols., London, 1907.

Burton, W. W., *The State of Religion and Education in New South Wales*, London, 1840.

'A Bushman' (J. Sidney), *A Voice from the Far Interior of Australia*, London, 1847.

Byrne, J. C., *Twelve Years' Wanderings in the British Colonies from 1835 to 1847*, 2 vols., London, 1848.

Caldwell, Robert, *The Gold Era of Victoria*, etc., London, 1855.

Cambridge, Ada, *Thirty Years in Australia*, London, 1903.

Campbell, Archibald, *A Voyage round the World from 1806 to 1812*, etc., Edinburgh, 1816.

Castella, H. De, *Les Squatters Australiens*, Paris, 1861.

Clacy, Mrs Chas, *A Lady's Visit to the Gold Diggings of Australia in 1852-53*, etc., London, 1853.

Clarke, Marcus, *The Term of His Natural Life*, London, 1925 edn.

Clarke, Percy, *The 'New Chum' in Australia: or, the Scenery, Life, and Manners of Australians in Town and Country*, London, 1886.

'A Clergyman Thirteen Years Resident in the Interior of N.S.W.' (Rev. John Morison), *Australia As It Is: or, Facts and Features, Sketches and Incidents of Australian Life*, etc., London, 1867.

Collins, David, *Account of the English Colony in New South Wales*, etc., London, 1798.

'Tom Collins' (Joseph Furphy), *Rigby's Romance*, Sydney, 1946.
Such Is Life, Sydney, 1948.

Corbyn, C. A., *Sydney Revels of Bacchus, Cupid and Momus*, etc., Sydney, 1854.

Cox, William, *Narrative of the Proceedings of*, etc. (Nat. Lib. Pamphlets, vol. I, No. 20).

Craig, W., *My Adventures on the Australian Goldfields*, London, 1903.

Croll, R. H. (ed.), *Smike to Bulldog: Letters from Sir Arthur Streeton to Tom Roberts*, Sydney, 1946.
Tom Roberts, Father of Australian Landscape Painting, Melbourne, 1935.

Crombie, Andrew, *After Sixty Years or Recollections of an Australian Bushman*, Brisbane, 1927.

Cunningham, P., *Two Years in New South Wales: a Series of Letters, comprising Sketches of the Actual State of Society in That Colony*, etc., 2 vols., London, 1827.

Curr, Edward, *An Account of the Colony of Van Diemen's Land*, etc., London, 1824.

Curr, E. M., *Recollections of Squatting in Victoria Then Called the Port Phillip District (from 1841 to 1851)*, Melbourne, 1883.

Davidson, G. F., *Trade and Travel in the Far East*, etc., London, 1846.

De Beaumont, George, *Ireland, Social, Political and Religious*, 2 vols., London, 1839.

Demarr, James, *Adventures in Australia Fifty Years Ago*, etc., *during the Years 1839-1844*, London, 1893.

Egan, Pierce, *Tom & Jerry; Life in London; or the Day & Night Scenes of Jerry Hawthorn Esquire and His Elegant Friend Corinthian Tom in their Rambles and Sprees through the Metropolis*, London, 1869 edn. (1st pub. 1821).

'An Eight Years' Resident' (Ebenezer Thorne), *The Queen of the Colonies; or, Queensland As I Knew It*, London, 1876.

Eldershaw, F., *Australia As It Really Is, in Its Life, Scenery, and Adventure*, etc., London, 1854.

Emerson, E. S. ('Milky White'), *A Shanty Entertainment*, Melbourne, n.d. (1904).

Ferguson, Dugald, *Vicissitudes of Bush Life in Australia and New Zealand*, London, 1891.

Flanagan, R., *History of New South Wales*, etc., 2 vols., London, 1862.

Fowler, Frank, *Southern Lights and Shadows*, etc., London, 1859.

Gane, D. M., *New South Wales and Victoria in 1885*, London, 1886.

'Garryowen' (Edmund Finn), *Chronicles of Early Melbourne 1835 to 1852, Historical, Anecdotal, and Personal*, 2 vols., Melbourne, 1888.

'A Gentleman Just Returned from the Settlement', *An Account of the English Colony at Botany Bay*, etc., London, 1808.

Gerstaecker, F., *Narrative of a Journey Round the World*, etc., 3 vols., London, 1853.

Gordon, P. R., *Fencing As a Means of Improving Our Pasture Lands*, Sydney, 1867.

Graham, Rev. John (ed.), *Lawrence Struilby: or Observations and Experiences during Twenty-Five Years of Bush Life in Australia*, London, 1863.

Griffith, Charles, *Present State and Prospects of the Port Phillip District of New South Wales*, Dublin, 1845.

Hamilton, J. C., *Pioneering Days in Early Victoria*, Melbourne, n.d. (1913).

Harney, W. E., *North of 23°: Ramblings in Northern Australia*, Sydney, n.d. (1949).

Taboo, Sydney, 1943.

'An Emigrant Mechanic' (Alexander Harris), *The Emigrant Family: or, The Story of an Australian Settler*, 3 vols., London, 1849.

A Guide to Port Stephens, etc., London, 1849.

Settlers and Convicts (ed. C. M. H. Clark), Melbourne, 1953 (1st pub. 1847).

A Converted Atheist's Testimony to the Truth of Christianity, London, 1852.

Harris, W. K., *Outback in Australia: or, Three Australian Overlanders*, etc., Newcastle (N.S.W.), 1913.

Haygarth, H. W., *Recollections of Bush Life in Australia during a Residence of Eight Years in the Interior*, London, 1848.

Henderson, John, *Excursions and Adventures in New South Wales; with a Picture of Squatting Life in the Bush*, etc., 2 vols., London, 1851.

Henning, Rachel, *Letters of* (Introduction D. Adams), Sydney, 1952.

Henty, R., *Australiana or My Early Life*, London, 1886.

Heywood, B. A., *A Vacation Tour to the Antipodes*, etc., London, 1863.

Hodgkinson, Clement, *Australia from Port Macquarie to Moreton Bay*, etc., London, 1845.

Holt, Joseph, *Memoirs of* (T. C. Croker, ed.), 2 vols., London, 1838.

Hood, John, *Australia and the East*, etc., London, 1843.

Howitt, Richard, *Impressions of Australia Felix*, etc., London, 1845.

Howitt, William, *Land, Labour and Gold: or, Two Years in Victoria*, etc., 2 vols., London, 1855.

Hungerford, Tom, *The Ridge and the River*, Sydney, 1952.

Riverslake, Sydney, 1953.

Sowers of the Wind, 1954.

(ed.) *Australian Signpost*, Melbourne, 1956.

Inglis, James, *Our Australian Cousins*, London, 1880.

'Ironbark' (G. H. Gibson), *Ironbark Chips and Stockwhip Cracks*, Sydney, 1893.
Ironbark Splinters, 1912.
Southerly Busters, 1878.

Jessop, W. R. G., *Flindersland and Sturtland: or, the Inside and Outside of Australia*, 2 vols., London, 1862.

Johnson, J. Pitts, *Plain Truths Told by a Traveller Regarding Our Various Settlements in Australia and New Zealand*, etc., London, 1840.

Jones, D. G. (?), *Bushmen, Publicans and Politics*, Deniliquin, 1869.

Joyce, Alfred, *A Homestead History* (ed. G. F. James), Melbourne, 1949 (2nd edn.).

Keate, George, *An Account of the Pelew Islands*, etc., *in 1783*, etc., London, 1789.

Kelly, William, *Life in Victoria, or Victoria in 1853, and Victoria in 1858*, etc., 2 vols., London, 1859.

Kirby, James, 'of Minyip, etc.', *Old Times in the Bush of Australia: Trials and Experiences of Bush Life in Victoria, during the Forties*, Melbourne, n.d. (1895?).

Knight, J. J., *In the Early Days*, etc., Brisbane, 1895.

Lambert, Eric, *The Twenty Thousand Thieves*, London, 1952.
The Veterans, London, 1954.

La Meslée, E. Marin, *L'Australie Nouvelle*, Paris, 1883.

Lancelott, F., *Australia As It Is: Its Settlements, Farms, and Gold Fields*, 2 vols., London, 1852.

Landor, E. W., *The Bushman: or, Life in a New Country*, London, 1847.

Lang, J. D., *Emigration: Considered Chiefly in Reference to*, etc., Sydney, 1833.
Freedom and Independence for the Golden Lands of Australia, etc., Sydney, 1857 (2nd edn.).
Historical and Statistical Account of New South Wales, etc., 2 vols., London, 1834.
Transportation and Colonization; or, etc., London, 1837.

Lawson, Henry, *Poetical Works of*, Sydney, 1947 edn.
Prose Works of, 2 vols., Sydney, 1935.
While the Billy Boils, Sydney, 1896.

Lloyd, G. T., *Thirty-Three Years in Tasmania and Victoria*, etc., London, 1862.

Lumholtz, Carl, *Among Cannibals, an Account of Four Years' Travels in Australia*, etc., London, 1890.

Major, Thomas, *Leaves from a Squatter's Notebook*, London, 1900.

Manifold, John, *Selected Verse*, New York, 1946.

Marjoribanks, Alexander, *Travels in New South Wales*, etc., London, 1847.

Marshall, Alan, *I Can Jump Puddles*, Melbourne, 1955.

Marshall, J., *Battling for Gold, or Stirring Incidents of Goldfields Life in West Australia*, Melbourne, 1903.

Melville, Henry, *The Present State of Australia*, etc., London, 1851.

Meredith, Mrs Chas, *Notes and Sketches of New South Wales, During a Residence in that Colony from 1839 to 1844*, London, 1861 edn.

Moore, G. F., *Diary of Ten Years' Eventful Life of an Early Settler in Western Australia*, etc., London, 1884.

Moore, T. Inglis (ed.), *Australia Writes*, Melbourne, 1953.

Morris, E. E., *A Memoir of George Higinbotham*, etc., London, 1895.

Mudie, James, *The Felonry of New South Wales*, etc., London, 1837.

Mundy, G. C., *Our Antipodes; or Residence and Rambles in the Australasian Colonies with a Glimpse of the Goldfields*, London, 1855 (3rd edn.).

Myers, Captain John, *The Life, Voyages and Travels of*, etc., London, 1817.

Macalister, Charles, *Old Pioneering Days in the Sunny South*, Goulburn, 1907.

'Macarthur, James' (Edwards, Edward), *New South Wales: Its Present State and Future Prospects*, etc., London, 1837.

McCombie, T., *History of the Colony of Victoria from Its Settlement to the Death of Sir Charles Hotham*, London, 1858.

Mackaness, G. (ed.), *The Correspondence of John Cotton, Victorian Pioneer, 1842-49*, Sydney, 1953.

Mackay, George, *A History of Bendigo*, Melbourne, 1891.

Mackenzie, Rev. D., *The Emigrant's Guide: or Ten Years' Experience in New South Wales*, London, 1845.

Macqueen, T. Potter, *Australia As She Is and As She May Be*, London, 1840.

Nicols, Arthur, *Wild Life and Adventure in the Australian Bush: Four Years' Personal Experience*, London, 1887.

O'Connell, Jas F., *A Residence of Eleven Years in New Holland and the Caroline Islands* (ed. 'by H.H.W. from his verbal narration'), Boston, 1836.

Paterson, A. B., *Happy Despatches*, Sydney, 1934.

Pearce, Sir G. F., *Carpenter to Cabinet: Thirty Seven Years of Parliament*, London, 1951.

Peirce, A. B., *Knocking About: being Some Adventures of Augustus Baker Peirce in Australia*; ed. Mrs A. T. Leatherbee, Yale, 1924.

Petrie, Tom, *Tom Petrie's Reminiscences of Early Queensland Dating from 1837, Recorded by his Daughter*, Brisbane and Sydney, 1932 edn. (1st pub. 1904).

Polehampton, Rev. A., *Kangaroo Land*, London, 1862.

Rafaello, Carboni, *The Eureka Stockade*, etc. (ed. H. V. Evatt), Sydney, 1942.

Ranken, George (ed.), *Windabyne, a Record of By-gone Times in Australia, Related by Reginald Crawford*, etc., *in 1880*, London, 1895.

Read, C. Rudston, *What I Heard, Saw, and Did at the Australian Goldfields*, London, 1853.

'A Resident', *Girl Life in Australia: A Description of Colonial Life*, Liverpool, 1876.

'A Resident', *Social Life and Manners in Australia: Being the Notes of Eight Years' Experience*, London, 1861.

Roosevelt, Theodore, *Letters of* (ed. E. E. Morison), 8 vols, Harvard, 1951.

Rowland, Percy F., *The New Nation*, London, 1903.

'Rudd, Steele' (A. H. Davis), *On Our Selection*, Sydney, 1954 edn. (1st pub. 1899).

Russell, H. S., *The Genesis of Queensland*, etc., Sydney, 1888.

Sadleir, J., *Recollections of a Victorian Police Officer*, Melbourne, 1913.

Satgé, Oscar De, *Pages from the Journal of a Queensland Squatter*, London, 1901.

Scott, G. Firth, *Colonial Born*, London, 1900.

'Seagram Giles' (Driscoll, J. H.), *Bushmen All: A Romance of the Never Never*, Melbourne, 1908.

Sherer, J. (ed.), *The Gold Finder of Australia*, etc., London, 1853.

Sidney, Samuel, *Gallops and Gossips in the Bush of Australia*, London, 1854. *The Three Colonies of Australia*, etc., London, 1852.

Spence, W. G., *Australia's Awakening: Thirty Years in the Life of an Australian Agitator*, Sydney, 1909.

Stephens, John, *A Voice from Australia*, etc., London, 1848.

Stirling, A. W., *The Never Never Land: A Ride in North Queensland*, London, 1884 (2nd edn.).

Stivens, Dal, *Ironbark Bill*, Sydney, 1955.

Stoney, H. Butler, *Victoria: with a Description of Its Principal Cities*, etc., London, 1856.

Streeton, Charles. *Memoirs of a Chequered Life*, 3 vols., London, 1862.

Therry, R., *Reminiscences of Thirty Years' Residence in New South Wales and Victoria*, London, 1863.

The Times Special Correspondent, *Letters from Queensland*, London, 1893.

Townsend, J. P., *Rambles and Observations in New South Wales*, etc., London, 1849.

Trollope, Anthony, *Australia and New Zealand*, Melbourne, 1876 edn.

Tucker, James (?), *Adventures of Ralph Rashleigh* (ed. Colin Roderick, M.A., Ph.D.), Sydney, 1952.

Turnbull, John, *Voyage Round the World in the Years 1800, 1801, 1802, 1803 and 1804*, 3 vols., London, 1805.

Twopeny, R. E. N., *Town Life in Australia*, London, 1883.

Ullathorne, W., *The Catholic Mission to Australasia*, Liverpool, 1837 (2nd edn.).

'A University Man' (George Carrington), *Colonial Adventures and Experiences*, London, 1871.

Unwin, Mrs Cobden, *The Hungry Forties, Life Under the Bread Tax: Descriptive Letters and Other Testimonies from Contemporary Witnesses*, London, 1904.

(Walker, Thomas), *A Month in the Bush of Australia*, etc., London, 1838.

'Warung, Price', (Astley, William), *Tales of the Old Regime, and the Bullet of the Fated Ten*, Melbourne, 1897.

Wathen, G. H., *The Golden Colony; or Victoria in 1854*, etc., London, 1855.

(Waugh, David L.), *Three Years' Practical Experience of a Settler in New South Wales*, Edinburgh, 1838 (4th edn.).

Wentworth, W. C., *Australasia, A Poem Written for the Chancellor's Medal at the Cambridge Commencement, July 1823*, London, 1823.

　A Statistical, Historical and Political Description of New South Wales, etc., London, 1819.

Westgarth, William, *Victoria and the Australian Gold Mines in 1857*, London, 1857.

　Victoria, late Australia Felix, or Port Phillip District of New South Wales; Being an Historical and Descriptive Account, etc., Edinburgh, 1853.

'Whaks Li Kell' (Daniel Healey), *The Cornstalk: His Habits and Habitat*, Sydney, 1894 (1st pub. 1893).

Wilson, T. B., *Narrative of a Voyage Round the World*, etc., London, 1835.

Withers, W. B., *History of Ballarat*, Ballarat, 1887 (2nd edn.).

Wood, Thomas, *Cobbers*, London, 1938.

Woolley, John, *Schools of Art and Colonial Nationality: A Lecture Delivered at the Wollongong School of Arts, May 28th 1861*, Sydney, 1861.

Young, G. F., *Under the Coolibah Tree*, London, 1953.

II (a)

ARTICLES, THESES, ETC.

Buckley, K., 'Gipps and the Graziers of New South Wales, 1841-46', in *Historical Studies: Australia and New Zealand*, vol. 6, no. 24, May 1955.

Butlin, N. G., 'Company Ownership of New South Wales Pastoral Stations', in *Historical Studies*, etc., May 1950.

Crowley, F. K., 'Working Class Conditions in Australia 1788-1851', Ph. D. thesis, Univ. Melbourne, 7 November 1949.

Dallas, K. M., 'The Origins of "White Australia" ', in *Australian Quarterly*, vol. 27, No. 1, March 1955.

Goodrich, Carter, 'The Australian and American Labor Movements', in *The Economic Record*, November 1928.

Harper, N. D., 'Frontier and Section', in *Historical Studies*, etc., May 1952.
'Turner the Historian: "Hypothesis or Process?" ', in *University of Kansas City Review*, Autumn 1951.

Kiddle, Margaret, 'English Assisted Immigrants from Country and Town *c.* 1830-50', A.N.U. Seminar paper, 17 June 1954.
'Irish Paupers *c.* 1830-1850', A.N.U. Seminar paper, 20 May 1954.
'Scottish Lowland Farmers *c.* 1830-1850', A.N.U. Seminar paper, 13 May 1954.

Martin, A. W., 'Political Groupings in New South Wales, 1872-1889: A Study in the Working of Responsible Government', Ph. D. thesis, A.N.U., 1955.

Perry, T. M., 'The Spread of Rural Settlement in New South Wales 1788-1826', in *Historical Studies*, etc., May 1955.

Serle, Geoffrey, 'The Causes of Eureka', in *Historical Studies: Eureka Supplement*, December 1954.

Shaw, A. G. L., Article on Transportation in *Sydney Morning Herald*, 27 June 1953.

Smith, Bernard, 'European Vision and the South Pacific', in *Journal of the Warburg and Courtauld Institutes*, vol. 13, 1950.
'Interpretation of Australian Nature during the Nineteenth Century', B.A. thesis, Sydney University.

Ward, Russel, 'Collectivist Notions of a Nomad Tribe', in *Historical Studies*, etc., May 1955.

II (b)
REFERENCE AND INTERPRETATIVE BOOKS

Alexander, F., *Moving Frontiers*, Melbourne, 1947.

Australian Encyclopaedia, 2 vols., Sydney, 1926.

Baker, S. J., *The Australian Language*, Sydney, 1945.
Australia Speaks, Sydney, 1952.

Basedow, Herbert, *The Australian Aboriginal*, Adelaide, 1925.

Bean, C. E. W., *Official History of Australia in the War of 1914-18*, 12 vols., Sydney, 1936-1942.

Boxall, George E., *The Story of the Australian Bushrangers*, London, 1899.

Brown, Max, *Australian Son: The Story of Ned Kelly*, Melbourne, 1948.

Butler, J. R. M., *History of England, 1815-1918*, Oxford, 1928.

Byrne, Desmond, *Australian Writers*, London, 1896.

Clapham, Sir John, *Economic History of Modern Britain*, London, 1926.

Coghlan, T. A., *Labour and Industry in Australia*, etc., 4 vols., London, 1918.

Cole, G. D. H., and Postgate, Raymond, *The Common People, 1746-1946*, London, 1946.

Collier, James, *The Pastoral Age in Australia*, London, 1911.

Crawford, R. M., *Australia*, London, 1952.

Curr, E. M., *The Australian Race*, etc., 2 vols., Melbourne, 1886.

Elkin, A. P., *The Australian Aborigines: How to Understand Them*, Sydney, 1948 (4th edn.).

Ellis, M. H., *Lachlan Macquarie: His Life, Adventures and Times*, Sydney, 1947.

Fairchild, H. N., *The Noble Savage, A Study in Romantic Naturalism*, Columbia University, 1928.

Ferguson, J. A., *Bibliography of Australia*, 4 vols., Sydney, 1941, 1945, 1951, 1955.

Fitzpatrick, Brian, *The Australian People*, Melbourne, 1946.
The British Empire in Australia, Melbourne, 1941.
British Imperialism and Australia, 1783-1833, London, 1939.
The Australian Commonwealth, Melbourne, 1956.

Gabriel, R. H., *The Course of American Democratic Thought*, New York, 1940.

Gollan, R. A., *Radical and Working Class Politics: A Study of Eastern Australia, 1850-1910*, Melbourne, 1960.

Graham, John A., *Early Creswick—The First Century*, Melbourne, 1942.

Grattan, C. Hartley, *Australia*, Univ. California, 1947.
Introducing Australia, Sydney, 1949 (2nd edn.).

Greenwood, Gordon (ed.), *Australia: A Social and Political History*, Sydney, 1955.

Gregg, Pauline, *Social and Economic History of Britain, 1760-1950*, London, 1950.

Gregson, Jesse, *The Australian Agricultural Company, 1824-1875* (Sydney), 1907.

Halsbury's *Laws of England, Being*, etc. (ed. Viscount Hailsham), London, 1938 (2nd edn.).

Hammond, J. L. and Barbara, *The Bleak Age*, London, 1947 (revised edn.).
The Rise of Modern Industry, London, 1925.
The Village Labourer, 1760-1833, London, 1913.

Hancock, W. K., *Australia*, London, 1945 edn.
Politics in Pitcairn and other Essays, London, 1947.
Survey of British Commonwealth Affairs, vol. 2, 1918-1939, Oxford, 1940.

Hauser, Arnold, *The Social History of Art*, 2 vols., London, 1951.

Hayek, F. A. (ed.), *Capitalism and the Historians: Essays by T. S. Ashton*, etc., University of Chicago, 1954.

Hobson, J. A., *Imperialism*, London, 1948 edn.

Ingleton, G. C., *True Patriots All*, Sydney, 1952.

Kiddle, Margaret, *Caroline Chisholm*, Melbourne, 1950.

LaNauze, J. A., *Political Economy in Australia: Historical Studies*, Melbourne, 1949.

Lovejoy, A. O., and Boas, G., *Documentary History of Primitivism and Related Ideas in Antiquity*, Baltimore, 1935.

Madgwick, R. B., *Immigration into Eastern Australia, 1788-1851*, London, 1937.

Miller, E. Morris, *Australian Literature*, 2 vols., Melbourne, 1940.

Mitchell, A. G., *The Pronunciation of English in Australia*, Sydney, 1946.

McCaughey, Patricia, *Samuel McCaughey*, Sydney, 1955.

Palmer, Helen G., *The First Hundred Years*, Melbourne, 1954.

Palmer, Vance, *The Legend of the Nineties*, Melbourne, 1954.

Pike, L. O., *History of Crime in England Illustrating the Changes of the Laws in the Progress of Civilization*, etc., 2 vols., London, 1876.

Plekhanov, G. V., *Art and Social Life*, London, 1953 edn.

Radzinowicz, Leon, *History of English Criminal Law and Its Administration from 1750*, London, 1948.

Riegel, Robert E., *America Moves West*, New York, 1951.

Roberts, S. H., *History of Australian Land Settlement*, Melbourne, 1924.

Saveth, Edward N., *American Historians and European Immigrants, 1875-1925*, University of Columbia, 1948.

Serle, P., *Dictionary of Australian Biography*, 2 vols., Sydney, 1949.

Shann, E. G., *Economic History of Australia*, Sydney, 1948 edn.

Shaw, A. G. L., *The Story of Australia*, London, 1955.

Smith, Bernard, *European Vision and the South Pacific 1768-1850*, London, 1960.
  Place, Taste and Tradition, Sydney, 1945.

Spengler, Oswald, *The Decline of the West*, 2 vols., London, 1928.

Taylor, G. R. (ed.), *The Turner Thesis Concerning the Role of the Frontier in American History*, Boston, 1949.

Turnbull, Clive, *These Tears of Fire*, Melbourne, 1949.

Turner, F. J., *Early Writings of Frederick Jackson Turner with a List of All His Works* (ed. E. E. Edwards), University of Wisconsin, 1938.
  The Frontier in American History, New York, 1948 edn.
  The Significance of Sections in American History, New York, 1950.

Turner, H. G., *History of the Colony of Victoria*, etc., 2 vols., London, 1904.

Webb, W. P., *The Great Plains*, Oxford, 1931.

White, Charles, *History of Australian Bushranging*, 2 vols., Sydney, 1903.
  Story of Australian Bushranging, Nos. 1-7, Bathurst, 1891-93.

Willard, Myra, *History of the White Australia Policy*, Melbourne, 1923.

Willey, Basil, *The Eighteenth Century Background: Studies on the Idea of Nature in the Thought of the Period*, London, 1949.

III

SOURCES OF, AND WORKS ON, BALLADS

Anderson, Hugh, *Black Bull Chapbooks*, Nos. 1, 2, 3, etc., Ferntree Gully, 1952 ff.
  Colonial Ballads, Ferntree Gully, 1955.
  Goldrush Songster, Ferntree Gully, 1957.

Bradshaw, Jack, *Highway Robbery under Arms without Shedding Blood*, etc., Sydney, n.d. (1868).
  True History of the Australian Bushrangers, etc., Sydney, n.d. (c. 1925).

Chanson, George, *The Sydney Songster No. 1: A Collection of New, Original, Local and Comic Songs, as Sung at the Sydney Concert Rooms*, etc., Sydney, n.d. (1866).

Elliott, Brian, *Singing to the Cattle*, etc., Melbourne, 1947.

Forbes, Alexander, *Voices from the Bush*, Rockhampton, 1869.

Jones, Percy, 'Australia's Folk Songs', in *Twentieth Century: an Australian Quarterly Review*, vol. I, No. 1.

Manifold, John, *Bandicoot Ballads*, Nos. 1, 2, 3, etc., Ferntree Gully, 1949 ff.

'*Native Companion*' *Songster*, Brisbane, 1889.

Palmer, Vance, and Sutherland, Margaret, *Old Australian Bush Ballads*, Melbourne, 1951.

Paterson, A. B., *The Man from Snowy River and Other Verses*, Sydney, 1895.
  A Bushman's Song, Sydney, 1896.
  Waltzing Matilda, Sydney, 1903.
  Old Bush Songs, Sydney, 1905, 1930.
  Saltbush Bill, J.P., and Other Verses, Sydney, 1917.
  Collected Works of, Sydney, 1921.
  Collected Verse of, Sydney, 1953.

Queenslanders' New Colonial Camp Fire Song Book, etc., Sydney, 1865.

Stewart, Douglas and Keesing, Nancy,
  Australian Bush Ballads, Sydney, 1955.
  Old Bush Songs, Sydney, 1957.

Thatcher, C. R., Ms. Papers (P.L.V.).
  Victoria Songster, etc., Melbourne, 1855.

Tibbs, *Tibbs' Popular Song Book, containing the latest hits on 'Bushy in Town'*, etc., Sydney, n.d. (c. 1887).

Wannan, Bill, *The Australian: Yarns, Ballads, Legends and Traditions of the Australian People*, Melbourne, 1954.

Wiseheart, *Wiseheart's Merry Songster; or Gems of Comicality*, Nos. 1, 2, 3, 4, 5, etc., Dublin, 1832.
  Wiseheart's New Comic Songster, Nos. 1, 2, 3, 4, 5, etc., Dublin, 1832.

Index